Contents

Focus on information in disasters

Annexes

Information:
a life-saving resource

Looking back over the events of 2004, it is striking how many of the year's disasters could have been avoided with better information and communication. For tens of thousands of people, disaster arrived suddenly, unannounced.

The tsunami, which wrecked so many lives, homes and livelihoods last December, looms large in this year's report. Although scientists across the region had the technology to register the massive earthquake off Sumatra which triggered the tragedy, they lacked the means to tell people what was coming or what to do.

Yet informal networks succeeded where official warnings failed: Vijayakumar Gunasekaran, based in Singapore, heard of the tsunami's devastating impact on the radio early on the morning of 26 December. He phoned a warning through to his family in Nallavadu on the eastern coast of India, in time for villagers to evacuate all 3,630 residents to safety.

Early warning is the most obvious way in which accurate, timely information alone can save lives. In the Caribbean, during 2004's hurricane season, most countries successfully alerted their populations of approaching storms and saved many lives as a result. The key to their success was putting *people*, not just technology, at the centre of their warning systems.

In Cuba, disaster awareness is taught as part of the school curriculum and evacuation drills are held every year before the hurricane season. In Jamaica, Red Cross volunteers like Patricia Greenleaf go from street to street issuing warnings by megaphone, 48 hours before hurricanes are due to hit. Building awareness from the bottom up is as valuable as transmitting information from the top down.

As well as saving lives, information reduces suffering in the wake of disaster. Tracing lost family and friends, knowing how much compensation you're entitled to or where you're going to live, simply understanding why disaster struck: such information means an enormous amount to survivors left homeless and traumatized.

In Aceh, Indonesia, Red Cross volunteers helped reunite 3,400 tsunami survivors with their families – often using satellite phones. In Sri Lanka, many people feared the waves were a divine punishment. The Belgian Red Cross helped dispel these myths by explaining the science behind the disaster.

Once fed and sheltered, disaster survivors are hungry for information on how to get back to work, how to participate in reconstruction, how to influence the recovery agenda of aid organizations and governments. In Tamil Nadu, the Indian state hit

International Federation
of Red Cross and Red Crescent Societies

hardest by the tsunami, local civil society groups formed a coordination cell to capture people's priorities across 100 disaster-struck villages and report back on what aid officials were planning. Maintaining communication with affected people is a crucial way in which aid organizations can promote transparency, accountability and trust.

Good information is equally vital to ensure disaster relief is appropriate and well-targeted. After the tsunami, women's specific needs were often overlooked. Large quantities of inappropriate, used clothing clogged up warehouses and roadsides across South Asia. Assessing and communicating what is *not* needed can prove as vital as finding out what is needed – saving precious time, money and resources.

Meanwhile, far from the media spotlight, various chronic crises silently steal lives and livelihoods. The Sahel region of West Africa has suffered near-famine, triggered by drought and locusts, which put the lives of 9 million people at risk by mid-2005. Despite timely warnings, the plight of the Sahel was overshadowed by events in Darfur and the Indian Ocean. Promoting better media coverage of the world's neglected humanitarian disasters is a vital priority if global aid is to be apportioned more fairly.

Local journalists can make an enormous difference to the lives of people living in crisis. In Afghanistan, a long-running radio soap opera combines entertainment with life-saving advice on how to avoid disease or landmines. Evidence shows that people adopt less risky behaviour after listening to these programmes.

So the record of the international aid community is mixed. Information alone can save lives. But there are gaps in the way we gather and share this powerful resource. Fortunately, this year's report reveals that there is much good practice on which to build. I would like to see three things happen.

First, aid organizations must recognize that accurate, timely information is a form of disaster response in its own right. It may also be the only form of disaster preparedness that the most vulnerable can afford.

Second, in our dialogue with journalists, donors and the wider public, we must put more emphasis on highlighting the plight of people caught up in the world's neglected disasters.

Finally, we must put far greater priority on communicating with people affected by disaster. Not only will this lead to more efficient aid assessment and delivery, but more crucial still, by giving vulnerable people the right information, they can take greater control of their own lives.

Markku Niskala
Secretary General

International Federation
of Red Cross and Red Crescent Societies

Data or dialogue? The role of information in disasters

The very first thing you need to do is climb into a helicopter. You can't get to see how many people are buried but you get an eagle-eye view… You can see which airfields are working, which bridges are down. After 3–4 hours in a helicopter, I had a complete overview of the geographical extent of the disaster [earthquakes in El Salvador, 2001], the logistics involved, the population centres – also where not to send people. Then you must get on the ground to get the quality.

Iain Logan, former head of disaster operations, International Federation

Today's technology and resources for international disaster response have opened up new possibilities for gathering and giving information. Newcomers can quickly get an overview of the disaster zone by helicopter surveys. They can find the history and context from a quick trawl on the Internet. But is this progress? Does it reveal the truth? What vital information is left out?

Local organizations are likely to have a good understanding of disaster-affected people but, because they lack access to helicopters, their perceptions may be devalued or come too late to influence the critical early decisions of international organizations. If relief agencies rely on technology, the Internet or the media, will they ignore processes of participation and consultation?

Responding to the Indian Ocean tsunami disaster, aid agencies distributed impressive amounts of relief aid. But despite this, some needy groups were missed. In some cases, aid went to men and the specific needs of women were not met. In other cases, aid went to dominant social groups, sidelining tribal people and outcastes. Information about them was lacking.

Information technology has helped aid agencies gather and store information, but do people affected by disasters get enough information? Do they get warnings of disaster? Are they told what aid agencies are planning on their behalf? Are they involved in making decisions? Do they know their entitlements from government? Are organizations as good at sharing information with affected people as with donors? The answers to these questions reveal much about the underlying power relationships between aid givers and receivers.

It's not only technology that raises new possibilities and questions. As more relief funds flow through private channels and as media reporting becomes more immediate, outside pressures can distort the truth. Agencies compete to spend funds

Photo opposite page: Information is a form of disaster response in its own right – and it may be the only type of preparedness that the most vulnerable people can afford.

Yoshi Shimizu/ International Federation

in places the public have chosen to respond to. The media gather the stories that are of 'human interest'. Whose interest – viewers or people in need?

Other disasters lie 'forgotten', unreported and underfunded. The tsunami, played out in front of the eyes of billions of television viewers, provoked a response on a scale never before witnessed in human history. But it wasn't the worst disaster in history. Over ten times as many people have died in the conflict and disease that continue to ravage the Democratic Republic of the Congo (DRC), eliciting little international response. Information about 'forgotten' disasters does exist, but it is poorly communicated to the wider public and often ignored by decision-makers.

Information bestows power. Lack of information can make people victims of disaster and targets of aid. People affected by disasters have few opportunities to challenge the information overlordship of powerful relief agencies. Aid flows from givers to receivers. Information flows from receivers to givers. The aid agencies are empowered to write reports, make responses, raise further funds and learn lessons. But the people affected by disasters often get little more than pots, pans and bowls of food.

That's not to say that disaster survivors are passive victims. In the absence of official early warnings, people affected by the tsunami used mobile phones to warn others. They found sources of help through civil society networks or web sites. They exchanged information between themselves, electronically and face-to-face – with far greater openness than many international organizations. Are aid agencies missing out on people-to-people communication?

The information perspective cuts across sectors, standards and principles offering an unconventional, fresh view of disasters. Instead of focusing on the relief items, budgets and policies that contribute to disaster response, the information perspective focuses on the exchanges and human relationships that underpin agency activity.

This year's *World Disasters Report* considers the quality of communication that takes place between those involved and what impact it has on people caught up in crisis. The theme may sound abstract, but it has very tangible implications. The right kind of information leads to a deeper understanding of needs and ways to meet those needs. The wrong information can lead to inappropriate, even dangerous interventions.

Information is also a vital form of aid in itself. People need information as much as water, food, medicine or shelter. Information can save lives, livelihoods and resources. It may be the only form of disaster preparedness that the most vulnerable can afford. And yet it is very much neglected. Aid organizations have focused on gathering information for their own needs and not enough on exchanging information with the people they aim to support.

International Federation of Red Cross and Red Crescent Societies

Types of information

Information is a slippery concept. It includes everything from facts to deep understanding, and may include lies and deception. The selection of information is an area in which power relationships operate vigorously. Disaster expert Ben Wisner suggests there is a hierarchy of information quality:

- **Data.** Basic, unorganized facts, usually in a statistical form, such as wind speed, rainfall intensity, death tolls.
- **Information.** Organized data, descriptions such as "a class 2 hurricane is approaching".
- **Knowledge.** Combines information with understanding into accepted fact, bringing awareness and the ability to predict events.
- **Wisdom.** Capacity to make value judgements based on experience, understanding and principle.

The *ALNAP Review of Humanitarian Action in 2003*, published by the Active Learning Network for Accountability and Performance in Humanitarian Action (ALNAP), made a similar distinction between data, information and knowledge. While information sharing is "external", learning is "internal" and involves "the application and interpretation of information".

Gathering data is a one-way process. Acquiring knowledge and wisdom involves exchanging and analysing information in the light of experience, through dialogue or multiple channels of communication (see Figure 1.1). Giving information – rather than just taking it – is not only a direct form of help, but leads to better communications and deeper analysis. If affected people understand an aid agency's capacity and perspectives, they can give better advice. It is the dialogue rather than the data that is the challenge.

This chapter examines how information is handled in relation to different aspects of early warning and disaster response. It then analyses thematic issues, including consultation and participation, information sharing, mapping risk and human security, the role of media, and the impact of information and communication technology.

Early warning: saving lives and money

Experience from the Caribbean reveals a wide variation in the impact of hurricanes and floods, depending largely on levels of knowledge and preparedness (see Chapter 2). The key success factor is that information must not rest in the hands of a few officials with evacuation plans, but be spread throughout communities at risk before and after the event. Good levels of education in Cuba, from teaching about hurricanes in schools to annual evacuation drills, have contributed to a high awareness of

Figure 1.1 Turning data into knowledge and wisdom requires exchanging and analysing information in the light of experience, through dialogue and multiple channels of communication. Local populations, NGOs, governments and international aid organizations should all participate in this process.

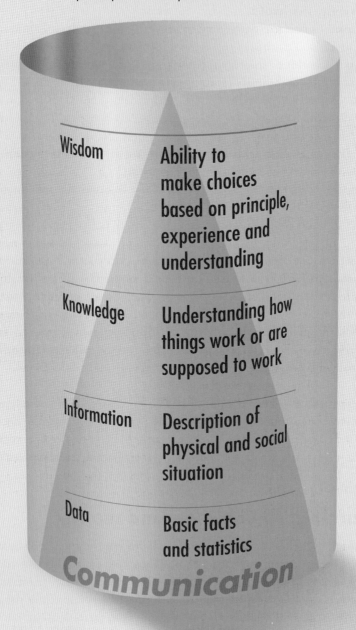

Wisdom — Ability to make choices based on principle, experience and understanding

Knowledge — Understanding how things work or are supposed to work

Information — Description of physical and social situation

Data — Basic facts and statistics

Communication

Sources: B. Wisner, J. Walter

International Federation of Red Cross and Red Crescent Societies

disasters and far lower death tolls from hurricanes than in neighbouring countries (see Chapter 2, Table 2.2).

Early warning information must be as accurate, timely and credible as possible, for people to trust and act on it. They need to know exactly where to go for safety and which route to take. Success rests on information from all sides being brought together. Local communities need a close relationship with systems of governance at all levels. Cuba has done well because these systems cooperate effectively, whereas Haiti, undermined by political violence and environmental degradation, suffers many more deaths.

There also needs to be more interaction at the global level. Officials tend to design early warning systems that overlook the needs and contributions of people on the ground. As John Twigg argued in a recent publication on disaster risk reduction: "Emergency planning manuals highlight the importance of officially validated forecasting and warning information issued from a central point... But in the modern age command and control of information is unrealistic. The public are increasingly *consumers* of information from different sources, choosing what information to use and where to obtain it."

The lack of an official early warning of the tsunami disaster is a reminder that scientific knowledge alone is not enough: information only becomes useful as a result of human interaction or communication. The people with some of the best information about the oncoming disaster were scientists in the Pacific who were unable to communicate with those in the tsunami's path. Slow-moving bureaucracy also cost many lives: the meteorology department of one regional power received the news of the earthquake off Sumatra one minute after it struck, tracked the devastating course of the tsunami, but failed to issue a warning to its own people at risk.

Ironically, the 'primitive' tribes of the Andaman and Nicobar Islands realized that disaster was approaching from the behaviour of birds and animals, and the appearance of the sea. They fled from coastal areas to higher ground. Hundreds of lives were saved in India when a migrant worker phoned a warning through from Singapore to his home village (see Box 1.1). And a 10-year-old English schoolgirl, Tilly Smith, is reported to have saved over 100 lives in Thailand when she raised the alarm after recognizing the signs of an approaching tsunami from a geography lesson two weeks earlier.

However, local knowledge is not always reliable. The inhabitants of Gonaives in Haiti felt protected by nearby mountains from the onslaught of Tropical Storm Jeanne in September 2004. Few of them had any idea that those same mountains were channelling deadly flows of floodwater and debris towards the town, leading to over 1,800 deaths (see Chapter 2).

Vijayakumar Gunasekaran, the 27-year-old son of a fisherman from Nallavadu village, Pondicherry on the eastern coast of India, works in Singapore. He followed the news of the earthquake in Aceh, Indonesia as it unfolded over the radio and television in Singapore on the morning of 26 December 2004. As the seriousness of the disaster in Aceh sank in, he began to worry about the safety of his family living along the Indian coastline facing Aceh. He decided to phone home.

Muphazhaqi, his sister, answered the phone. When he asked what was happening in Nallavadu, she said that sea water was seeping into their home. Vijayakumar realized at once that his worst fears were rapidly materializing. He asked her to leave their home quickly and also to warn other villagers to evacuate the village. "Run out and shout the warning to others," he urged his sister.

Her warning reached a couple of quick-thinking villagers who broke down the doors of the community centre set up by the M.S. Swaminathan Research Foundation where a public address system, used to announce sea conditions to the fishermen, was housed. The warning from Vijayakumar, corroborated at this time by a second overseas telephone call from Gopu, another villager working abroad, was broadcast across the village using the loudspeaker system. The village's siren was sounded immediately afterwards for the people to evacuate.

No one was killed Nallavadu, home to some 3,630 people, as a result of the timely warnings. While all lives were saved, the tsunami destroyed 150 houses and 200 fishing boats in the village. ■

Mobile phones and the Internet have opened up new possibilities for early warning and disaster preparedness. In many parts of Asia and Latin America, there is a mobile phone in most villages and word can spread very fast. Meanwhile, the use of mobile phones and the Internet is growing faster in Africa than anywhere else, according to the United Nations (UN). In Viet Nam, the UN Development Programme (UNDP) has distributed wind-up radios to fishermen so they can receive early warnings of oncoming windstorms broadcast by the Voice of Viet Nam, while out at sea. But the global potential for linking phones and radios into systems of early warning has not yet been fully developed.

Information management at the local level is vital in providing early warning, whether the source of the disaster is far away or nearby. In Coyolate river basin in Guatemala, community volunteers have since 1997 operated simple rain gauges and collected information in order to predict floods. They send this information to a local forecasting centre via solar-powered radios. The system can only forecast floods a few hours in advance, but because it is local and credible it is effective. In 1998 it led to the evacuation of an area in advance of Hurricane Mitch, saving many lives.

Early warning messages also flow to governments and aid agencies advising them to take action before a hazard such as drought deteriorates into a disaster. But the key

International Federation
of Red Cross and Red Crescent Societies

question is whether information translates into understanding and action. The threat of last year's locust plagues in the Sahel and north-west regions of Africa was first reported in June 2003, but the global response was very slow. By early 2005, 9 million people across the region had been plunged into a serious food crisis. Donors admitted that just US$ 1 million could have contained the locust threat in July 2003, but delays in response meant that 100 times more money was needed to address the consequences. The problem was not so much lack of information as a lack of communication and understanding between scientists, the governments concerned and donors (see Chapter 3).

Assessment: capturing needs or targeting resources?

Assessment should be the basis for disaster response. Over 300 aid organizations are signatories to the *Code of Conduct for the International Red Cross and Red Crescent Movement and NGOs in Disaster Relief* which states: "We will base the provision of relief aid upon a thorough assessment of the needs of the disaster victims and the local capacities already in place to meet those needs." Similarly, the Sphere handbook strongly and repeatedly emphasizes that disaster response must be based on first-hand analysis.

Yet numerous evaluations, including those undertaken after the Gujarat earthquake in India and floods in Mozambique, have criticized a lack of thoroughness in assessments. The same has been the case yet again in the response to the tsunami (see Chapter 4). In his evaluation of the International Federation's response in Aceh, conducted during February 2005, Abhijit Bhattacharjee found that: "The response so far has been influenced more by the media needs and the perception of donors... rather than by the *expressed* needs of the affected community."

Aid managers in tsunami-affected countries acknowledged that this was a problem. More staff should have been assigned to assessment teams rather than hurrying to organize the first planeloads of supplies. Initial relief distributions were often based on informed guesses. As a result the needs of some vulnerable groups – for example, pregnant and lactating women in Sri Lanka, low-caste workers supporting the fishing industry in India and homeless people sheltering with host families in Aceh – were missed (see Chapters 4 and 5). The demand for quick decisions, driven by competition between agencies, often takes precedence over establishing accurate information on needs.

A study published by the United Kingdom's Overseas Development Institute in 2003 concluded that even where proper assessments are made, policy-makers often bypass them. Decisions about the response are based on preconceptions about the role of the agency rather than gathering local information. "Needs assessment, at least in the formal sense, often plays only a marginal role in the decision-making of agencies and donors. Assessment is often taken to be a 'front-end' process, which culminates in the design of a response and appeal for funds. Initial assessments, especially of rapid-onset or fast-evolving situations, depend as much on assumptions, estimate and prediction as they do on observed fact," noted the study.

The danger is that, after asking questions about needs, the agency decides to do what it always does. This may lead to inappropriate aid, and it can easily lead to lack of trust between aid agencies and local people. Information may become distorted, as people adjust their answers to what they think the agency has to offer. This makes it difficult for agencies to develop a deeper relationship later.

Of course, detailed needs assessments may not be possible in the first hours of a sudden-onset disaster, when saving lives is of greater importance than gathering information. But basing relief on assumptions can be dangerous, as seen in Darfur, Sudan last year, when the tarpaulins distributed to protect homeless people from the weather attracted raiding parties from local militia. Agencies need to develop better ways of combining emergency response with needs assessments which are both rapid and participatory (see Box 1.2). In practice, this means maintaining a balance between the desire for results, pressure from competition and respect for the views and requirements of people in need.

Coordinating and sharing information

A second area of concern is the duplication of surveys, which arises when aid organizations fail to coordinate. Duplicating assessments is inefficient and may cause distress to vulnerable people. Examples of inter-agency assessments in response to the tsunami were rare. In Nagapattinam, the Indian district hit hardest by the tsunami, more than 300 organizations competed for projects in 40 villages. Oxfam became so concerned about the negative effects that it took up the issue of ensuring overall quality of the response as a major focus of its own work.

The Sphere Project specifies that "information is gathered using standardized procedures and made available to allow for transparent decision-making". But in practice, agencies do not follow standardized procedures and reports are not made available. In Aceh, there was so much competition between agencies over beneficiaries that they even concealed information from each other. Less than a quarter of the 200 agencies known to be in the province had provided the UN's coordinating body with activity reports by late January. Coordination is easily undermined by competition, and has been one of the most challenging and least successful aspects of the tsunami response.

The aid system is bad at sharing information within itself, let alone with disaster-affected people, who are left very much to their own devices. The International

International Federation
of Red Cross and Red Crescent Societies

Federation has developed an online knowledge-sharing tool called FedNet, which provides web-based discussion forums and information to anyone within its 181 members worldwide. The UN has, since 1999, set up Humanitarian Information Centres (HICs) to coordinate information during disasters. But their stated purpose is to provide information management within the humanitarian community, rather than create a holistic system that includes local organizations and affected people. HICs often lack the staff needed to go out and gather the information, while persuading aid agencies to share their information has proved a challenge, especially in sudden-onset disasters (see Chapter 4, Box 4.4).

Civil society groups, rather than the international system, are generating good practice. After the 2001 earthquake in Gujarat, a local network of organizations, Abhiyan, set up an information base at the district headquarters and advised aid agencies about areas of need, basic requirements for starting to work and coordination arrangements. Abhiyan's information centres throughout the district gave information to local people as well as outsiders.

When the tsunami struck Tamil Nadu, Abhiyan helped a group of non-governmental organizations (NGOs) to set up a similar network, known as the Nagapattinam NGO coordination cell, which was especially effective at conveying information between affected people and disaster responders. Groups of volunteers visited 100 villages across the district every day to find out people's needs and key issues. This information was collated centrally and presented to the government and aid agencies to help guide their interventions. Information about response and recovery was fed back to the villages on a daily basis (see Chapter 5).

Consultation, participation and transparency

Under the Red Cross Red Crescent's Code of Conduct, the flow of information between aid agencies and people should be regulated by principles of consultation, participation and transparency. These principles are emphasized in Sphere's common standards and have been absorbed into the internal policies of most established aid agencies. But a review of the aid response in Aceh six weeks after the tsunami struck by McCluskey and Choudhury for the Joint Quality and Accountability Initiative, representing the Sphere Project, ALNAP and others, found that there had "been no consistent consultation with beneficiaries [and]... there appeared to be no formal (and very limited informal) feedback mechanisms".

The review revealed that relief workers appreciated the importance of consultation, but were not clear what kinds of information should be shared and discussed. In addition, "some aid workers felt that it would have been inappropriate and inconsiderate to ask people 'what they need', in the first weeks after such extreme trauma".

Box 1.2 Participatory assessments reveal risky assumptions

We had to take important decisions based on little reliable information. But when you see 50,000 people huddled together, with nothing except the clothes on them, you know what they need.

International assessment team leader,
Aceh, Indonesia, January 2005

The basic needs of people affected by disaster may seem evident to an experienced aid worker. However, it can be dangerous to plan responses without taking into account the specific context, particularly during conflicts. During 2004, displaced people in Darfur, Sudan were living in the open with little to protect them from the elements. With the rainy season approaching, the need for waterproof tarpaulins seemed 'obvious'. But a little probing revealed a more complex situation.

When armed militias raided camps for internally displaced people (IDPs) in early 2004, they looted tarpaulins and other household goods, as well as attacking IDPs themselves. During interviews with IDPs, many were worried about this side effect of international aid, although they desperately needed better shelter. Some even requested that valuable items such as tarpaulins should not be distributed. But they only voiced such concerns after relatively lengthy (30-60 minute) interviews.

Two lessons emerge: first, the importance of understanding the historical, political and social context; second, the need to undertake in-depth interviews with affected people, even in urgent situations.

During sudden crises, there is an imperative to act quickly, as lives may be in danger. But it is always possible to speak to some affected people. Given time constraints, only a few interviews will be possible, so interviewees must be carefully selected. The first step is to identify areas most affected, using secondary information and key informants. Second, the most vulnerable groups are selected through rapid, on-the-spot consultation with different stakeholders. Finally, random sampling is used to select individual and group informants.

Each of these three steps can be done in less than an hour, though with more time the accuracy of the process will be improved.

After sudden-onset disasters, the initial assessment, to decide early deployments of people and materials, should be done within one day. This won't be 100 per cent accurate and the situation is likely to change rapidly, making information quickly out-of-date. So during the first few days, relief workers must implement a flexible, continuous process of assessment and programme adjustment. Agencies should not delay the initial deployment of resources until perfect information is received. But they should adjust activities as the quality of information improves. Assessment and implementation must run in parallel.

So much for the theory, but how well are needs assessments conducted in practice? Despite efforts, response continues to dominate assessment. This is often because organizations are specialized in a particular sector and deploy preconceived responses. Reviews of the response to the tsunami show that many agencies launched aid flights containing standard relief materials, based on rough guesses of numbers affected and experience of what this meant in terms of needs in similar contexts.

Responding with limited second-hand information can be risky. For example, some of the emergency response units sent by the International Federation to address water, sanitation and health needs in tsunami-affected countries were more suited to helping affected people concentrated in large numbers, rather than people spread thinly along hundreds of kilometres of coastline, as was the case in Sri Lanka.

Organizations accept the risk of getting initial aid partially wrong when weighed against

International Federation
of Red Cross and Red Crescent Societies

the benefits of getting it partially right. They do this because:

- Life-saving activities in rapid-onset disasters have a short window of opportunity.
- Preventive action must be put in place rapidly to prevent disease outbreaks.
- Access to areas may be difficult, so assessments and initial response have to happen simultaneously.
- Organizations feel under pressure to use the resources made available as rapidly and appropriately as possible.

As the situation stabilizes, assessments can become more rigorous and detailed. Eventually it becomes feasible to undertake medium-term (6–12 month) planning. Project staff should, however, continue to monitor the situation so they can identify changes promptly and, where necessary, instigate further assessment and analysis. As assessments become more detailed during recovery, they should generate more participation from affected people and promote a deeper understanding of vulnerability and capacity.

Slow-onset disasters provide such an opportunity. However, agencies often don't spend the time necessary to understand the complexity of these situations. A good example was 2002's food crisis in southern Africa. Initially, most organizations saw it as drought-induced and only later realized that multiple factors, including HIV/AIDS and poor governance, eroded the ability of people to cope. More time spent at the onset of the crisis ensuring the participation of affected people in assessments could have resulted in a better response.

But participation remains contentious in needs-assessment practice. Often organizations simply consult people to extract information rather than truly engage them in the assessment process and its conclusions. Once assessed, affected people are rarely informed of the results, which can have a negative impact since they may rely on assistance that doesn't come. Also damaging are repeated assessments by different organizations of the same population, particularly if they receive no assistance or explanation.

One solution could be joint assessments. These have advantages beyond reducing 'assessment fatigue', such as removing agency bias and improving the consistency of results through a pre-agreed methodology. Joint assessments may also improve coordination in planning and implementing projects, as well as enabling staff and logistical resources to be shared during the assessment. They can be organized along sectoral or geographical lines. However, such collaboration is only feasible if organizations share common values and operational principles and if they use the same, or compatible, assessment methodologies.

Collaboration won't work if assessments are mandate-specific or if organizations' principles are not compatible. Some organizations won't risk losing their neutrality and independence by conducting joint assessments with actors perceived as prejudiced or politically tainted. And joint assessments can lead to a 'false consensus' where dissenting voices are diluted, a point made by Darcy and Hofmann in their 2003 study on measuring needs. Nevertheless, if collaboration is not feasible it is still essential to know who else is making assessments and where.

The debate on needs assessment has progressed well, with the Good Humanitarian Donorship initiative, the revised Sphere handbook, the UN's consolidated appeals process and the International Federation's forthcoming *Guidelines for emergency assessment* all committed to improving the theory and practice of assessments. Transparency is emerging with increased documentation of methodologies used by different organizations. Increasingly, these methodologies are based on an understanding of capacities as well as vulnerabilities, which will require greater participation of affected people in the assessment process. ∎

As a result, aid agencies lacked sufficient feedback about the views of communities and often had to make immediate decisions without consultation. In several cases, the failure to gather even 'mission-critical' information led to very poor aid delivery, "including reports of large scale food distributions containing serious nutritional imbalances, and many reports of expensive water purification and supply equipment being inappropriate, under utilised or defunct".

McCluskey and Choudhury concluded: "There is certainly a high level of interest and appreciation of communication, but the ideal has been compromised by the a) perceived urgency of the response, b) high amounts of 'un-restricted' funds available, c) lack of activity or strategic planning, d) the need to quickly stake claim to 'operating niches', and e) the limited knowledge of process and value of consultation and feedback at different stages of an emergency."

Agencies may have developed ways of gathering data, but this is not enough. After the tsunami's waves forced Sri Lankans into camps, soldiers were put on patrol to protect them. By a sensitive process of consultation with women and girls, Oxfam discovered that they felt threatened. Some soldiers watched them as they bathed, or made indecent comments. Oxfam took up the issue with the military authorities, which then imposed better discipline. This became the basis for a campaign on women's protection, designed to encourage others to speak out. However, it took several months for the issues of women's protection and needs in Sri Lanka to be properly addressed (see Chapter 5).

While the value of consulting with disaster-affected people may be recognized, the benefits of learning from them seem to be less apparent. Of the 37 field workers ALNAP interviewed for its 2003 review – both men and women, international and national staff – not one mentioned learning from affected people. ALNAP concluded: "The lack of learning about and from affected populations and other local actors when all agencies strive for a participatory approach – at least in their policies – seriously undermines the credibility of humanitarian action."

Despite several years' work on accountability in aid, it has proved difficult to set up channels through which affected people can comment on aid agencies' work. During the food shortages in Zimbabwe in 2003, Save the Children UK found that children felt marginalized in decision-making processes. So they set up feedback committees through which children could make their views known (see Box 1.3). And following the monsoon floods which swept Nepal in 2004, the Nepal Red Cross Society undertook a 'participatory action learning' process to capture feedback from affected people while the disaster response was ongoing (see Box 1.4).

Processes of 'public auditing', in which stakeholders collectively review the progress of aid projects and hold managers to account, have often been highly successful. In

International Federation
of Red Cross and Red Crescent Societies

Nepal, the UK's Department for International Development (DFID) used this method, not only to involve local people but also to allow rebel forces an opportunity to understand, and hopefully respect, development activity.

Holding aid agencies to account in disaster situations has proved far more difficult. One challenge is that the information presented to affected people must be relevant and comprehensible. Handing out annual reports or web site addresses won't yield useful results. Accountability depends on a highly sensitive process of transparency, taking into account the interests and capacities of people involved. Few agencies have yet given this the time and priority that it requires to succeed.

Yet, as the *ALNAP Practitioners' Handbook* says, "Transparency is a prerequisite for trust." It urges aid workers to "remember that communication is a two-way process, requiring that all parties get to know one another. Humanitarian aid workers tend to focus their attention on gathering data from the affected population, often omitting to explain who they are, what they do and why. Yet transparency is essential for successful communication, negotiation and participation."

Giving as well as getting

Aid agencies have not got used to the idea that they should give information to affected populations, as well as getting it from them. Information has not been recognized as an issue in itself. It rarely appears in agency objectives or procedures. But disasters are times of great uncertainty and this uncertainty may be the most painful part of the experience. Parvita, a widow from India who survived the tsunami, told the *World Disasters Report*: "I don't want another cooking pot – I have as many as I will ever need. I want to know where my family is going to be living in another month's time!"

Aid agencies did a great deal of analysis for themselves about relocation options after the tsunami, but did they do enough to ensure this information reached affected people? A study in Guinea by ALNAP found that: "Providing regular information on the number of available places for resettlement, details of application procedures and the status of ongoing applications will reduce misunderstandings and should significantly lessen any negative effects of resettlement, repatriation or camp closures."

There is mounting evidence that, as well as having direct practical value, information given to survivors about the nature of a disaster can help them come to terms with their experiences. Astier Almedom of Tufts University in the United States studied the psychosocial needs of Eritrean refugees from her country after two decades of war. She concluded: "Information on what is happening and why mitigates the worst effects of war and displacement. The fact that information on the escalation of hostilities and

Box 1.3 Zimbabwean children claim right to reply

Jessica Pedzura, 17, lives in Mutorashanga, an impoverished mining community afflicted by food shortages in northern Zimbabwe. In late 2003, Save the Children UK (SCF) began distributing emergency food aid there to 10,000 people a month.

Although the programme was largely aimed at 'children in need', Jessica said the first the children knew of it was when maize was delivered to a distribution point some miles away. Asking children about when, where and how aid should be delivered wasn't part of the agency's agenda. Jessica and her friends were simply 'beneficiaries'. Her teacher said, "It has been tradition to look down upon our children and just simply pour information into them as if they don't think. We tend to forget that they are human beings, people who can make meaningful contributions. They have knowledge with them which they can only express and share with others if given the support to do so."

SCF evaluated the programme and found that many in the community, including children, felt marginalized by the way the programme had been implemented. Recipients had not been adequately informed about their rights, entitlements and responsibilities. Community meetings, meant to help identify the needy, were flawed because villagers were reluctant to dispute undeserving cases for fear of being victimized later. Children complained that distribution points were too far away and carrying the heavy loads exhausted them. Distributions took place on weekdays, disrupting their education. "We had the impression that the agency was not particularly interested in what we had to say," said Jessica.

So, in September 2003, SCF began a pilot project to capture children's feedback more systematically, based on three principles. First, complaints had to be channelled through an objective, independent mechanism, because communities feared complaining to the very agency staff against whom they might have a grievance. Second, SCF had to explain the principles, practice and structures of food aid, to ensure the feedback was relevant. Third, children had to lead information collection and dissemination, because they were principal beneficiaries and previous experience of child participation showed they could identify issues that adults were unwilling or unable to see.

Jessica, selected by her peers as chairperson of one of seven children's feedback committees, recalled her training and the role committees were expected to play: "The workshops were a mixture of fun and learning. We learnt about the food aid programme, where the food came from, which mode of transport was used, how and when it was stored until transported to the final destination, how ration sizes were calculated. We also learnt about the criteria to select beneficiaries and who they should be. As to our future tasks, we understood that this was to hear problems faced by children, to report any exploitation and whether the food was taken to the correct families. We were also going to teach others, both adults and children, some of the things we had learnt at the workshop. After all this work we would then give our feedback as to what was going on to an ombudsperson, someone independent of the organization who would present our complaints and recommendations to a hearing committee. We were informed that not only Save the Children was represented but that a government officer, another NGO and a donor were also present on this board. After their discussions, Save the Children would then inform us about their solutions to the problems we had seen."

Over the next eight months, 70 children collected feedback from their peers, which proved invaluable in identifying problems and suggesting solutions. Children said information flows between aid personnel and the community were weak, fuelling speculation that local food aid officers employed by SCF were concealing something. Why could only five people per family receive rations? Did SCF want to penalize large families? In fact, the agency needed to maximize the number of households benefiting from a limited supply of maize. Children reported that one member of staff was quick-tempered and unwilling to answer questions. They recommended all staff be trained in communication skills, later put into practice.

Another observation concerned situations where children living with guardians were denied their rations or forced to work long hours for a share of the aid. They complained of guardians selling off food to buy beer or other commodities. Sometimes they had to give a portion of their rations to 'adult helpers' in return for transport to distant distribution points. The children called for a much more vigorous promotion of their rights within the community, through which they hoped to make the welfare of vulnerable children everyone's responsibility, thereby limiting cases of abuse.

Jessica believed considerable progress was made: "Our community now knows a lot more about abuse and I believe awareness is now higher about the rights of children. I have not heard of ill treatment of foster children in Mutorashanga since the children's feedback committees were established, and I think this is because of more awareness."

The project experienced some difficulties. Some local leaders felt the process was politically subversive. It is a short step, claimed one observer, from inviting people to express their views about food aid to their asking why food shortages had arisen at all and what their elected representatives were doing about it. Power politics between adults and children surfaced. Some guardians and community chiefs were concerned that children participating in community decisions would undermine adult authority. These worries largely abated, because of the practical solutions children came up with and the respectful way they communicated with their elders.

The responsibility of conveying the views of their peers was intimidating for some children. But despite initial reservations, all reacted positively to the chance to acquire skills of communication, information gathering, representation and democracy. Rather than simply improving food aid delivery, the project empowered children to embrace responsible decision-making, a capacity they will hopefully carry with them long after the emergency is over. As the mother of one child committee member said, "The children were equipped with information on child rights. They managed to get feedback from their peers and keep it confidential. They gained leadership skills and learned to respect one another, especially children in more difficult circumstances. My own daughter has changed the way she used to treat her stepbrother. She encourages everyone in the family to be more sensitive to his needs."

The project's success has prompted SCF to set up committees in other parts of the country, which will eventually provide significant feedback on both emergency and development programmes. As Zimbabwe heads for another year of food crisis, promoting the realization of humanitarian accountability remains a priority. ■

the need to flee for safety was given by trusted sources helped. Many believed that a sense of staying together and keeping track of the news by listening to 'Dimtshi Hafash', the popular national radio station, had protected them from 'Chinquet' (mental oppression)."

The Belgian Red Cross found that giving out scientific information after the tsunami was helpful in dispelling the idea that the event was a punishment from god, and this in turn helped people to recover more quickly (see Chapter 5). Similarly, after the Gujarat earthquake, the Self Employed Women's Association (SEWA), a large community-based women's organization, spread information about earthquakes to counteract the belief of some survivors that they had been cursed by god and that efforts to recover were useless.

Some neglected sections of the population may be particularly in need of information. Children are easily bewildered by disasters, but adults often forget to tell them what is happening. An International Federation team, visiting families in Sri Lanka affected by the tsunami, found "only very few activities to provide information and support to children. Adults are all busy with their own experiences". Save the Children also recognized this need and developed programmes to help children understand what happened. But there may be other social groups that remain neglected.

Some aid organizations have become involved in helping people trace relatives and friends missing after disaster, but the systems usually take time to become established, while the most acute needs are in the first few days. In response to the tsunami, the ICRC deployed mobile 'family links teams' to reunite survivors and relatives, often by satellite phone. The names of 47,000 missing or wanted people were registered and distributed on posters and via the Internet (see Chapter 5, Box 5.4). The French NGO Télécoms sans Frontières provided free mobile phone services so that tsunami survivors could talk with friends and relatives, but this only operated for a short time in a few locations. Food was distributed everywhere, but not mobile phones.

All aid agencies are likely to gather information about individuals after a disaster or have the capacity to do so. But they tend to focus on getting their own programmes running and, by the time they turn their attention to tracing, local people may have found their own solutions. It is an area in which agencies could be more effective.

Local media often play a critical role in providing information during disasters but receive very little help from outside. In Sri Lanka, a local radio station reported that they were deluged with requests to broadcast information about missing people. The station dedicated programme time to interviews and exchanges with survivors in relief camps (see Chapter 5, Box 5.2).

International Federation
of Red Cross and Red Crescent Societies

In Aceh and Sri Lanka, it was a media organization, Internews, rather than aid agencies, which supported locally-based reporting of humanitarian information after the tsunami. With local broadcast capacity devastated, Internews assembled out-of-work Acehnese journalists to produce a two-hour emergency radio programme on rehabilitation and reconstruction, called *Peuneugah Aceh* (News from Aceh). They distributed over 180 digital radio receivers to local radio stations and camps for displaced people. In Sri Lanka, the organization set up two mobile radio production units to train local journalists and produce daily tsunami-related reports in local languages (see Chapter 7, Box 7.6).

Radio is a relatively old-fashioned medium of communication, but is often more accessible for poor people than other media, especially for women in their homes. With wind-up or solar-powered radios, listeners don't need electricity or batteries. Skilfully produced programmes can go beyond simple exchanges of information by using role modelling and entertaining soap operas to promote greater awareness of risks such as landmines or infectious diseases. In Afghanistan, evaluations of the BBC's long-running radio soap opera *New Home, New Life* have shown that listeners change their attitudes and behaviour after hearing the drama (see Chapter 7).

With greater focus on information, aid agencies could make creative use of these opportunities to convey sophisticated messages.

Mapping risk in disaster and conflict

Under the Red Cross Red Crescent's Code of Conduct, aid agencies must strive to reduce future vulnerability and not just address the immediate results of disaster. Gathering and sharing information is a basic component of disaster risk reduction.

In India, the Gujarat-based Disaster Mitigation Institute (DMI) was asked to develop disaster mitigation-related posters for schools, but found that these were ignored unless accompanied by an ongoing process of dialogue, discussion and training. Working with children, teachers and parents, DMI developed risk plans for each school and helped local communities map their own risks and devise preparedness systems. Because these were developed in a participatory way, the information had already been internalized and the various obstacles and eventualities foreseen.

DMI observed: "The aim is to ensure that disaster mitigation efforts are not top-down, but rather based on information that comes directly from the community. Information that may be put on maps includes showing which buildings suffered severe earthquake damage, hazard prone areas such as areas subject to flooding, and villagers' desire for improved infrastructure (bus stops, water facilities etc). The key actors in this process go beyond the government, donors and experts to include vulnerable families, local organizations, traditional leaders and local practitioners."

In complex emergencies, especially conflicts, the quality and type of information needed are much higher. Risk mapping cannot only consider direct threats and logical responses, but also a changing pattern of tensions and relationships. Risks can be increased or reduced by factors such as inequality and social division. Different factors interact with each other and may vary depending on whether they are viewed locally, nationally or internationally. Conflict also involves propaganda, which implies deliberate distortion of information. In conflict it may not be enough to find out the 'truth'; perception also matters. An expanding literature has drawn particular attention to the way in which aid agencies become part of the political economy of conflict.

DFID has developed a methodology for analysing conflict based on drawing up 'maps' of causes, which can be superimposed on a similar map of responses. This shows how aid interacts with conflict, reveals gaps and helps agencies to devise strategies that integrate an understanding of conflict. Instead of making a few superficial adjustments based on general 'conflict-sensitive' or 'do no harm' principles, the methodology models the complexity of information about a specific conflict. ActionAid, Tearfund and others have now developed this into a participatory format linked to conventional methods of risk mapping.

Such methods are beginning to yield significant results. In Nepal, DFID found that it was perceived to be too close to urban elites who constituted a specific 'side' in the conflict. In order to be neutral, it needed to monitor who were its staff, where they were working and with whom. This led to a new approach to transparency and accountability which included, among other things, pledges to improve communication by producing an annual report on DFID's performance and impact in English and local languages.

Violence often pervades societies in countries not torn by war. Development in South Asia, for example, is characterized by high levels of violence against certain social groups. This is not 'conflict' but part of ongoing risk in the lives of poor people. As economist Amartya Sen has shown, the problem is not so much poverty or even disaster but 'downside risk' – the danger that, as a result of a personal crisis or national disaster, poor people may slide into total destitution. While rapid responses after disaster may be necessary, they won't remove the underlying insecurity, the endless series of threats and shocks that vulnerable people experience. Putting this centre-stage under the name 'human security', Sen has combined development and relief perspectives, peaceful situations and conflict, into a single concept.

In doing so, Sen has demonstrated that the artificial distinctions made by aid agencies between relief and development, conflict and peace, reflect a desire to oversimplify the management of information – above all to take an aid agency perspective rather than

Box 1.4 Participatory action learning during Nepal floods

During July 2004, unusually heavy monsoon rains lashed Nepal, causing devastating landslides in hill areas and floods in the plains. Nearly 200 people died and 800,000 were affected across a third of the country. Parts of southern Nepal were submerged for two weeks and 68,000 homes were damaged or destroyed. The Nepal Red Cross Society (NRCS), which has nationwide reach, led the relief effort.

Before the disaster, the NRCS had initiated community-based disaster preparedness (CBDP) activities in half the flood-affected districts. While relief operations were ongoing, the NRCS, supported by the International Federation, launched a 'participatory action learning' (PAL) process, to assess how CBDP helped communities during the floods. Through field-based interviews with affected people, the NRCS learned much about the positive and negative aspects of their preparedness and response operations.

As part of their preparedness, villagers collected a few kilos of rice and wheat from every household each month. This pre-positioning of food supplies proved vitally important to stranded villagers during the disaster. And while NRCS had stockpiled 30,000 'non-food family packs' in their warehouses, survivors said it was food not family packs that they most needed immediately after the disaster. Meanwhile, the PAL team found that village 'teacher sponsors', who had been recruited as volunteers to promote disaster preparedness, played a key role during the floods. Some spontaneously carried out needs assessments and relief distributions.

In areas benefiting from CBDP, women were actively involved in rescue and response. They used megaphones to warn people to evacuate. They were the ones stockpiling food. Women said they felt more powerful after taking part in CBDP and the training motivated them to send their children to school and to increase their awareness of health, sanitation and first aid. "We now know there is strength and support in unity," said one woman in the village of Dhabauli.

However, women felt their priorities during the disaster response, such as accessing safe drinking water and clean, private sanitation, especially if pregnant, were not sufficiently understood by relief teams. Part of the problem was that men, including village leaders, conducted the needs assessments. They also said that women were not sufficiently represented within NRCS management.

In Kolhuwa village, the community, with support from the NRCS, had constructed an embankment to protect them from the river. Their village was left unscathed, but their embankment diverted floodwaters towards the far bank, flooding another unprotected village. Since then, the NRCS has begun to assess the wider, unintended impacts of disaster mitigation structures.

For Sanjeev Kafley, NRCS's disaster management director at the time of the floods, a key lesson was that needs assessment and relief distribution have to go together. "Seeking only information may lead to frustration and lack of cooperation among people affected, putting relief workers' security at risk," he said.

Teija Lehtonen, of the Finnish Red Cross, who initiated the PAL, points out differences between PAL and normal evaluations: "It's the process that counts and not just the end product. The key issue is the ownership of the process by the NRCS; they wrote the terms of reference. It's important that they accept the criticism as they've conducted the PAL and written the report." In April 2005, the NRCS began to address the gender issue by conducting a course to train women as leaders in disaster response. ∎

the perspective of people in need. Big organizations need simple methods of handling and presenting information, but this can lead to distortions in strategy.

Some agencies are grappling with the problem of handling complex information in a way that reflects multiple perspectives. In Darfur, Tearfund developed a three-step method to strengthen communities in a conflict situation. The first stage was to map the capacities and vulnerabilities of local people through a participatory process, using focus groups and discussions. This information was processed in a formal workshop involving Sudanese people, notably Tearfund local staff. Drawing on the DFID methodology, the workshop mapped security, political, economic and social aspects of the situation at different levels. The results were absorbed into Tearfund's strategy and fed back into discussions with villagers.

One of the key outcomes for Tearfund was a better understanding of villagers' attitudes towards their attackers, especially their capacity to understand the attackers' point of view. Desertification in the north and uncertainty about land rights had put unbearable pressure on particular herding groups, which were easily manipulated by others. Underlying the war was a common interest in creating a sustainable balance between the interests of farmers and pastoralist herders. This opened the way for dialogue and, more distantly perhaps, reconciliation.

The problem is that the quality of information arising from such processes may outstrip the capacity of the agency to handle it. It remains to be seen whether organizations will adapt to cope with such systems or make do with what is more easily absorbed.

Media's partial picture of global needs

Media reports draw attention to events, people or issues considered to be of interest to their users. The Indian Ocean tsunami dominated the headlines partly because Western tourists were affected. Such has been the power of the media that around £350 million (US$ 640m) was raised by the British public alone (via the Disasters Emergencies Committee appeal). This figure was ten times more than the amount raised for the Darfur crisis, which by May 2005 had caused an estimated 180,000 deaths and forced another 2 million people from their homes. At the same time, in western Africa, over 3 million people in Niger were left desperately hungry after protracted drought and locust swarms – but a UN appeal for just US$ 16 million to feed them had attracted only a fifth of the funds two months after being launched (see Chapter 3). According to Médecins sans Frontières (MSF), the "top 10 most under-reported humanitarian stories" of 2004 accounted for just one minute of the 14,561 minutes of nightly news reporting on the three major US television networks (see Chapter 6, Box 6.1).

Some aid agencies readily admit that some of the tsunami money would be better spent elsewhere. A week after the disaster, MSF France closed its overflowing appeal

International Federation
of Red Cross and Red Crescent Societies

and drew attention to less high-profile disasters that desperately needed aid funding, such as deaths from tuberculosis or the suffering in Chechnya. In the Democratic Republic of the Congo, the International Rescue Committee has used mortality surveys to demonstrate that 3.8 million people have died in the crisis since 1998. By early 2005, people were still dying at a rate of 1,000 a day, but the story received little media attention. As the BBC's Fergal Keane said, "Congo is seen as too dangerous, remote and mystifying by many in the mainstream media."

Aid agencies have blamed the media for not drawing attention to the world's 'forgotten crises', but very few have steadfastly focused on the places and people in greatest need. Instead, agencies have tended to follow the flow of events and resources. Evidence suggests that the media are actually giving more coverage to humanitarian disasters than in the past, but there is insufficient dialogue between agencies and the media. Aid organizations have not handled the media as effectively as they might or provided exactly the kind of information they need (see Chapter 6).

The root of the problem may lie in a competitive attitude between aid agencies and a fear that telling the truth about global needs will cause public confusion and disengagement. But the tsunami has shown that this process can reach an absurd level with huge amounts of aid targeted to high-profile disasters, while other crises go totally neglected. Better public information and understanding may be the answer. But only by cooperating together can agencies begin to tackle this issue, and they will not get far without engaging the media.

Dialogue with donor governments is also critically important. Donors base funding decisions on many factors other than media coverage or available information: security, accessibility and national interest all play a part. But as the *translators* of humanitarian need to the wider world, aid organizations could do far more to communicate the urgency of neglected crises to donors, the media and the wider public.

The impact of technology

Information technology presents new possibilities but does not necessarily bring about change. Data on web sites may be inaccessible to vulnerable communities simply because of language barriers or lack of Internet access. Some technology is not yet widely available because of cost. But this limitation is eroding rapidly and agencies need to focus on the opportunities opening up. If language is a problem, web sites can be made available in local languages. If cost is the problem, then aid organizations could sponsor access to technology.

The tsunami may mark a turning point. New forms of people-to-people communication have shown their effectiveness, without involving international agencies. One example is the case of 'blogs' (web-logs). According to Rasika Dhavse, writing for *Indiatogether.org* on 17 January 2005, "As media channels broke the news soon after the tsunamis hit the coasts, bloggers had already started making use of their spaces by putting up detailed information about this natural phenomenon. They kept up the work with compilations of the latest death toll, names of missing persons, aid agencies, links to updated news about relief and rescue, the areas that are being sidelined by the media, the kind of relief materials urgently needed on the ground, requests for aid, and so on." Dhavse added that bloggers, who are not under pressure from the deadlines and competition that journalists face, tend to provide more realistic information.

Aid agencies could help make blogging sites more effective by providing information about themselves or specifying what information they are looking for. They could make the technology more widely available and use it as part of disaster preparedness. But there are also risks. People with enough time and money to run a blogging site are likely to belong to relatively elite social groups. They may use the site to attract attention to particular areas and people for inappropriate reasons. But local organizations and partner agencies could be encouraged to participate and maintain quality.

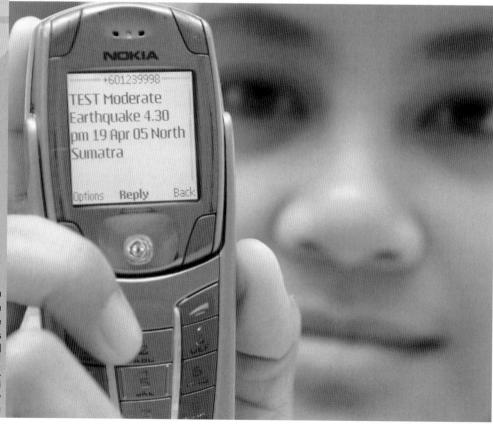

Advances in information technology provide exciting opportunities for early warning and risk reduction.

© REUTERS/Bazuki Muhammad, courtesy www.alertnet.org

International Federation of Red Cross and Red Crescent Societies

Relief and risk reduction have been revolutionized by mobile phones, but local organizations are sometimes at a disadvantage compared to richer international agencies. After Gujarat's 2001 earthquake, the women's union SEWA distributed 200 mobile phones to its staff, using its own resources. Instead of returning to headquarters, they were able to stay in the field for long periods, communicating with each other while travelling. Mobile phones were given to local volunteers in affected villages. Aid organizations could be more active in funding such initiatives as a form of capacity building.

SEWA also used satellite TV to conduct video-conferences with its staff across the earthquake-affected region and to interview officials in front of an audience of affected people. When invited to meet the finance minister in Delhi, SEWA took a video camera and transmitted the proceedings live to hundreds of its members, 1,000 kilometres away in Gujarat. Villagers could even put their views directly to the minister.

A group of international and local organizations have collaborated to create RANET, an initiative "to make weather, climate, and related information more accessible to remote and resource poor populations", especially in West Africa. RANET combines conventional technology, including community radio and satellite transmissions, with unconventional sources of power, including solar and wind energy, so that systems can be established in areas without mains electricity. But RANET provides more than just early warning. "Weather and climate information is not enough for communities to make decisions about resource management or long-term development. For instance, while providing agro-meteorological bulletins, often community farmers require crop prices, general agricultural practice tips, and animal husbandry information," it observes.

Improved forms of communications technology can open up new ways of reducing vulnerability. SEWA plans to link its disaster preparedness centres to commodity markets so that farmers can get instant information about crop prices and prospects. This will help them assess the risk of selling crops in advance to merchants or waiting until harvest.

All these possibilities come with a cost tag attached. They are unconventional and largely invisible ways of helping. They do not fit into agency definitions, sectors and processes. But greater support from international agencies is essential if local organizations are to reap the full benefit. Information and communications technology must be recognized as a form of aid in itself.

Conclusions and recommendations

There is plenty of money in the international disaster relief system for responses to high-profile disasters, but not for those that take place off the media radar. There is status and profile for agencies that exploit the myth of helpless victims. The need to get information takes precedence over the need to give it. Information from the perspective of vulnerable people, about ongoing struggles for human security, attracts less attention than stories about what Westerners and their aid agencies are doing. Competition rather than information often drives the international response. The system is top-down and excludes information that flows the other way.

But there are factors that limit or go against the trend. The Red Cross Red Crescent's Code of Conduct calls on agencies to involve local people in decision-making. The Sphere Project's humanitarian standards have created what is in effect a 'right to information'. The first common standard is that: "Women and men of all ages from the disaster-affected and wider local populations, including vulnerable groups, receive information about the assistance programme, and are given the opportunity to comment to the assistance agency during all stages of the project cycle."

Secondly, local organizations are becoming more pervasive, more competent and more demanding. They are beginning to pick up on some of the promises and demand their fulfilment. Techniques such as 'public auditing' practised at the local level may come back to haunt international agencies. One day they too may have to face a barrage of questions from well-informed, confident 'beneficiaries'.

Thirdly, the spread of technology is putting more power into the hands of vulnerable people and their communities. The tsunami disaster has shown that if aid agencies do not provide what people most need, such as early warning and family tracing, they will provide it for themselves.

Information, of course, is a form of power. Within the global disaster system, flows of information reflect a power relationship based on concepts of giver and receiver. Do aid organizations use information to accumulate power for themselves or to empower others?

Ways forward include:
- Recognizing information as a form of disaster response in its own right.
- Communicating the urgency of neglected crises to donors, the media and the wider public.
- Sharing information from disaster assessments.
- Promoting public auditing at all levels of disaster response.
- Supporting better access to information and communications technology for vulnerable communities.
- Building information-sharing partnerships with local government and civil society networks.

Principal contributor to Chapter 1 was Tony Vaux, who worked with Oxfam for 27 years, including nine years as the organization's global emergencies coordinator. He is now an independent consultant specializing in disaster response evaluation and conflict issues. Box 1.1 was taken from 'Phone call saved scores of Indian villagers from tsunami' by Chin Saik Yoon, which appeared in the December 2004 Digital Review of Asia Pacific. *Box 1.2 was contributed by Jeremy Loveless and Hisham Khogali of the International Federation. Chris McIvor, of Save the Children UK, contributed Box 1.3 and Jonathan Walter, editor of the* World Disasters Report, *contributed Box 1.4.*

Sources and further information

Active Learning Network for Accountability and Performance in Humanitarian Action (ALNAP). *The Case of Guinea.* London: ALNAP Global Study on Beneficiary Consultation and Participation, 2004. Available at http://www. alnap.org/alnappubs.html

ALNAP. *ALNAP Practitioners' Handbook.* Draft. London: ALNAP. Available at http://www.alnap.org/alnappubs.html

ALNAP. *ALNAP Review of Humanitarian Action in 2003.* London: ALNAP, 2004. Available at http://www.alnap.org/alnappubs.html

Almedom, A. 'Factors that mitigate war-induced anxiety and mental illness', *Journal of Biological Sciences*, No. 36, 2004.

Darcy, J. and Hofmann, C.-A. *According to need? Needs assessment and decision-making in the humanitarian sector.* HPG Report 15. London: Overseas Development Institute, 2003.

Department for International Development (DFID). *Conducting Conflict Assessments: Guidance Notes.* London: DFID, 2001.

DFID. *Nepal Country Assistance Plan.* London: DFID, 2004.

Disasters Emergency Committee (DEC). *Independent Evaluation: The DEC Response to the Earthquake in Gujarat.* London: DEC, 2001. Available at http://www.dec.org.uk/index.cfm/asset_id,905/index.html

DEC. *Independent Evaluation: The DEC Response to the Floods in Mozambique.* London: DEC, 2000.

Disaster Mitigation Institute (DMI). *Learning at Disaster Mitigation Institute.* Experience Learning Series No. 26. Ahmedabad, India: DMI, 2004.

International Federation. *Code of Conduct for the International Red Cross and Red Crescent Movement and NGOs in Disaster Relief.* Geneva: International Federation, 1995. Available at http://www.ifrc.org/publicat/conduct/index.asp

International Federation. *World Disasters Report.* Geneva: International Federation, 2002.

International Federation. *Guidelines for emergency assessment.* Geneva: International Federation, forthcoming.

International Federation. *Psychosocial assessment as part of the Federation's Field Assessment and Coordination Team in Sri Lanka*. Unpublished report, 2005.

Le Billon, P. *The Political Economy of War: an annotated bibliography*. HPG Report 1. London: Overseas Development Institute, 2000.

McCluskey, J. and Choudhury, Z. *Assessment and Scoping Report, Aceh, Indonesia*. Joint quality and accountability initiative. 4-13 February 2005.

Save the Children (UK). *Children's Feedback Committees in Zimbabwe – An Experiment in Humanitarian Accountability*. Harare: SCF-UK, 2005.

Sen, Amartya. *Human Security Now – protecting and empowering people*. Commission on Human Security. New York, 2003.

Sphere Project. *Humanitarian Charter and Minimum Standards in Disaster Response*. Oxford: Oxfam, 2004.

Twigg, J. *Disaster Risk Reduction – mitigation and preparedness in development and emergency programming*. HPN Good Practice Review Number 9. London: Overseas Development Institute, 2004.

Web sites

ALNAP **http://www.alnap.org**
Digital Review of Asia Pacific **http://www.digital-review.org/ahp01.htm**
Good Humanitarian Donorship **http://www.reliefweb.int/ghd/**
India Together **http://www.indiatogether.org**
International Federation **http://www.ifrc.org**
Médecins sans Frontières **http://www.msf.org**
RANET **http://www.ranetproject.net**
Reuters Alertnet **http://www.alertnet.org**
SEWA **http://www.sewa.org**
Tearfund **http://www.tearfund.org**

Run, tell your neighbour! Hurricane warning in the Caribbean

"Oh man! How this Ivan has made us work," said one 54-year-old Havana resident, speaking to a reporter from the *Miami Herald* on 14 September 2004. "I am dead," he added, explaining how he'd prepared for the most intense hurricane to hit the Caribbean since records began. "I took everything up off the floor, nailed things in place and to the wall and all the doors and drawers shut. I put paper and plastic over everything. I took all the lamps off the ceiling, moved all the furniture to the walls, put things up in the closet… I hurt everywhere."

In early 2004, experts had predicted that the 2004 Atlantic hurricane season was set to be one of the worst in decades. They were not wrong. From August to November, 15 tropical cyclones raked the region, nine of which were hurricanes (see map). At least 2,000 people were killed during a six-week period – most of them in Haiti, but 152 of them in the United States. Hundreds of thousands were left homeless. Economic losses totalled over US$ 60 billion. Insurers carried half of this amount, making 2004 "the most expensive hurricane season ever for the insurance industry", according to Munich Re.

In mid-August, Charley swept across Cuba and slammed into the United States. Two weeks later, Hurricane Frances, a storm the size of Texas, span through the Bahamas and prompted the biggest evacuation in Florida's history, as nearly 2.5 million people fled their homes. In early September, 'Ivan the Terrible', a category 4-5 hurricane packing winds of around 250 kilometres an hour (see Table 2.1), damaged or

Table 2.1 The Saffir-Simpson hurricane scale

Category	Maximum sustained winds – kilometres per hour (miles per hour)	Storm surge – metres (feet) above normal	Potential damage
1	118–153 (74–95)	1.2–1.5 (4–5)	Minimal
2	154–177 (96–110)	1.8–2.4 (6–8)	Moderate
3	178–209 (111–130)	2.7–3.7 (9–12)	Extensive
4	210–250 (131–155)	4–5.5 (13–18)	Extreme
5	> 250 (> 155)	> 5.5 (> 18)	Catastrophic

Photo opposite page: José Rubiera, Cuba's chief weather forecaster, tells Cuban president Fidel Castro about the path of Hurricane Ivan during a live television broadcast in Havana (12 September 2004.

© REUTERS/ Ismael Francisco, courtesy www.alertnet.org

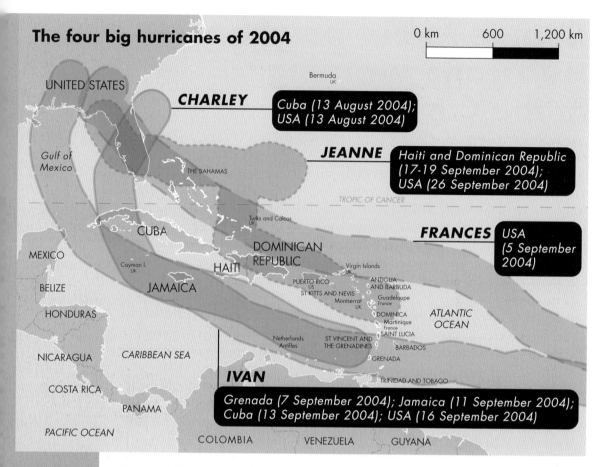

The four big hurricanes of 2004

0 km · 600 · 1,200 km

UNITED STATES

Bermuda
UK

CHARLEY Cuba (13 August 2004);
USA (13 August 2004)

Gulf of
Mexico

THE BAHAMAS

JEANNE Haiti and Dominican Republic
(17-19 September 2004);
USA (26 September 2004)

TROPIC OF CANCER

Turks and Caicos
UK

CUBA

DOMINICAN
REPUBLIC

FRANCES USA
(5 September
2004)

MEXICO

Cayman I.
UK

HAITI

JAMAICA

Virgin Islands
UK

PUERTO RICO
US
ST KITTS AND NEVIS
Montserrat
UK

ANTIGUA
AND BARBUDA
Guadeloupe
France
DOMINICA
Martinique
France
SAINT LUCIA

ATLANTIC
OCEAN

BELIZE

HONDURAS

NICARAGUA

CARIBBEAN SEA

Netherlands
Antilles

ST VINCENT AND
THE GRENADINES

BARBADOS

GRENADA

COSTA RICA

PANAMA

IVAN

TRINIDAD AND TOBAGO

Grenada (7 September 2004); Jamaica (11 September 2004);
Cuba (13 September 2004); USA (16 September 2004)

PACIFIC OCEAN

COLOMBIA

VENEZUELA

GUYANA

destroyed 90 per cent of Grenada's buildings, before inflicting further damage on the Cayman Islands, Jamaica and the United States. Then in mid-September, Jeanne dumped record rains on Haiti and the Dominican Republic, leading to deadly floods and mud torrents.

This chapter analyses the impact of three of the fiercest hurricanes – Charley, Ivan and Jeanne – on the islands of the western Caribbean. Haiti suffered by far the greatest human toll: over 1,800 dead and 800 missing, according to the country's civil protection directorate. Yet Cuba, Jamaica and the Dominican Republic, while hit very hard physically and economically, suffered relatively low death tolls. Why? Geography and politics play their part. But much of the difference between living and dying comes down to knowledge and warning.

What information was available, when and how was it shared? What level of local awareness and preparedness was there? And were people at risk able to take action to protect themselves? The chapter reveals that local organization and awareness working from 'below' are just as important as timely and accurate high-tech warnings from 'above'.

✚C International Federation
of Red Cross and Red Crescent Societies

Cuba: leading the way

Civil defence in Cuba is seen as a matter of national security, whether the adversary is natural or human. During 2004's hurricane season, the country again proved how effective it is in protecting human life from the worst of the weather. When Charley swept into Cuba on 13 August 2004, 70,000 houses were severely damaged and four people died. When Ivan brushed the country's western tip a month later, over 2 million people were evacuated but no one lost their lives.

Cuba has a world-class meteorological institute, with 15 provincial offices. They share data with the United States National Hurricane Center (NHC) and produce their own computer models that project storm tracks. During each hurricane season, the media begin to alert the population 72 hours before a storm's projected landfall. Provincial and local civil protection committees are mobilized and begin checking evacuation plans and shelters. National television, radio and newspapers all play a key role in publicizing the potential threat (see Box 2.1). Cubans call this the "informational phase".

When the storms are 48 hours away, authorities can target warnings at areas most likely to be affected. Then local and neighbourhood committees begin to check on

Box 2.1 Cuban met office meets the media

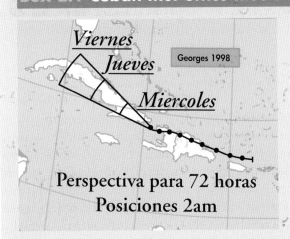

Viernes
Jueves   Georges 1998
Miercoles

Perspectiva para 72 horas
Posiciones 2am

The illustration above shows a 'cone of error' superimposed on a map of Cuba, as shown on national TV and on front pages of newspapers, shortly before Hurricane Georges hit in 1998. It gives the forecast for the next 72 hours. When any storm approaches the island, the forecasting of its precise track is open to a margin of error. On average the error is over 700 kilometres when the storm is five days away, decreasing to less than 150 km the day before it arrives.

The Cuban meteorological institute explains this to the general public through broadcast and print media so they understand the uncertainty involved in forecasting and accept evacuation or other preparedness measures within a fairly large 'risk area'. The literacy among ordinary Cubans is so high that most of them understand and value these explanations. During the last 48 hours before a hurricane hits Cuba, there are frequent radio and TV bulletins – plus old footage and photomontages from previous hurricanes – to emphasize the warning. ■

Graphic courtesy of José Rubiera, director of Cuba's National Forecasting Center.

vulnerable people, making sure that anyone in dangerous locations or with special needs – such as blind people or pregnant women – can evacuate. Within 12 hours of the hurricane striking, everyone who needs to be evacuated should be in shelters, homes must be secured, windows boarded up and neighbourhoods cleared of loose debris that can fly around and cause damage. These are the legal norms and requirements in Cuba, and they were enforced during Charley and Ivan.

In Cuba, evacuation orders are mandatory – an important distinction from neighbouring countries. Public transport is provided to get people to shelters. Local branches of the *Federación de Mujeres Cubanas* (Federation of Cuban Women) help persuade reluctant people to accept evacuation, so it is only rarely that the police or army have to step in.

Designated shelters include schools and other public buildings, which are provided with food, water, blankets and, in some cases, entertainment. "We have a building in the Ministry of Fisheries where we take pregnant women and breastfed babies," says Juan Francisco Perdomo, head of civil protection for Santa Fe, a seafront town of 21,000 people on the western outskirts of Havana. "This shelter is in front of the main hospital, just in case of an emergency... The shelter has 25 beds. During Charley three babies were born, two girls and a boy."

The danger of hurricanes is taught in schools and each year in May, before the beginning of the hurricane season, there are reminders and drills for the public. Most adults are reasonably well educated, so it is easy for them to understand what officials and weather scientists tell them.

This sounds too good to be true, but several independent studies on the ground have concluded that the system actually works as it is designed to. During a recent study for the *World Disasters Report*, researchers interviewed local government officials in Santa Fe, which during Hurricane Charley recorded gusts of up to 250 km/h. Santa Fe has 203 neighbourhood 'Committees for the Defence of the Revolution'. They keep records on vulnerable people, such as those aged over 65, the disabled, parents with newborns and people living in low-lying areas, so that it is easy to evacuate them to one of the council's five shelters on higher ground. Santa Fe has a dedicated disaster management unit of 22 people who coordinate efforts and have access to four vehicles and megaphones for reinforcing the warnings that are broadcast on television and radio.

Cuba is highly organized and what happens at the local and neighbourhood levels in Santa Fe are the fourth and fifth tiers of a system of government and civil defence that ascends through municipality and province to the national apex. Hence, Santa Fe's officials are directly coordinated and supported, via two-way radio, by the municipal-level civil defence, which receives weather updates by e-mail.

International Federation
of Red Cross and Red Crescent Societies

The municipality has advance, written agreements with bakeries, electricians, family doctors and others who can be called upon if needed. Municipal authorities also take the larger picture into account. For example, when in flood, the nearby River Jaimanita could isolate part of Santa Fe, so during the 2004 hurricane season, the municipality sent an additional medical brigade into that area in case it was temporarily isolated.

Santa Fe's officials don't rely only on national and provincial weather forecasters, but draw on the experience and expertise of residents. "I was a sailor and know the coastal zone very well; in Santa Fe I can feel when there is a risk from the sea approaching," says Carlos Beltran, vice president of the popular council. "In the case of Charley, we started an early mobilization before the national warning and, after this, we were totally ready." Another resident, Pilolo, is a blind man known for being able to predict a storm surge by the direction of the wind and the smell of the salty air. This knowledge is respected and used by civil protection authorities.

When Hurricane Ivan approached less than a month later, again the full Cuban alert system went into high gear. Because Ivan was so powerful, ten times more people were evacuated than during Charley. Ivan's path spared much of Cuba in the end, but the precautions paid off: no one died.

Cuba's record at protecting its people from hurricanes is impressive. However, José Rubiera, director of Cuba's National Forecasting Center, is not complacent. When asked by the United Nations (UN) International Strategy for Disaster Reduction (ISDR) if there was room for improvement, he replied: "We have to improve our educational and information systems. Four people died in Hurricane Charley, which is too many. Some people are still not reacting correctly to the alerts. There is a lack of vigilance. When we asked the people to evacuate the Havana dykes at 9 in the morning, some people delayed until 1 pm, so it was too late when the big waves hit the coast."

Jamaica: preparedness pays off

After Hurricane Ivan ploughed through Grenada, Jamaica braced itself for the worst. On 10 September, the day before it arrived, the prime minister went on national radio and television. He reminded Jamaicans what had happened when Hurricane Gilbert scoured the island for eight hours from east to west in 1988: 45 dead, half a million made homeless, a billion dollars of damage. He added that, a few days earlier, Ivan had killed 39 people in Grenada. Jamaica's meteorology office benefits from the forecasting models of the United States' NHC, which have become more and more accurate. Twelve hours before Ivan hit, forecasts of where the storm would make landfall were good to within 50 km – very accurate indeed.

Jamaica is divided into administrative areas called parishes, which are further divided into local government councils. In the parish of Saint Thomas to the east of the capital

Kingston, many people had already heard or seen the alerts put out by the Jamaican meteorology office and the national Office of Disaster Preparedness and Emergency Management (ODPEM). They had also seen reports from Grenada on CNN and other TV channels.

In the town of Yallahs, in Saint Thomas parish, Joshua Davis called together his volunteers who constitute one of the Jamaica Red Cross's community-based disaster response teams. They went from street to street issuing warnings – the 'final mile' so critical in ensuring that high-tech advice is converted into precautions on the ground (see Box 2.2). They warned local residents by cell phone; they checked that the

Box 2.2 Jamaica's community disaster response teams

"I was glad that I could warn them before the storm," says Patricia Greenleaf simply. Patricia is a member of the Jamaica Red Cross's community disaster response team (CDRT) for Cedar Valley. Along with dozens of other volunteers, she went from street to street issuing warnings by megaphone, 48 hours before Hurricane Ivan hit. They encouraged marginalized groups and people with special needs, including the elderly and mentally impaired, to hang a white flag or piece of material outside their home to signal that they needed help when the time came for evacuation.

Hurricane Ivan, the most powerful storm the Caribbean had seen for 50 years, had just pounded Grenada with winds of up to 250 kilometres an hour, killing 39 people and damaging or destroying 90 per cent of the island's buildings. The Jamaica Red Cross put all its branches and 12,000 volunteers on high alert. They opened 1,000 community shelters across the country.

When 'Ivan the Terrible' struck Jamaica on 11 September 2004, Patricia's team was ready. They had prepared a local map detailing potential risks and resources. They knew where Cedar Valley's most vulnerable people lived. They had drawn up a community response plan with the local Red Cross branch. They were already trained to carry out light search and rescue, emergency first aid and rapid assessment. And they were equipped with medical kits, megaphones, shovels, rope, waterproof boots and helmets. Despite widespread damage to property, no one in Cedar Valley died during the storm.

Across the country, 15,000 people sought refuge in 285 shelters. In Ivan's wake, the CDRT teams produced needs assessments and helped the Red Cross assist over 10,000 families with food and other emergency aid.

The Jamaica Red Cross has so far trained and certified 57 people as CDRT members in eight teams across the country. The development of CDRTs began in September 2003, with vulnerability and capacity assessments in eight communities at risk from windstorms and flooding. Community representatives took part in group exercises covering the key elements of disaster management, such as hazard recognition, risk reduction and networking with government and non-governmental agencies. The training encouraged them to take responsibility for their own communities' safety, through providing people with hurricane early warning and promoting resilience to disasters. ■

International Federation
of Red Cross and Red Crescent Societies

shelters were ready; they borrowed private vehicles to evacuate the blind and disabled. "We look for the most indigent, the most vulnerable, those who do not have anybody," says Davis, "and we know that we are the ones that are going to have to take them out and get them to the shelters."

By law, all schools in Jamaica become shelters and the prime minister had reminded school principals to hand over keys to ODPEM representatives in their areas. By the time the parish-level Red Cross director phoned to check, Joshua could report that preparations were already under way.

Meanwhile, the Saint Thomas parish disaster committee sent volunteers to watch rivers for signs of flooding and despatched others to issue special warnings to people who lived on slopes that they knew could slide during torrential rains. Further to the west, Saint Catherine parish staff collected the elderly and street people and took them to shelters or the local infirmary.

Since Hurricane Gilbert, there has been much improvement in Jamaica's ability to prepare for hurricanes and to warn its people. Cell phones have made a big difference. ODPEM has implemented a national disaster management plan through its local government disaster committees. It has mapped flood and landslide hazards in partnership with the national authorities responsible for water, mines and geology. And it has developed a model community-based flood warning system, which builds on the experience of other similar initiatives in the region (see Box 2.3).

In addition, according to ODPEM's director Barbara Carby, a public awareness programme is maintained year-round. "Anniversaries of major disaster events are used each year to focus attention on the hazard that caused the disaster," says Carby. "On the anniversary, the public is given information on prevention, preparedness, mitigation and response via electronic and print media." June – just before the hurricane season – is 'disaster preparedness month', during which awareness days, practice drills and displays are organized for schools and businesses. And ODPEM has developed a close relationship with Jamaican media, which gives it free prime-time access on many stations.

These factors helped keep the death toll during Hurricane Ivan down to 17. No one died in Yallahs or in neighbouring Cedar Valley, although two-thirds of inhabitants lost the roofs of their houses. Nevertheless, there was an element of luck. Ivan was even larger than Gilbert, but it only hit the south coast and centre of the island – and most of Ivan's rain fell into the sea.

A number of challenges remain. Despite a history of hurricanes, people still resist evacuation. According to Joshua Davis, some young Jamaicans just laugh at warnings. Others are reluctant to leave their possessions at home. Meanwhile, a basic level of

In 1998, Hurricane Mitch unleashed torrential rains over Honduras and Nicaragua, which triggered flooding and landslides, killing more than 20,000 people. However, this widespread pattern of death and injury was not seen in one municipality, La Masica, in the Atlantida province of Honduras. Although a nearby river, the Lean, flooded the town, causing much economic damage, none of the municipality's 25,000 people was killed.

The reason was that an early warning and risk management project, with the full involvement of La Masica's inhabitants, had been initiated a couple of years prior to Mitch. With collective memories of the impacts of Hurricane Fifi in 1974 and a series of other serious flooding incidents since then, the population of La Masica had sought to improve their preparedness and planning for such events. In the process, they managed to attract international attention and support for their work.

The project adopted participatory methods for risk mapping and the establishment of a local risk management organization that was well supported at both political and grass-roots levels. Local people observed the river flow, using simple flood meters, and reported back via radio. Many of those involved were local women. They made emergency plans for responding to reports of rising water radioed in by observers upriver.

Their success in preventing any deaths with low-cost technology and local participation contrasts with the major failure during Hurricane Mitch of a real-time flood warning system, installed in Honduras with international support at a cost of more than US$ 700,000. The system's river gauges were washed away and the satellite-based information system was not operating at the time, due to technical problems. La Masica's simple approach, based on people and radios, proved more resilient than the international system, based on sophisticated technology. ∎

literacy and education is important for understanding and acting on warnings – but some of Joshua's volunteers cannot read maps. And, with budget cuts of 12 per cent planned for the national disaster management system, the country may struggle to continue improving public safety in the face of future storms.

Dominican Republic: past experience proves unreliable

The Dominican Republic shares the island of Hispaniola with its neighbour Haiti. As in Haiti, extensive coastal plains give way inland to mountain ranges. When Jeanne – which had abated from a hurricane to a tropical storm – parked itself over the north of the island from 16 to 17 September, it dumped record amounts of rain. Rivers burst their banks and thousands of people sought sanctuary on rooftops. In all, 23 Dominicans died from the storm, 40,000 were rescued and nearly 2 million of the country's 8.5 million residents were affected.

The day before the storm arrived, the meteorological institute issued a warning and provided maps showing the storm's likely path, which were hand-delivered to municipal civil defence officials. National radio broadcast the warning and local radio stations relayed the message to their audiences. The Dominican Red Cross deployed five teams to make contact with local authorities and advise communities about the probable impacts of Jeanne.

News quickly reached even the smallest settlements – by a wide variety of means. Some people received long-distance phone calls from relatives living in Puerto Rico, an island hundreds of kilometres to the east, who had seen the storm approaching the Dominican Republic on television. Modern cell phone technology is in many places replacing traditional early warning technologies.

Rodney Pena is head of civil defence for Ramon Santana, a small town of 9,000 people, which lay directly in the hurricane's path. "The local civil defence waits for orders from the provincial director via cell phone," says Pena, "because there are no telephone lines in the community and the civil defence does not have radios in Ramon Santana." However, as Jeanne approached, Pena's boss also sent him a messenger with a map showing the hurricane's predicted track. Local mayors then took the message further into rural areas, on horseback or by motorcycle.

Recent disasters were in the forefront of people's minds. In September 1998, Hurricane Georges tore through 17 Caribbean islands, killing around 4,000 people – including 500 in the Dominican Republic. And in May 2004, just four months before Ivan, heavy rain triggered devastating landslides in Jimani, on the country's mountainous border with Haiti, which left 414 Dominicans dead, 274 missing and 13,000 homeless.

Both these disasters had been clouded by allegations of national government inaction and neglect. So officials were keen to demonstrate their professionalism. Meanwhile, most ordinary people believed the warnings for Jeanne, especially as they came from sources other than just the government.

However, people focused on the wind hazard, assuming that whatever flooding took place would be similar to what they had experienced on previous occasions. Some decided not to evacuate, because they had never been flooded before or lived in houses that could stand up to the wind. This proved to be a big mistake. In Ramon Santana, for example, the rainfall was intense – at one point, 100 millimetres fell in just 24 hours. The local River Soco flooded more severely than at any time in the past century.

Fortunately, the town's leaders, including the civil defence director, fire chief, police chief and two church leaders, kept vigil all night. They monitored the river and when it began rising to a dangerous level, they sounded the alarm. The town's main siren didn't work as the electricity grid had been turned off as a precaution. So they used an ambulance siren to wake people who had not yet evacuated. The siren also woke those who had returned home from the shelters after the wind died down, thinking that the danger was over. Some, like 93-year-old Angel Volquez, had to be physically carried away to a shelter by police, since he insisted that, during his long life, the family home had never been flooded.

In rural parts of Ramon Santana district, people did not hear the ambulance siren and awoke to find their wind-safe houses – including one belonging to a US baseball star – beginning to flood. They sought shelter as best they could. A family of 11 spent the rest of the night up a tree, until a local teacher rescued them on a homemade raft. Remarkably, no one was killed in Ramon Santana, although 4,000 people had to be rescued and 200 homes were destroyed.

Following Hurricane Georges, the Dominican Republic passed a new emergency law and created a nationwide civil defence system that cooperates with churches, non-governmental organizations (NGOs), youth groups and neighbourhood associations to get warnings out. Despite a lack of short-wave radios and telephone connections, a combination of local knowledge and efficient social networks allowed warnings to spread rapidly before Tropical Storm Jeanne.

However, some still did not get the warnings promptly. At Ramon Santana's school, for example, teachers didn't know of the approaching hurricane until mothers came to take their children home early. Some people didn't understand or trust the warnings. And past experience can prove a fickle guide. It may lead to greater hazard awareness, but it can mislead if something surprising like the River Soco flood occurs. Several of the country's 23 deaths happened when people tried to cross swollen rivers or were hit by flying debris when they left shelters – deaths which could have been avoided by even a basic level of risk awareness.

Haiti: one storm, two stories

Marie Luis Mondestin lost her first son to the flood. Like many Haitians, he never learned to swim. Mondestin told her story to Associated Press in late September 2004: "It was around 11 in the evening when suddenly the waters just shot up. He was trying to help us save things and then all of a sudden he just panicked and swallowed a whole load of water." Too poor to own a radio, Mondestin said she knew the storm was coming to Haiti but was not told it could affect Gonaives.

The torrential rains that Tropical Storm Jeanne poured on the northern flanks of Hispaniola ignored political frontiers. On the Haitian side, the deluge funnelled a deadly torrent of floodwater, mud and debris through mountain ravines and onto the plains. The coastal town of Gonaives was inundated. Witnesses reported that the flood rose by two metres in half an hour. At least 1,800 people died; another 800 remain missing. In all, 80 per cent of the town's 250,000 inhabitants were affected. Why did the same storm carry away 100 times more Haitians than Dominicans? Did the government know what was coming? Were people warned? Were they prepared?

First consider geography. Almost all of Haiti's steeply mountainous territory has been deforested. Jeanne's rains lashed nearly barren slopes, with just 1.4 per cent of their original tree cover. While flash flooding sometimes happens even on well-forested slopes, deforestation undoubtedly exacerbates the risk.

In political terms, Jeanne could not have come at a worse time. The sudden departure of Haiti's president, Jean-Bertrand Aristide, seven months earlier had left great instability and rioting in its wake. Early warning systems require a system of local government that can prepare people for an emergency, pass on warnings from the national centre, monitor events as they unfold locally, and assist in evacuation and sheltering. While in theory Haiti has such a system, during 2004's political violence, much of it didn't function.

Civil society and international organizations play an important role in supporting local government. For example, as Hurricane Ivan approached Haiti earlier in the 2004 season, the Haitian National Red Cross Society took primary responsibility along the southern coast for warning, evacuation and shelter. As Ivan approached, the Red Cross installed satellite telephones in three urban centres along a peninsula in the south of the country. The United Nations Development Programme (UNDP) had partnered with the Red Cross and others to invest in public education and preparedness in the same region. However, these organizations were not active further north. So people were successfully evacuated and sheltered as Ivan passed harmlessly to the south of the island, but not when Jeanne wrought her destruction on the island's north-western shores only weeks later.

Worse still, Gonaives was an epicentre of the political violence that led to the overthrow of Aristide. Consequently, its basic services – education, health and security – deteriorated, in a country where these were already scarce. Attempts to organize local disaster preparedness had been suspended or destroyed as offices were looted and officials fled. This left the town's people extremely vulnerable to natural hazards. Maintenance of the canals that drain the seaside town had long been abandoned. Refuse clogged them, making the flooding even more severe.

The national meteorological centre lacks resources: Haiti is the only country in the Caribbean that doesn't post its own hurricane warnings, depending entirely on forecasts and warnings issued by other islands and the United States' NHC. Haiti's civil protection office is relatively young (dating from 1999) and weak – its emergency operations centre wasn't working when Jeanne hit. While the civil protection office alerted its provincial offices of Jeanne's approach, the advance warning never made it as far as Gonaives. Even once the storm struck, most residents felt they would be protected from the wind by the very mountains channelling the deadly deluge towards them. They weren't prepared, because they had no idea what was about to hit them.

Haiti is no stranger to disasters. Four months before Jeanne, flash floods in the south smothered the town of Fonds Verretes with boulders and mud. Officially, 1,191 died; another 1,484 are still reported missing. In the past 60 years, a string of hurricanes has claimed the lives of around 17,000 Haitians. Clearly Haiti needs help to reinforce its preparedness and warning systems from top to bottom. UNDP has been working with the country's civil protection for several years, but with very little impact at the local level. Only 30 of 572 local authorities have any kind of disaster committee.

Nevertheless, there is potential to resurrect some basic elements of local warning and preparedness. Fishermen, for example, know the signs of an approaching storm, while farmers in the Arbonite Valley above Gonaives can tell by changes in the colour of river water when a flash flood is coming. Remnants remain of neighbourhood mutual aid arrangements that grew up in the years of 'popular organization' (1986–1994), during resistance to military dictatorship and the early days of Aristide's presidency. In the past, local marketplaces have been successfully used to disseminate hurricane warnings. Even traditional experts in sending long-distance messages by blowing on a

Tropical Storm Jeanne dumped colossal quantities of rain on both Haiti and the Dominican Republic. While 2,600 Haitians were reported dead or missing after devastating floods and landslides, 23 Dominicans died. Along with deforestation, the lack of early warning and preparedness proved fatal in Haiti.

Marko Kokic/
International Federation

International Federation
of Red Cross and Red Crescent Societies

conch shell have been incorporated into local government warning schemes. So too have local Catholic, Protestant and voodoo priests. But intensifying political violence and rapid urbanization have undermined much of this local expertise.

Secrets of success

Hurricane warning should be easy. The scientific understanding of hurricanes has grown rapidly in the past decade. Communications media, including the Internet, cell phones, radio and television, have seen explosive growth. However, conveying accurate, credible warnings to people at risk – in time for them to take preventive action – takes more than technology. What are the vital links in the early warning chain which make the difference between life and death in the face of some of the planet's most ferocious storms?

In all countries of the Caribbean the same pieces – with different names – have to come together:

- Hurricane forecasting.
- National warning.
- Local government diffusion.
- Civil society participation.
- Popular understanding and action.

Hurricane forecasting

Each national meteorological office (met office) in the Caribbean utilizes the US NHC's resources, which include satellite-based storm tracking, airborne data from planes that fly though hurricanes and computer modelling, which predicts the direction and speed of storms with more accuracy every year. Some countries, such as Cuba, supplement these forecasting tools with their own radar and computer models. Islands also share forecasts. NHC experts visit all countries in the region, apart from Cuba, each hurricane season. In turn, experts from Caribbean countries spend time at the NHC in Florida. Cuba is abreast of the latest advances at the NHC and shares its expertise with US forecasters and others through its membership of the World Meteorological Organization's hurricane forecasting committee.

However, challenges remain, particularly in terms of forecasting hurricane intensity. Hurricane Charley was a category 2 storm when it hit Cuba. But it suddenly intensified to a category 4 storm just before it hit Florida. Forecasters couldn't enter the data from the coming storm into their computer forecasting models quickly enough. "We've got a long way to go before we can really make skilful use of the data to predict the intensification of storms," said Chris Landsea, a meteorologist with the United States National Oceanic and Atmospheric Institution (NOAA), in an interview with *National Geographic News* in November 2004.

National warning

In theory, then, all Caribbean nations have access to accurate forecasts at least 72 hours – sometimes up to five days – in advance of a hurricane's landfall. The met office should then report to the national office of civil protection or a national disaster committee, so that a decision can be made to alert the population.

At national level, a distinction is made between 'early warning' that a storm may be three to five days away and a 'warning' that a dangerous storm may hit within 24 hours. While early warning should signal preparations for action, the warning itself should trigger local preventive action.

Cuba and Jamaica have stronger national systems than the Dominican Republic and Haiti, with a clearer chain of command, which integrates other government departments effectively. However, things have improved in the Dominican Republic. In 1998, the government provided warning of Hurricane Georges only as it began to hit the capital. In 2004, the authorities issued a warning 48 hours in advance, providing more than enough time for citizens and local teams to prepare.

Local government diffusion

Local government provides the vital link between national-level warnings and communities at risk. All four countries have systems three or four layers deep. Cuba and Jamaica have fully decentralized systems, comprising not only elected local councils but also officials from civil protection and other government departments. Critically, they have resources available for local-level warning and evacuation. In Haiti, while such a structure exists on paper, outside the nine provincial capitals, local government barely functions. In the Dominican Republic, there is more happening at local government level, but resources are scant and communications patchy.

While national radio and television may broadcast the warning to the most isolated corners of the country, it is local government that must team up with the national Red Cross and NGOs to ensure that people understand the warnings, shelters are ready, evacuation proceeds on time and people take appropriate action.

Furthermore, warnings must include localized detail. It is often not the storm surge at the coast or the wind that kills, but flash flooding and landslides (see Box 2.4). These 'secondary hazards' can be forecast, but this requires investment in hazard mapping and training local government and civil society to use the maps to issue supplementary, localized warnings. Cuba has 15 provincial met offices that add local detail to the national storm warnings. The other three countries do not. In the Dominican Republic and Jamaica, much of this kind of supplementary

International Federation
of Red Cross and Red Crescent Societies

Box 2.4 **Floods and landslides: the real killers**

Flash flooding – triggered by the torrential rains that often accompany hurricanes – has killed thousands of people in the Caribbean, from 1963's Hurricane Flora in Cuba to Tropical Storm Jeanne in Haiti in 2004. In hurricanes, far more people are killed by flooding and landslides than by wind-related hazards, such as being hit by flying objects, falling trees or collapsing houses.

Flood and landslide hazards are local. They need to be assessed by detailed hazard mapping months or years before a hurricane. They can also change dramatically as trees are cut or as land use and drainage are modified by human actions. As a result, such hazards prove harder to predict and warn of than high winds and coastal storm surges.

In Cuba, a nationwide proposal for mapping landslide hazards, at scales also appropriate for provincial and local warning and land use planning, has been developed in cooperation with international donors. To date, however, most hazard mapping is at the national scale, and thus not readily applicable for local actions to reduce risk. For example, Oxfam has produced flood and landslide maps for Haiti, but at the national scale.

In Jamaica, cooperation between the national disaster management office and the national authorities for water, mines and geology are an example of good practice. Working together, they have used donor funding to set up model community flood warning systems and to begin flood and landslide hazard mapping.

Engineering can help: Cuba, Japan and Hong Kong (China) have all reduced flood and landslide hazards through stabilization of slopes, check dams and drainage designs. ∎

warning already takes place, based on common sense and unwritten local knowledge. But this local improvisation needs to be formalized and supported with resources.

Local government is responsible for ongoing public education about hurricanes, plus preparedness efforts to reduce losses when the next hurricane hits. If local government is weak, the chain of warning and preparedness breaks apart.

Civil society participation

Nowhere, can the government do everything. Civil society must pitch in. But this means people must trust the government. In Haiti, political violence has rapidly eroded trust in government. Violence has hampered the ability of the authorities to improve people's lives, further reducing their respect and trust for local government – a vicious circle. Where government and civil society do not trust each other, hurricane warnings may be blocked or ignored.

In the Dominican Republic and Jamaica, youth associations, women's organizations, churches, the Red Cross and a wide variety of other NGOs take part in hurricane warning, evacuation and shelter management. When Hurricane Mitch hit Honduras in 1998, a community-based flood early warning system in La Masica municipality proved more resilient than the high-tech alternatives (see Box 2.3).

Since Mitch, National Red Cross Societies have worked with dozens of communities across the Caribbean to create risk maps and evacuation plans for their local areas. "The main issue is how to sustain these activities at least for the medium term," says Xavier Castellanos, regional disaster preparedness delegate for the International Federation. "Governments should put emphasis on community education programmes with sufficient budgets," he adds.

Popular understanding and action

Vital to Cuba's success in preventing storms from becoming disasters is the detailed comprehension of hurricane early warning possessed by ordinary people. Throughout the rest of the Caribbean, however, lack of education and literacy often prevents people from understanding warnings. Wind speeds and national alerts mean little to most of them. Even well-meaning volunteers may not know how to read maps.

Many people simply trust their own experience and the oral history of hurricanes in their local area. This local knowledge can be reliable or it can betray – witness the false sense of security that mountains and windproof homes gave people in Haiti and the Dominican Republic. Outreach and public awareness campaigns are essential, as is the integration of hurricane knowledge into school curricula.

In Haiti, constant interaction with the diaspora in Florida, and elsewhere on the east coast of the United States and Quebec, Canada, has dramatically increased cell phone use and access. Although this technology may not reach the poorest of the poor, it has considerable coverage and could be used to spread early warnings – as happened in Jamaica.

Can Cuba's example be copied?

Since the *World Disasters Report 2002* highlighted Cuba's achievement in protecting life during Hurricane Michelle the previous year, academics and policy-makers have debated whether Cuba's approach can be applied anywhere else.

Cuba's success is summarized by José Rubiera, the country's chief weather forecaster, who told the UN's ISDR recently: "Our system works very well because there is a strong political will to implement disaster reduction. We are very good at forecasting hurricanes. People have faith in our meteorological system and take seriously the information we give them... [They] also have a strong background in meteorological information; they have been trained at school from an early age. They are well aware about the meaning of the information we provide them and know exactly what they have to do according to the alert we are launching."

International Federation
of Red Cross and Red Crescent Societies

While there cannot be a universal recipe for effective early warning, some essential ingredients of the Cuban approach are not only relevant but also replicable:

- Generation of and access to excellent hurricane warning and prediction information.
- A system of governance and civil protection from national to local level, which is coherent, well-coordinated, proactive, responsive and accountable.
- Ongoing risk awareness, practice drills and preparations, based on universal educational access and literacy.
- Close integration of the media into the warning system.
- Strong neighbourhood organizations and participation of youth, women's and professional organizations.
- Investment in public transport, shelters and emergency provisions.

None of this depends on a particular political ideology. Despite Cuba's difficulties since the fall of their main economic partner, the Soviet Union, the country's warning and preparedness system has improved. Cuba lost more than 1,000 lives in landslides due to a hurricane in 1963, but recorded 18 deaths in the six major hurricanes affecting the island from 1996 to 2004. Clearly wealth is not the key ingredient; according to Audrey Mullings, a Jamaican Red Cross volunteer, "The best thing to learn from Cuba is that you don't need a lot of money to make things work."

What is needed, however, is the commitment of government at all levels to early warning. A wide variety of pluralistic economic and political systems are already developing early warning structures along the lines of Cuba's good practice. However, countries committed to reducing the role of the state in public life and allowing market forces to decide priorities (such as access to public transport for evacuation rather than dependence on privately-owned vehicles) may find it harder to take this path. Cuba can offer lessons to neighbours whose populations are more vulnerable to hurricanes (see Table 2.2). Caribbean islands are not the only places at risk: some coastal cities, such as New Orleans for example, could also be disasters waiting to happen (see Box 2.5).

Towards people-centred early warning

The Indian Ocean tsunami of December 2004 sparked a vigorous discussion of the need for 'people-centred' early warning systems. The World Conference on Disaster Reduction in Kobe, Japan witnessed arguments for both high-tech and low-tech solutions. Satellite imaging, rapid electronic communications and a host of other technologies vied for attention with community representatives who emphasized the need for ordinary people not only to understand the warnings that might result from new systems, but to have a chance to help design them.

The evidence provided by the Caribbean's 2004 hurricane season comes down on both sides – a balance of technology and local activism. The excellent hurricane forecasting

On 15 September 2004, Hurricane Ivan was heading straight for New Orleans, a city below sea level, situated in a bowl between the Mississippi River's levies and a lake. Natural wetland protection from hurricanes has been destroyed over the years by development, deposition of silt and chemical contamination from the oil industry.

The night Ivan approached, 20,000 low-income people without private vehicles sheltered in their homes below sea level. A direct hit would have drowned them. A US Army Corps of Engineers computer simulation has calculated that 65,000 could die in the city, in the event of a direct hit by a slow-moving category 3 hurricane.

Fortunately, Ivan veered away from the city at the last moment, but still killed 25 people elsewhere in the south of the United States. At present, there is no plan for the public evacuation of low-income residents who do not own cars. Churches, however, have begun to develop their own evacuation plans, partnering church members who have vehicles with those who do not. ■

This box is based on a presentation by Shirley Laska, Director, Center for Hazard Assessment, Response, and Technology, University of New Orleans, entitled "New Orleans and Ivan and Beyond", made at the United States National Academy of Sciences on 8 March 2005.

available in the Caribbean is necessary, but not sufficient, to prevent disasters. In the most successful cases – Cuba and Jamaica – there is functional local government, proactive voluntary activity and evidence of great improvisation and local knowledge.

The technological fixes are in many ways the easy part of building an early warning system. The real challenge lies in making it people-centred. The following recommendations may help point the way towards achieving this:

- **Make warnings intelligible.** More must be done to translate hurricane warnings into language that people understand. People at risk need to know what to do when they get a hurricane warning, where to go and which route to use. Increasing basic literacy will help as will linking disaster preparedness to the oral history of hurricanes in specific areas.
- **Make warnings specific.** The majority of deaths in hurricanes are from flooding and landslides. National hurricane warnings must be supplemented with local warnings of specific and secondary hazards. This requires prior flood and landslide mapping.
- **Encourage local ownership.** Early warning systems are more likely to succeed in conveying their message the 'final mile' if people at risk participate in designing and maintaining them. This means communities – not just national experts – must take part in mapping local hazards, conducting practice drills and building local awareness.
- **Supplement local knowledge.** Personal experience and oral history are important, but not always reliable, as in Gonaives where people felt protected by

Table 2.2 Deaths from hurricanes during 2004

	Charley	Frances	Ivan	Jeanne	Others	Total
Bahamas		2		0		**2**
Barbados			1			**1**
Cayman Islands	0		2			**2**
Cuba	4		0			**4**
Dominican Republic			4	23		**27**
Grenada			39			**39**
Haiti				1,800+		**1,800+**
Jamaica	1		17			**18**
Puerto Rico				1		**1**
Trinidad and Tobago			1			**1**
United States	30	47	57	5	13	**152**
Venezuela			3			**3**
Total	**35**	**49**	**124**	**1,800+**	**13**	**2,000+**

Note: Includes deaths directly and indirectly caused by hurricane impacts. No data means the hurricane did not hit that country, while a zero figure means the hurricane hit but no deaths were reported.
Sources: US National Hurricane Center (NHC), Governments of Haiti and Dominican Republic

the mountains. Experience must be discussed critically and supplemented with public education on secondary risks and their causes.

■ **Spread awareness through schools.** Children who are aware of hurricane hazards – from storm surges and winds to flooding and landslides – spread awareness through their families and neighbourhoods, and become more receptive as adults. Cuba includes hurricane knowledge in the school curriculum. Jamaica and the Dominican Republic are following suit.

■ **Link warning to risk reduction.** We have only discussed warnings issued days or hours before the storm strikes. But rapid, uncontrolled urbanization and environmental degradation send their own longer-term warnings. Everywhere, but especially in Haiti, investment to tackle the root causes of disaster vulnerability is urgently needed – before history repeats itself.

Principal contributors to this chapter were Ben Wisner, Victor Ruiz, Allan Lavell and Lourdes Meyreles. Ben Wisner, who also contributed Boxes 2.1, 2.4 and 2.5, is an independent researcher affiliated with the Development Studies Institute at the London School of Economics, the Benfield Hazard Research Centre (University College London) and the Disaster Prevention Research Institute at Kyoto University, Japan. Victor Ruiz is an independent consultant and sociologist based in the Dominican Republic. Allan Lavell, who also contributed Box 2.3, is the coordinator of the risk and disaster research programme at the Secretariat General of the Latin American Social Science Faculty

(FLACSO) and the Latin American Network for the Social Study of Disaster Prevention. Lourdes Meyreles is a sociologist who coordinates FLACSO's Dominican Republic programme. Ruth Chisholm, the Jamaica Red Cross's director of emergency services and communication, contributed Box 2.2.

Sources and further information

Castellanos Abella, E. and Van Westen, C.J. "Development of a system for landslide risk assessment in Cuba" in *Proceedings of the International Conference on Landslide Risk Management,* 31 May–3 June 2005, Vancouver, Canada.

Collie, Tim. "We know that this is destroying the land, but charcoal is what keeps us alive", *South Florida Sun-Sentinel,* 7 December 2004. Available at http://www.latinamericanstudies.org/haiti/charcoal.htm

Davis, Ian; Sanderson, David; Parker, Dennis and Stack, Jayne. *The Dissemination of Warnings.* London: DFID, The Royal Society, The Royal Academy of Engineering and The Institution of Civil Engineers, 1998.

Diaz, Henry and Pulwarty, Roger (eds.). *Hurricanes: Climate and Socioeconomic Impacts.* Berlin: Springer Verlag, 1997.

Drye, Willie. "2004 U.S. Hurricane Season Among Worst on Record", *National Geographic News,* 30 November 2004. Available at http://news. nationalgeographic.com

Douglas, Erol. *Pedro River Community Flood Warning System.* Kingston, Jamaica: UNDP, 2004.

Leatherman, Stephen. *Lessons Learned between Hurricanes: From Hugo to Charley, Frances, Ivan and Jeanne.* Florida International University, A Disasters Roundtable Workshop, National Academies, Washington DC, United States, 8 March 2005.

Lawrence, Miles and Cobb, Hugh. *Tropical Cyclone Report: Hurricane Jeanne.* US National Hurricane Center, 7 January 2005. Available at http://www.nhc. noaa.gov/2004jeanne.shtml

Longshore, David. *Encyclopedia of Hurricanes, Typhoons, and Cyclones.* New York: Checkmark Books, 2000.

Murray, Kevin and Miller, Jake. "Haiti: A Flood of Injustice", *Grassroots International,* 27 September 2004. Available at http://grassrootsonline.org/Haiti_Flood.html

Pelling, Mark. "Patrimonial Regimes and the Maintenance of Constructive Civil Society: Santo Domingo, Dominican Republic" in *The Vulnerability of Cities.* London: Earthscan, 2004.

Pielke Jr, Roger and Pielke Sr, Roger (eds.). *Storms.* 2 Vols. London: Routledge, 2000.

République d'Haïti, *Rapport National sur la Prévention des Catastrophes.* Préparé dans le cadre de la Conférence Mondiale sur la Prévention des Catastrophes, Kobe, Japon. August 2004.

Rubiera, José. Presentation at the World Conference on Disaster Reduction, Kobe, Japan, January 2005. Available at http://www.unisdr.org/wcdr/thematic-sessions/presentations/session2-3/imc-dr-rubiera.pdf

Smarth, Luc. "Popular Organizations and the Transition to Democracy in Haiti" in M. Kaufman and H. Dilla Alfonso (eds.), *Community Power & Grassroots Democracy,* pp. 102-125. London and Ottawa: Zed Books and IDRC, 1997.

Steward, Stacy. *Tropical Cyclone Report: Hurricane Ivan.* US National Hurricane Center, 16 December 2004. Available at http://www.nhc.noaa.gov/ 2004 ivan.shtml

Surgeon-Rogers, Tonna-Marie. *Global Analysis of UNDP's Support to National Disaster Risk Management Systems: Caribbean Regional Report.* September 2004.

Thompson, Martha with Gaviria, Izaskun. *Weathering the Storm: Lessons in Risk Reduction from Cuba.* Boston: Oxfam America. Available at http://www.oxfamamerica.org/newsandpublications

United Nations Office for the Coordination of Humanitarian Affairs (OCHA). *Evaluación de la Capacidad Nacional para la Respuesta a Desastres.* Santo Domingo, Dominican Republic: OCHA, 2005.

Wisner, Ben; Blaikie, Piers; Cannon, Terry and Davis, Ian. *At Risk: Natural Hazards, People's Vulnerability and Disasters.* 2nd edition. London: Routledge, 2004.

Zschau, Jochen and Kueppers, Andreas (eds.). *Early Warning Systems for Natural Disaster Reduction.* Berlin: Springer Verlag, 2003.

Web sites

Caribbean Disaster Emergency Response Agency **http://www.cdera.org**
Caribbean Net News **http://www.caribbeannetnews.com**
Disaster Center **http://www.disastercenter.com**
Haiti Support Group **http://haitisupport.gn.apc.org**
Havana Journal **http://havanajournal.com**
Munich Re **http://www.munichre.com**
National Hurricane Center (United States) **http://www.nhc.noaa.gov**
National Oceanic and Atmospheric Administration (United States)
    http://hurricanes.noaa.gov
National Weather Service (United States) **http://www.crh.noaa.gov**
Second International Conference on Early Warning **http://www.ewc2.org**
The Jamaica Observer **http://www.jamaicaobserver.com/news**
UNISDR's Platform for the Promotion of Early Warning
    http://www.unisdr.org/ppew
World Meteorological Organization **http://www.wmo.int/meteoworld**

CHAPTER 2

Locusts in West Africa: early warning, late response

Fatimitu Mint Eletou had nothing left but a prayer. After several years of drought followed by a plague of locusts, she prayed that her garden would grow enough food to feed her five children and ailing 87-year-old mother. The family lives in a dark mud-walled room 1.2 metres wide and 1.8 metres long in southern Mauritania. There was nothing in her storeroom to keep them going until the vegetables ripened.

Fatimitu's story, reported in February 2005 by the United Nations (UN) Integrated Regional Information Network (IRIN) for Africa, was not unique. Over 9 million people faced severe food shortages this year across the nine countries of the Sahel, because of poor harvests following years of drought and the 2004 locust plague. But who cares? Even in the best of times, in Niger at least, 40 per cent of children are malnourished.

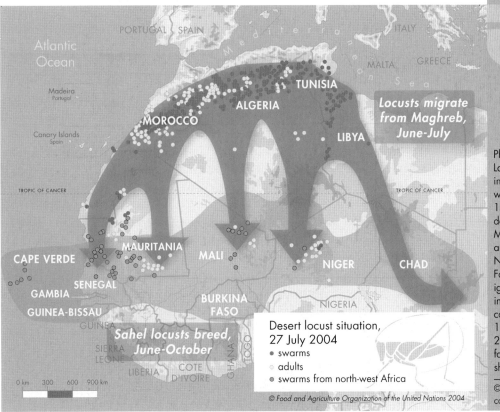

Locusts migrate from Maghreb, June-July

Sahel locusts breed, June-October

Desert locust situation, 27 July 2004
● swarms
○ adults
● swarms from north-west Africa

© Food and Agriculture Organization of the United Nations 2004

Photo opposite page: Last year's locust invasion of the Sahel was the worst for 15 years. Swarms devoured half of Mauritania's cereal crop and 40 per cent of Niger's animal fodder. For nine months, donors ignored warnings, increasing the costs of controlling the plague 100-fold. By June 2005, 9 million people faced severe food shortages.

© REUTERS/Pierre Holtz, courtesy www.alertnet.org

Appeals for food aid were ignored. In April 2005, the aid agency Oxfam reported that its appeal for West Africa had raised "precisely nothing". In May, the UN launched an emergency food appeal for impoverished Niger. Their stores empty, villagers were forced to scavenge anthills hoping to find stray grains of food. Over 3 million people urgently needed life-saving support. Two months after the launch of the US$ 16 million appeal, just 22 per cent of the money had been raised. Jan Egeland, the UN's under-secretary-general and emergency relief coordinator, described the crisis of hunger unfolding in Niger as "the number one forgotten and neglected emergency in the world".

High-profile crises like the Iraq war and Indian Ocean tsunami have left other critical humanitarian stories underreported and forgotten. The Sahel food crisis was one of the most urgent. But it could have been avoided. So how did the situation become so acute? You would think that after thousands of years of knowledge about what causes them, locust plagues would be relegated to history books and religious texts.

Locust warnings began to emerge from the region in June 2003 (see Figure 3.1). By that October, the UN's Food and Agriculture Organization (FAO) – responsible for coordinating international locust control efforts in Africa for over 50 years – was warning of a plague and calling for better control measures. In February and June 2004, FAO launched appeals for aid, but donors were sluggish to respond. Two months later, the Sahel was gripped by its worst locust invasion since the late 1980s.

No plant escapes a hungry locust. Black clouds of them blotted out the sun in Nouakchott, the Mauritanian capital, and devoured the lawn of the local football stadium during the quarter-final match of the President of the Republic Cup in October 2004. Gambia declared a state of emergency. Egeland said the plague represented a greater threat to livelihoods than "any of the wars in the African region, Darfur included". The livelihoods of some 150 million people were being consumed before the eyes of an indifferent world.

This is what happens when old threats have been forgotten and alarm bells go unheeded. For nine months, donor governments failed to respond to early warnings of an impending plague. The aid community failed to convey the urgency of the invasion to donors and the general public. Despite some real efforts by North African governments, regional mechanisms lacked the resources and often failed to communicate or cooperate sufficiently until the situation was out of control. And local populations lacked the knowledge and means to respond effectively and swiftly.

Beyond the lack of information and communication is an even more worrying bias of the international aid system towards political and financial interests, rather than human need. "It shouldn't be like that because we should give according to needs. But

International Federation
of Red Cross and Red Crescent Societies

Figure 3.1 Sahel locusts: evolution of a crisis

Locusts/Season/Crops	Date	Humanitarian situation and action
Wet winter in NW Africa triggers cycle of locusts and disaster	January–March 2003	
Locusts born in unusually large numbers in Morocco and Algeria	March–May 2003	Moroccan and Algerian governments try to control swarms with spraying
Locust invade Sahel	June 2003	Regional anti-locust organization voices concern about situation in Morocco, Algeria and Mauritania
Locust swarms invade Sahel – Mauritania hit first – Sahel rains	July 2003	US$ 1m spent now could have contained the threat
Locusts breed Sahel rains	August 2003	
Locusts breed Sahel rains	September 2003	
Rains and explosion of desert foliage create **ideal locust breeding conditions**	October 2003	**FAO warns donors** of impending plague – calls for control efforts to be reinforced
New 'hopper' locusts born in Sahel	February 2004	**FAO appeals for US$ 9m** to support local control launched – appeal 'ignored'
Hoppers born	March–May 2004	
	June 2004	**FAO appeals for US$ 100m** – warns donors situation 'extremely critical'
Sahel rains	July 2004	
Sahel rains – **Height of locust invasion** Swarms devour 1.6m hectares – destroying 50 per cent of Mauritania's cereal crop, 40 per cent of Niger's animal fodder	August 2004	Donors earmark US$ 32m/FAO adds US$ 10m Mauritania has '10 per cent of resources' needed to fight invasion/Situation nearly 'catastrophic'/Press coverage of crisis begins/4m hectares sprayed with pesticide/Regional meeting of 13 countries 'declares war'
Sahel rains	September 2004	
	October 2004	Jan Egeland/Situation worse than any African war, livelihoods of 150m at risk/**FAO receives US$ 45m to date** – plus US$ 30m in pledges
Swarms fly north	November 2004	
Swarms die in Atlas Mountains	December 2004	
	January 2005	Food prices soar, livestock prices plummet
	February 2005	Livestock dying
	March 2005	1 in 3 children malnourished
	April–June 2005	**9 million people severely affected**, infant mortality hits record levels, migration sparks conflict Oxfam and UN appeals 0 per cent funded
'Lean period' until harvest in October	July–October 2005	

that is not happening now," said Jan Egeland to reporters in June 2005. He added, "overt discrimination percolates down to whether a country is French-, Portuguese- or English-speaking".

This chapter looks at the role of information during 2004's locust plague. What information was available and when? How was it shared? How aware were donors, aid agencies and governments of the threat? What were the consequences for affected populations? The chapter reveals what kinds of information aid agencies should be gathering about slow-onset disasters and how it should be communicated to garner greater donor and public support.

Rain solves one disaster, sparks another

Since the end of the 1960s, West Africa has been experiencing a harsh, persistent drought. In 2002, the rainfall deficit reached 50 per cent in some parts of the region. However, rains during 2003 and 2004 solved one disaster but sparked another. The moisture created ideal breeding conditions for the desert locust and four generations bred rapidly, one after another (see Box 3.1).

The trigger for the locust plague was an excessively wet winter during early 2003 in the Maghreb countries of north-west Africa. That spring, locusts were born in unusually large numbers in the mountains of Morocco and Algeria. Government authorities moved swiftly but failed to control locust populations (see Box 3.2). Complicating control efforts in the area was a strip of no man's land, some 30–50 kilometres wide, along Morocco's long, contested border with Algeria. As neither side dared fly planes near the zone, it became an unintended refuge for desert locusts.

The swarms did force the often-hostile neighbours to communicate. "If we can control this zone, we can break the cycle," said Brahim Boudarine, the provincial agricultural director for the Moroccan government in a *New York Times* article at the time. He added that the two sides remained in telephone contact and that both had vowed to treat swarms close to the border.

Despite overcoming political obstacles and carrying out considerable control operations, Algerian and Moroccan officials failed to prevent the swarms from heading south and invading the Sahel at the onset of its rainy season, in July 2003. Mauritania was the first country hit.

Meanwhile, in June 2003, the Desert Locust Control Committee for West Africa, a regional body established in 2000 by FAO with the governments of Algeria, Chad, Libya, Mali, Morocco, Niger, Senegal and Tunisia, had already expressed concern about the locust situation in Morocco, Algeria and Mauritania.

International Federation
of Red Cross and Red Crescent Societies

Box 3.1 From Jekyll to Hyde: the lifestyle of a locust

Normally, the desert locust is a solitary, unthreatening insect found in the desert and brush regions of North Africa (Morocco, Algeria, Tunisia, Libya, Egypt), the Sahel region (Burkina Faso, Cape Verde, Chad, Gambia, Guinea Bissau, Mali, Mauritania, Niger and Senegal), the Arabian Peninsula (Saudi Arabia, Yemen, Oman) and parts of Asia to western India. In West Africa, locusts normally originate in the Sahel, invade north-west Africa and reproduce. Their offspring then return south in a cycle that has been known to last years.

After a long period of drought followed by abundant rains, as vegetation blooms in areas of the desert where the locusts breed, over-crowding and competition for food can trans-form the insect from a local pest into a plague. Professor Jeff Lockwood from the University of Wyoming explains: "The stress of overcrowd-ing acts like the drug that transformed Dr. Jekyll into Mr. Hyde. The locusts undergo a physical change. Their wings and jaws grow longer, stronger. They change colour. They begin trav-elling in monstrous swarms."

At night, the swarms perch on any avail-able vegetation and eat. By morning, the fields are bare. Early morning is the ideal moment to spray them with pesticides, as they sit on the plants for hours before taking off.

Swarms contain some 40 to 80 million locusts per square kilometre. One swarm in the 2004 plague was reported to be some 60 km long. But it is not only their numbers; the voracious appetite of locusts causes havoc. Each locust measures 4.6–6 centimetres long and weighs two grams, but eats its weight in food in 24 hours. Stephen Simpson, an Oxford University entomologist, is quoted in the British newspaper The Guardian as saying: "A single swarm will eat in a day the same amount of food as the population of London will eat in a week."

According to Lockwood: "They become clouds of terror, like a tornado. Most of the land they pass over doesn't suffer any dam-age at all. But where the tornado or the locust swarm touches down, there are devastating effects. If it's your village or district that the locusts descend into, you may be facing famine or at least hunger."

Swarms can travel up to 100 km a day. In addition, locusts do not depend for their sur-vival on abundant vegetation. When food is scarce, they will eat their dead, ensuring the destructive cycle of the swarms continues. And although locusts normally live only three to five months, females can lay some 100 eggs four times in a lifetime, leaving behind a wasteland sown with a potentially greater disaster. ■

In September 2003, a team from the Mauritanian National Centre for Locust Control went out on a routine 3,500-km survey of the country's southern and central regions. They had been making this trip for the past 20 years, but this time there were some worrying developments. "We began seeing desert locusts every 100 metres where there had been only a few the month before," reported Mohamed Lemine, an FAO locust expert based in Mauritania.

When abundant rainfall during the Sahel's rainy season finished dousing the region in October 2003, bringing an explosion of desert foliage, FAO experts in Mauritania and Rome knew they had the ideal breeding conditions for the Sahel's own generation of locusts.

Donors dither, locusts breed

FAO wasted no time. The same month, October 2003, the FAO's Desert Locust Information Service (DLIS) issued the first of many warnings to the donor

International Federation
of Red Cross and Red Crescent Societies

community of an impending plague and advised that control efforts, such as spraying the swarms with pesticides, be reinforced. In February 2004, an FAO appeal for US$ 9 million to support local control efforts was launched, but failed to raise any funds. Donor efforts were concentrated elsewhere, particularly in the Sudanese region of Darfur. Calls for international help from FAO couldn't compete with the international media spotlight on Darfur.

BBC reporter Pascale Harter wrote: "The worst development in the Maghreb region this year [2004] has been the international community's pitiful response to the locust plague in Mauritania. Appeals in February 2004 by FAO for a measly US$ 9 million to fight the beginnings of a locust invasion were ignored. While donors dithered, the locusts multiplied."

From February 2004 onwards, young locusts ('hoppers') began to emerge from eggs laid by the earlier swarms. By July, FAO warned that the locust situation in West Africa had become "extremely critical". It urgently appealed for additional aid totalling US$ 100 million for control operations in Mauritania, Senegal, Mali, Niger and Chad.

In August, international donors had earmarked only US$ 32 million for locust control campaigns, while FAO added US$ 10 million more from its own funds. But government officials in Mauritania and Mali, the two most affected countries at that time, reported they had nowhere near enough pesticides or spraying equipment. One news report said: "At the moment, the fight against the plague of locusts looks more like an effort to drain the ocean."

Mohamed Abdallahi Ould Babah, the head of Mauritania's Centre to Fight Locusts, told reporters in August: "We're racing against the clock but it's an unfair race because we have only 10 per cent of the resources we need to win it." He claimed that his country still needed US$ 20 million to fight the swarms.

Around this time, the international press started showing dramatic images of helpless farmers beating pots or swinging sticks to try and chase away the millions of locusts eating their crops. Reports were filed saying the swarms would soon threaten Darfur, providing a useful link with a major news story and ensuring some international media coverage.

When beating pots failed, farmers turned to other traditional methods such as burning rubber tyres. They hoped the thick smoke would drive the ravenous insects away. Some farmers pooled their own money together to buy pesticides, but they lacked the equipment to spray it. In any case, the size of the swarms and the lack of material resources to control them meant that traditional methods were never going to be enough.

CHAPTER 3

Costs soar as war declared

By now, the only way to control the swarms effectively was to drop large amounts of conventional pesticides over large tracts of land. By August 2004, some 10 million acres (4 million hectares) were treated in Algeria, Mauritania, Morocco, Libya and Tunisia. But in Mali, for example, the sole helicopter assigned to the country's locust programme only started spraying at the end of August. The reason: lack of fuel, pesticides and equipment.

Meanwhile, quotes from leading UN officials, in particular Clive Elliott, FAO's leading locust expert, hinted at some frustration with the donor community. In early August, Elliott said: "It takes a while for the penny to drop in terms of realizing that the situation really is serious. Unfortunately the locusts get on with their reproduction and each generation they go through makes the problem worse."

Despite the agitation for action by the UN and other non-governmental organizations (NGOs) such as Oxfam, together with international media reports, locust swarms devastated 1.6 million hectares of farmland in Mauritania, devouring 30–100 per cent of farmer's crops and raising the spectre of a major regional food crisis.

Though spraying helped to control the swarms to a degree, it came too late for many farmers, especially those in isolated geographical areas who had lost most of their crops to the locusts before spraying started. Gambia, where more than 70 per cent of the population are dependent on farming for their survival, declared a state of emergency. "The situation is about to become catastrophic in the next few days," said Mauritanian Mohamed Abdallahi Ould Babah in August.

Finally, at the end of August, Senegal's Agriculture Ministry held a regional crisis meeting of 13 West African countries at risk from the locust swarms, plus the international donor community. It was just short of a year since FAO had issued its first warning. Senegal's president, Abdoulaye Wade, opened the meeting by declaring war on the locusts and calling for a full-scale military operation to stop them. "I'm particularly stressing the need for the army to be mobilized because for me this is a real war. And the war is far from being won."

With the war declared, donors started to provide the long-requested funds to combat the locusts. But, during the long lapse between donors' pledges and the actual arrival of their cash, the insects got on with causing more damage.

On 6 October 2004, Jan Egeland vented the UN's collective frustration in an opinion piece for the *New York Times*: "In March, the Food and Agriculture Organization called for US$ 9 million to head off the impending locust invasion. Yet that appeal and subsequent warnings fell on deaf ears. Now that the infestation has spread, destroying millions of dollars' worth of crops in the process, the costs have risen tremendously, to more than US$ 100 million."

In the end, the Americans donated around US$ 7.5 million. In mid-October, the European Union announced a grant of US$ 64 million for medium-term locust control activities. At the close of the month, FAO had received nearly US$ 45 million, with pledges for an additional US$ 30 million. In addition, the World Bank set up a fund of up to US$ 100 million to strengthen locust control in the region, in the form of interest-free loans to individual countries.

By the end of 2004, the control measures of the Moroccan and Algerian governments in particular, plus a cold winter in the Atlas Mountains, brought the plague under control. But that was by no means the end of the disaster.

Villagers struggle to survive

In a region already afflicted by chronic poverty, poor health, political instability and recurrent drought, the invasion of these voracious insects had serious human consequences. The onslaught occurred during the 'lean period' just ahead of the annual harvests. Families had depleted their food reserves and invested available income from previous harvests into seeds, which were set to yield good results.

However, the locusts consumed almost half of Mauritania's entire national cereal crop, threatening the livelihoods and food security of millions of rural families. In Niger, locusts ate about 15 per cent of the country's cereals, but almost 40 per cent of the fodder on which livestock depend. During early 2005, subsistence farmers across the region were forced to eat the seed corn they were planning to plant later in the year and began to sell their valuable livestock to raise money to buy more food. But, as prices for millet and other staples soared, doubling in some parts, the resale value for cattle and livestock plunged.

The result was that, from April 2005 onwards, reports of severe malnutrition and food insecurity in the Sahel region were widespread. In Mauritania, the government estimated that one-third of the population – about 900,000 people – faced food shortages and were selling off valuable livestock to survive. Mohameden Ould Zein, Mauritania's director of food security, told IRIN that his organization had registered "a resurgence of diseases associated with food insecurity, like child malnutrition and acute respiratory infections". The French NGO, Action contre la Faim, reported that one in three children under the age of 5 suffered from malnutrition in Mauritania's north-eastern region of Kidal.

Similarly in Niger, the authorities said 3.9 million people, a third of the population, would not eat properly this year. With nothing left to eat, many villagers in Niger scavenged for wild plants to survive. "The population has adopted behaviour characteristic of a famine," explained Daddy Dan Bakoye, the head of statistics at Niger's Ministry of Agriculture, in an interview in May 2005.

Meanwhile, Gian Carlo Cirri, country director for the World Food Programme (WFP) in Niger, said a survey done by his organization had shown that 350,000 children under 5 faced serious malnutrition. "These results would normally indicate a people living in a war zone and yet we have not even entered the 'hunger season', the period each year leading up to the harvest when food is generally scarce," explained Cirri in a press release. "The next harvest is not due until the end of the rainy season in September/October so these statistics will only get worse over the next few months unless immediate action is taken."

A 19 per cent tax on basic goods including milk and flour, imposed in early 2005, didn't help the situation in Niger and incited considerable civil unrest. According to Abdoulaye Massalatchi, reporting for Reuters, the government said "it had been forced to do so by the demands of the International Monetary Fund". The taxes were subsequently lifted.

The desert locust grows 6cm long and consumes its own weight in food every day.

© REUTERS/Pierre Holtz, courtesy www.alertnet.org

International Federation of Red Cross and Red Crescent Societies

In Mali, teams from Oxfam visiting in October 2004 had found that the food and livelihoods of pastoral communities were precarious, with only two to four months of animal feed left. When they returned in May 2005, the situation had become much worse. Where there had been healthy animals the previous October, they found carcasses of donkeys and sheep. "Malnutrition affected around one child in three," reported Oxfam. "Infant mortality among the population, whose children had never received any sort of medical attention, had reached record levels this year. One family in five had lost a child in the last six months."

The locust invasion and drought were severely affecting 1.7 million people in Mali and another 3 million in Burkina Faso, during March 2005, according to the International Federation. Women were forced to sell their jewellery and spare clothes to buy food. Villagers collected tree leaves to prepare as their daily meal.

Migration causes conflict

A large proportion of the Sahel's rural population, particularly in Mali and Mauritania, are pastoralists who rely on livestock for food and income. Recurrent drought has made life very difficult for these communities and migration is a long-standing solution to their difficult situation. For example, in a survey done in the mid-1990s in Mali, the government estimated that 47 per cent of all rural households included at least one member who had migrated.

In May 2005, Oxfam noted widespread migration of men and whole families to urban centres in Mali. Rural livelihoods were threatened as farmers left home in search of food and work. The struggle for arable land between farmers and pastoralists has been explosive. The locust plague, which wiped out grazing lands in the dry northern areas, forced many pastoralists to head south with their livestock, moving into land traditionally used for farming.

The International Federation reported that tensions flared between farmers and migrating cattle-breeders desperately looking for fresh pasture. In Po province, Burkina Faso, an entire village of 500 homes was burned down after the livestock of unwanted new migrants invaded precious cropland in November 2004 (see Box 3.3). The consequences of this competition over land use could be dire. "Social upheaval," warned Hervé Ludovic de Lys, director of the West Africa office for the UN Office for the Coordination of Humanitarian Affairs (OCHA), speaking to the *New York Times*.

For those who remained at home, the localized nature of the hardship inflicted by the locusts made it difficult for aid agencies to measure the scope of the food emergency within these communities. An OCHA news story quoted Mame Dieng, a village chief in Rao district in northern Senegal, who lost his entire harvest to the locust swarms:

Box 3.3 "The sun suddenly disappeared behind a big cloud"

"If you want to do something to help us out of our misery, you have to hurry up. Because in a few weeks you will not find anybody in this village any more," explains Ibrahim Kone, the leader of a village in Burkina Faso afflicted by 2004's devastating locust plague.

Most of the village was already deserted, except for some elderly women and children sitting beside their straw huts. The 'workforce' had left to seek an income in the cities and more fertile areas to the south of the country.

Migration, especially into the forested areas inhabited by autonomous ethnic groups, has led to localized conflicts.

In the province of Po, one village of cattle-breeders swelled as relatives arrived from the locust-afflicted north of the country, desperate to pasture their livestock. When their cattle overran the fields of neighbouring farmers, the farmers took revenge. They burned down the cattle-breeders' entire village, destroying 500 homes and killing three people.

Zongo Yakouba, who lives in the deserts of Oudalan province, reported what he saw when the swarms struck: "On 27 September [2004], at ten past one, the sun suddenly disappeared behind a big cloud. We ran out of our hamlets to see what it was and found this cloud settling down on our millet fields, which were just about to be harvested. They were all yellow, big insects that we had never seen before."

Within minutes, the alarm had gone out across the whole village. Even the old women ran to the fields, banging cooking pots and drums, in a vain effort to prevent the locusts from eating their staple food for the next few months. But the noise didn't bother the feasting insects. After a couple of hours, with the millet stems stripped bare, the locusts formed a cloud again and took off into the sky in search of more sustenance.

Hoping to warn the local authorities of the threat to other villages, a community leader headed to the nearest city on his motorcycle. But the air was so thick with insects that the journey, which normally takes an hour, took him over twice as long. In any case it was too late: the locusts flew faster than he could ride his motorcycle through the sandy savannah.

Within two days, most farmers in the area had lost their crops and the local authorities were overwhelmed with requests for help.

Why were the farmers so taken by surprise? Had no one warned them, or hadn't they taken the warnings seriously? The fact that the villagers recollected the exact date and time of the locust invasion shows it was a traumatic experience, engraved on their minds. They remembered their grandparents telling them about some insects arriving all of a sudden and destroying the harvest, nearly 20 years ago. But nothing this bad.

The local authorities said they didn't receive any warnings from the central government, but this cannot be confirmed. When interviewed, local officials also seemed shocked by the swarms. They described the time and nature of the invasion very vividly, just as Zongo Yakouba had. But it's possible that even if the central government had warned them, they may not have taken the information seriously, as it related to a phenomenon beyond their experience. ∎

"Certain villagers in the region had begun to migrate to the big towns to look for work, driven by the need to maintain their livelihoods. Many of those who remained

International Federation
of Red Cross and Red Crescent Societies

behind will have to sacrifice their children's education, since they have no money to pay for it."

Affected countries lack resources to cope

The affected area included some of the poorest countries in the world, which lacked the resources to control this pest. It has long been established that disaster mitigation requires appropriate timing and careful planning. In the case of locusts, the only time plagues can be treated without using pesticides is 25 to 50 days after eggs have hatched. At this particular period, the locusts are wingless and crawling on the ground. To kill them, farmers need to dig trenches and bury them.

Moussa Niang, head of the Senegalese Integrated Programme for Podor (PIP) that trains locust awareness officers, explained in an IRIN interview: "It is absolutely necessary for people to understand the danger that locusts represent, so that they can help in our efforts."

Yet Niang explained that awareness officers had difficulties convincing people of the dangers of locusts until it was too late. And awareness-raising efforts could even be counterproductive. "We explain to them that the pesticides are toxic and how to protect themselves, for example, by not allowing their animals to graze in a field that has been sprayed for two to three days, to avoid poisoning," Niang said in the interview. Worried about their livestock, farmers failed to report swarms for fear that their farms might be sprayed and contaminated. And the locusts ate the entire crop.

"The state reacted [to the locust crisis] without involving the population. From the word 'go', the approach was wrong," said Niang.

One of the lessons learned from the 2004 plague was the weakness of national control teams and early warning systems. Although FAO officers in Rome, Dakar and elsewhere in the region, together with locust officers in the capitals of affected countries, used satellite images and geographical information systems to follow the locust swarms from the onset, they could do little to stop them. The lack of crop-duster aircraft, pesticides and know-how among national control teams across the region was dire.

The lack of resources at the national level was a result of both governments and donors diverting funds for locust control to other national programmes, according to Michel Le Coq, at the International Centre for Agronomic Research in Montpellier, France. Le Coq worried that a lack of accountability on how money was disbursed would once again bring national capacities to dangerously low levels. "Transparency on how money is spent is essential to maintaining quality control teams and mechanisms in place for the long term," he explained.

Regional cooperation falls short

Fighting the locust plague required significant regional cooperation, as the insect knows no boundaries. In addition, locust populations must be monitored every year, even when there is no activity.

Past history shows that despite repeated discussions on the subject, in 2004 there were few regional mechanisms to prevent the spread of the swarms. As Ludovic de Lys explained in a report by the UN's International Strategy for Disaster Reduction, "To the regional threat of locusts, which know no frontier, the answer has to be regional. Cross-border cooperation is desperately needed, but so far such instances are very rare."

Alhasanne Adama Diallo, director of the regional centre of the Specialized Hydrometeorological Institute of the Permanent Interstate Committee for Drought Control in the Sahel (CILSS) added his point of view: "The responsibility to reduce the impacts of such disasters in this part of the world [Sahel and Maghreb] lies in those neighbouring countries of the Sahara, namely Algeria and Morocco. The Sahel does not have the sufficient means (equipment and treatment products), or the finances to avoid such a disaster."

In the 1960s, a West African regional organization called the Joint Organization for the Fight against Locusts and Birds (OCLALAV) had carried out several successful anti-locust campaigns. A victim of its own achievements, complacency set in among regional governments and the organization effectively disappeared by the 1980s, due to a lack of financial and material resources.

The official explanation for this demise was that OCLALAV's activities and mandate were passed on to national centres. But Fode Sarr, one of the Senegalese government's regional directors for rural development, told IRIN, "Member states simply stopped paying their dues, depriving the organization of resources."

"The damage caused by the default of OCLALAV resulted in reduced regional cooperation, dealing a blow to one of the important building blocks of disaster risk management. It also meant less specialized information was being shared with regard to the extent and growth of the problem," explained the IRIN report.

Another regional body, the FAO's Desert Locust Control Committee for North Africa had the expertise, but lacked sufficient financial resources to assist national efforts early on. It was, however, crucial in supporting regional coordination and cooperation efforts.

Using US$ 30 million raised from the appeals of 2004, governments in the region together with FAO began re-establishing a regional mechanism called the Emergency

International Federation
of Red Cross and Red Crescent Societies

Prevention System for Transboundary Animal and Plant Pests and Diseases (EMPRES) to tackle the problem. In fact, FAO had been proposing this regional mechanism since the mid-1990s. But due to a lack of funds, it never became functional. On the back of the 2004 invasion, everyone hopes that the lessons learnt will not be quickly forgotten, and that this initiative does not encounter the same fate as its predecessor.

In addition to regional cooperation, more must be done to stop the erosion of national capacity during long periods of locust remission. Only a significantly improved capacity to monitor and control locusts will enable the Sahel to defend itself against the next invasion.

International agencies misunderstand the risk

"The tardiness of the international community to respond to the emergency is in large part responsible for the high costs of containment," said a report from the United States Agency for International Development (USAID). During a multi-donor meeting called by the French government in collaboration with FAO in Paris on 24 October 2004, there was agreement that only US$ 1 million would have been needed to contain the threat in July 2003, whereas the delayed response meant that, in the end, 100 times that figure was needed.

Whether the failure to respond to the locust invasion early on was the fault of donors or the aid community remains a controversial issue in the region. Some donors said FAO woke up too late to this crisis. They complained that FAO's warnings were not insistent enough. But what the institution failed to realize was that most donors and even governments in the region had forgotten how terrible a locust plague could be. Regina Davis, USAID's representative in West Africa, explained in one news report: "There were a very few people other than a selected number of specialists, who really understood the threat and scope of the locust invasions." The last plague in 1987–1989 was considerably smaller and those who were around then could not have known how much larger the swarms of 2004 would get.

According to the regional humanitarian coordinator for a major NGO: "At the time of the FAO's first warning in 2003, everybody had forgotten the risk, because the last major invasion was so long ago. No one had a clear understanding of what an invasion was and, therefore, downplayed the threat."

Clive Elliott at FAO said most donors did not react until the plague hit the headlines. The press campaign was what pushed them to respond. He believed that without the TV images broadcast in the living rooms of the developed world, donors would have reacted even more slowly and less generously. For the future, FAO is considering more aggressive communication efforts as soon as the first swarms emerge.

Once the invasion was at its peak, the communication efforts by UN agencies went into high gear. Video footage, photos, online journals and interviews with UN authorities were organized and disseminated to broadcast news organizations. But what kinds of information should aid agencies gather about slow-onset disasters in order to garner more timely donor and public support?

Chapter 6 of this year's *World Disasters Report* argues that NGOs and UN agencies need to capture media attention by supplying news agencies with good data based on solid fieldwork. In the case of the Sahel, aid agencies failed to do this early on – either for the 2004 locust crisis or the subsequent food crisis this year. In a press release about the region's food crisis in April 2005, for example, WFP wrote that "millions of people could be affected by hunger". A former BBC journalist asked: "What exactly do they mean by 'could be'? Are people starving or not?"

Joel Boutroue, a senior OCHA official, told reporters at the launch of the UN appeal in Dakar that "2005 is a key year in West Africa". He said that elections in several West African countries, combined with the food crisis, meant that the situation in the region was volatile. He added: "There's competition for funds and we need to sound the alarm a bit harder." But more than a month after that conference, the alarm remained silent.

Another senior aid official based in the region offered this analysis on communication efforts around the 2005 food crisis: until very recently, he said, aid agencies had failed to collect the necessary nutritional information about the food situation. Without this basic data, the entire flow of information was sketchy, piecemeal and anecdotal, leaving donors confused as to the scope of the disaster and media outlets uninterested as they didn't understand the problem (see Box 3.4).

"The current food crisis is an indictment of us all in the humanitarian response community," admitted Christopher Horwood, head of information analysis with the UN news agency IRIN. "We, too, fail to raise awareness of a serious food crisis until malnutrition levels reach catastrophic levels." IRIN produced a documentary film on the locust plague released in January 2005.

Yet, with slow-onset disasters, no matter how hard agencies try to sound the alarm, donors frequently fail to respond quickly to early warnings. Early warning systems are of little use if no one acts on them. One reason is the difficulty of knowing exactly when these often hidden and chronic disasters really begin and when they actually end, if ever. In addition, with no public pressure to act, governments can dither as the crisis gets worse. As Professor Jeff Lockwood from the University of Wyoming in the United States put it, "You don't usually grab a headline by saying, we prevented a problem. You usually get a headline by saying, there's a problem, and we engaged in a heroic effort to end it."

International Federation
of Red Cross and Red Crescent Societies

Properly financed and managed early warning

Funds remaining from appeals made to combat the locust invasion are being used to strengthen and maintain regional and national control mechanisms for early warning and response. But donors are concerned about the sustainability of these mechanisms, particularly at the national level, if there is a long period of remission. Donors and national governments in locust-prone countries need to ensure that funds used to reinforce control mechanisms are allocated with a long-term aim of maintaining the quality and capacities of these institutions. Importantly, this requires a political commitment within the region to transparent management and disbursement of funds.

Better data on impact

Data collection has tended to be piecemeal, making it difficult to get a sense of the scope of the problem both across the Sahel region and at a national level. Aid agencies could consider sharing data with one another to build up a bigger picture of the scope and extent of the problem and sharing this information with the international media and donors. Efforts should be made to ensure that, even if another plague does not occur for some time, records are kept of the impact of this latest invasion.

Stronger information campaigns

The UN learned the hard way that the best way to stir the donor community into action is to transmit calls for assistance through the world's media into the living rooms of voters in the developed world. Aid organizations should engage in more proactive and innovative multimedia strategies (including documentary films like IRIN's) to raise awareness of emerging humanitarian crises to as wide an audience as possible, in order to increase pressure on governments to respond. This is particularly important in the case of chronic and forgotten disasters such as famine in the Sahel.

Regional mechanism to create greater awareness of locust and famine threats

More efforts should be made to maintain awareness among donors, governments and local populations of the threat of locust plagues and famine, and how best to prevent future disasters. This could be enhanced by establishing a regional mechanism along the lines of the UN's Emergencies Unit for Ethiopia, which informs donors of potential food insecurity and appropriate responses. In the case of the Sahel, this regional mechanism could bring together the expertise of international humanitarian and development organizations to raise awareness, issue early warnings and coordinate the response. The major lesson from the 2004 plague is that most people had forgotten how devastating locusts could be. ∎

Past experience proves that aid agencies have to work hard to engage the media and donors in promoting hidden and chronic disasters, as well as early warning. Old methods of issuing appeals and press releases are not enough. This means developing multimedia strategies to convey the threat and its possible risks. But these same agencies face serious financial restraints and it is often the communication budget that is the first victim of cost-cutting measures. Yet without media attention, the public is not alerted to major humanitarian crises like the Sahel and, subsequently, the funding for aid agencies suffers.

History repeats itself

This chapter is about a locust invasion that had devastating consequences for many communities in the Sahel region. As a result, millions of people faced malnutrition, at best, and starvation, at worst. This could have been avoided if early warning alarm bells had been listened to. Once again, in mid-2005, aid organizations called for relief efforts to limit the food crisis that emerged as a result of the drought and locust invasion of 2004. And once again, many aid workers had the familiar feeling that their calls were falling on deaf ears.

Although some of the lessons learnt from the locust invasion were being addressed, such as the lack of regional preparedness, one of the most important seemed to have been ignored: that of responding immediately to early warning distress signals so disaster can be avoided. It is disturbing that, in mid-2005, history was repeating itself so soon.

Principal contributor to this chapter and Boxes 3.1 and 3.4 was Jean Milligan, a freelance writer specializing in humanitarian and development issues. The Food and Agriculture Organization of the United Nations contributed Box 3.2. Box 3.3 was contributed by Hanna Schmuck, the International Federation's regional disaster management coordinator for West and Central Africa, based in Dakar, Senegal.

Sources and further information

Ba, Diadie and Reuters. 'African leaders draw up battle plans to fight locusts', *The Guardian*, 1 September 2004.

Egeland, Jan. 'Spray Now or Pay Later', *New York Times*, 6 October 2004.

Harter, Pascale. African review of the year 2004, *BBC News*, 31 December 2004.

Le Coq, Michel. 'Institutional reorganization to facilitate preventive management of the Desert Locust', *Advances in Applied Acridology*, 2000, p. 19.

Le Coq, Michel. 'Recent progress in Desert and Migratory Locust Management in Africa. Are preventative actions possible?', *Journal of Orthoptera Research*, 2001.

McLaughlin, Abraham. 'In Africa, when it rains, it swarms', *Christian Science Monitor*, 14 October 2004.

Oxfam. *Food crisis in northern Mali: Oxfam sounds the alarm*. Oxfam, May 2005.

Rowley, J. and Bennet, O. *Grasshoppers and Locusts. The plague of the Sahel*. Panos Dossier. London: The Panos Institute, 1993.

Sample, Ian. 'Why is Africa swarming with locusts?', *The Guardian*, 9 September 2004.

Showler, Allan T. *The Desert Locust in Africa and Western Africa: Complexities of War, Politics, Perilous Terrain, and Development*. University of Minnesota, 2004.

Smith, Craig S. 'Rain on Sahara's Fringe is Lovely Weather for Locusts', *New York Times*, 21 July 2004.

UN Integrated Regional Information Networks (IRIN). *Mauritania: Villagers stare hunger in the face after locust invasion*. Bouchamo, 10 February 2005.

UN IRIN. *The Eighth Plague*, OCHA multimedia presentation, January 2005.

UN International Strategy for Disaster Reduction. *Platform for the Promotion of Early Warning Newsletter*. Issue 2004/2, December 2004.

Web sites

Action contre la Faim **http://www.acf-fr.org/**
All Africa **http://www.allAfrica.com**
Desert Locust Information Service
    http://www.fao.org/news/global/locusts/locuhome.htm
Emergency Prevention System (EMPRES) for Transboundary Animal and Plant Pests and Diseases **http://www.fao.org/EMPRES**
Food and Agricultural Organization **http://www.fao.org**
International Centre for Agronomic Research (CIRAD) **http://www.cirad.fr**
Mauritania's Desert Locust Centre **http://www.claa.mr/en/encentre.htm**
Oxfam **http://www.oxfam.org.uk**
ReliefWeb **http://www.reliefweb.int**
Reuters AlertNet **http://www.alertnet.org**
UN Development Programme **http://www.undp.org**
UN Emergencies Unit for Ethiopia **http://www.uneue.org**
UN Integrated Regional Information Networks (IRIN) **http://www.irinnews.org**
World Bank Group **http://www.worldbank.org**
World Food Programme **http://www.wfp.org**

CHAPTER 3

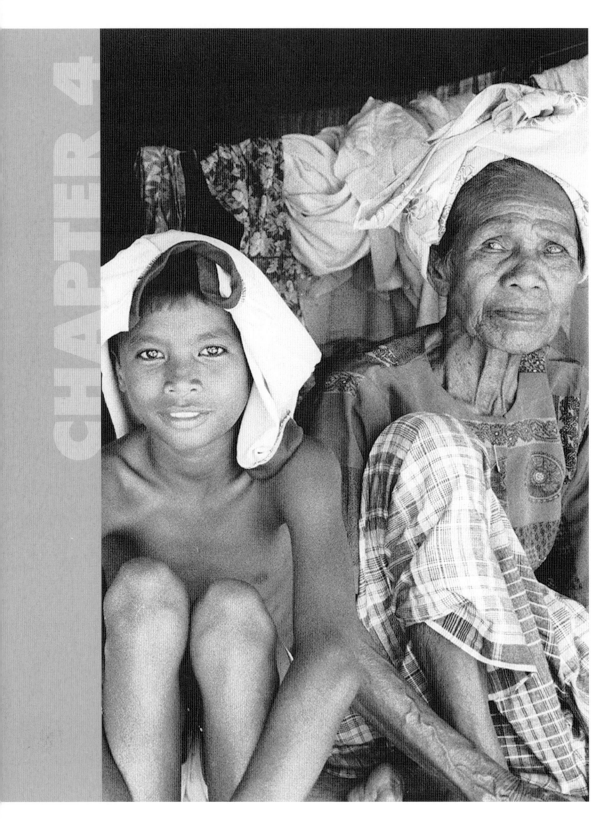

CHAPTER 4

International Federation
of Red Cross and Red Crescent Societies

Information black hole in Aceh

The small group of men can smell the open sea. Yet, surrounded on all sides by salt water, they are more than two kilometres inland. Five weeks after the tsunami of 26 December 2004, the impact remains inescapable. Here, amid a post-atomic bomb landscape, the marketplace of Banda Aceh once teemed with life, until waves as "high as palm trees" came crashing in, minutes after a massive offshore earthquake shook the seabed at 07:59 local time. The smallest of the men, black-bearded and deeply tanned, says his wife and five children are dead. He survived because, on that Sunday morning, he was riding his taxi-bicycle. Now he lives in a government building "with many other men". His face is expressionless. His companions murmur sympathetically, and finally one of them says, "Nothing like this has ever happened anywhere in the world."

But the world took its time grasping just what *had* happened in Aceh, a conflict-torn province at the northern tip of the Indonesian island of Sumatra. Two days after the disaster, Sri Lanka was still being described by media and aid organizations as the area "the most seriously affected by the tsunami". Soon it was clear that this distinction belonged to Aceh, close to the epicentre of the initial earthquake: some 164,000 people dead or missing, more than 400,000 displaced from their homes, not counting a further 390,000 who lost all means of subsistence. All in a province that numbered 4.5 million inhabitants before the disaster.

The tsunami rapidly became the most-reported natural disaster in history, prompting a flood of funding – both official and private – amounting to over US$ 9 billion across the region, according to Reuters. Destruction, death and, above all, international solidarity reached proportions seldom seen before. At least 200 humanitarian organizations – plus military forces from nearly a dozen different countries – converged on Aceh to offer their aid. The result was a messy relief operation, in which information circulated badly and coordination at times appeared non-existent.

On the positive side, the 'second tsunami' of post-disaster disease and deprivation which some were predicting never happened, thanks to enormous Indonesian and international efforts. And most emergency needs were met by the end of January, enabling agencies to target their efforts – and fat budgets – on recovery and reconstruction.

This chapter focuses on the flow of information in the first month after the tsunami. What operational data did disaster managers need during the immediate response? With local communications shattered, how did agencies assess needs? Where were the gaps? Did systems for gathering and sharing information work? How did a lack of information coordination affect the relief effort?

Photo opposite page: The first weeks of disaster response in Aceh were based mor on guesswork and experience than on accurate needs assessments. As a result, some vulnerable people missed out on relief. Aid organizations need to dedicate more resources – especially local and regional staf – to assess needs and consult with affected people, from the very outset of a disaster.

Yoshi Shimizu/ International Federation

News slow to emerge

Four hours after the tsunami hit, a senior government official and the chairman of the Palang Merah Indonesia (PMI – Indonesian Red Cross) boarded a special flight into Banda Aceh, the provincial capital. They grasped the scale of what two United Nations (UN) staff were to discover the following day: tens of thousands of corpses littering the streets, a third of the city's inhabitants perished, and administrative and medical personnel decimated.

So why was news of the catastrophe so slow to filter out? That night, Indonesia's president, Susilo Bambang Yudhoyono, declared a national disaster but, unlike Sri Lanka, did not immediately call for international aid. Indonesian television channels carried on broadcasting the evening's entertainment. Aceh – wracked by armed insurrection for the past 30 years – was under a state of 'civil emergency' and virtually sealed off. Telecommunications had completely collapsed. Apart from the military, no one had either satellite phones or radios. The military and police had themselves lost around 1,000 people, shattering the government's administration and security apparatus in the conflict-torn province.

Footage of the death and devastation in Banda Aceh started flowing the morning after the disaster, filmed by Metro TV, a private Indonesian network whose teams were on the ground within hours (see Box 4.1).

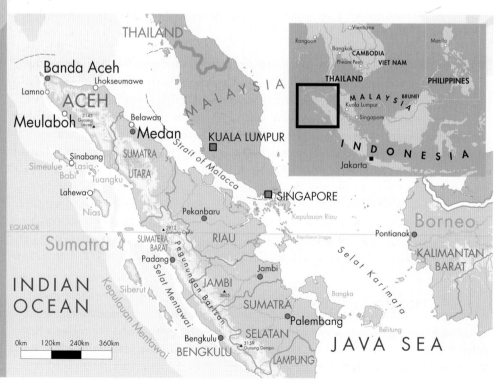

Box 4.1 **The scramble for accurate information**

Until Tuesday 28 December 2004, most media reported Sri Lanka as the country "worst hit" by the tsunami. Although press agencies repeatedly described Aceh as "the closest region to the earthquake's epicentre", this did not lead to the obvious conclusion. There were exceptions, of course. A few hours after the disaster on 26 December, Desi Fitriani, a journalist from Metro TV, a private Indonesian network whose owner is Acehnese, was able to fly from Jakarta to Banda Aceh with her cameraman. Because of the collapse of communications, they couldn't send any footage until the following morning. But then, the gruesome images of thousands of bodies lining the streets started reaching the outside world.

The same day, 27 December, two more television crews (Tim Palmer from the Australian Broadcasting Corporation and Sohaib Jasim from Al Jazeera, both based in Jakarta) arrived in Banda Aceh, after driving along the east coast of Aceh. Although the latter proved to be the less affected part, the journalists were, in Palmer's words, "overcome" by what they saw. They reported on dead children, clinics running out of medicine, and what appeared to be a total lack of government response. From 28 December, news started trickling out from the west coast, the worst-affected area. Metro TV and Al Jazeera reported there were only a few hundred survivors in villages and towns that used to have 10,000 inhabitants. The same day, a Metro TV cameraman flew to Meulaboh, the biggest city on the west coast, and reported on survivors lacking water and food. Meulaboh

was immediately nicknamed 'ground zero' of the tsunami by the media.

By 31 December, the message had got through: Aceh was "by far the hardest hit of any place", in the words of the *New York Times*. Over the following days, stories of massive casualties, slow aid delivery, logistical challenges and lack of coordination dominated. This often negative reporting was to influence aid agencies that had not yet reached Aceh. From 6 January 2005, journalists focused on the two hospitals still functioning in Banda Aceh, described as "overflowing", with the injured arriving mainly from the west coast, suffering from infected wounds that often required amputation. Although the human tragedies were painfully real, the numbers of injured people were actually quite limited. This type of reporting further increased the numbers of medical teams flying in and influenced their make-up, in a way that did not necessarily match needs.

Some humanitarians have complained that the media exaggerated the extent of the disaster in Aceh. "The media depicted the scenario as if half of Sumatra had sunk into the ocean," said one international aid worker, "and did not provide balanced information that the damage ranged between 500 and 2,000 metres along the coast only." An alternative conclusion, however, is not that the media necessarily misreported what was after all the worst natural disaster the world had witnessed for a generation, but that relief organizations should base their responses on more accurate needs assessments than journalists are qualified to make. ■

Locals respond first

Meanwhile, the inhabitants of Banda Aceh were coming to each other's assistance, despite enormous difficulties: wrecked buildings, streets strewn with debris, the lack of petrol for cars, no electricity, repeated aftershocks. Although nearly every family was affected, Red Cross volunteers, with the slowly increasing assistance of the army, removed bodies and distributed whatever drinking water and food was available (see Box 4.2).

In the absence of any central coordination, the first relief workers to arrive from outside managed as best they could. "We did a rapid assessment in town and found about 60 spontaneous IDP [internally displaced person] settlements, of all sizes: between three families and 4,000 people," explained Martin Unternaehrer of the International Committee of the Red Cross (ICRC), whose delegates started arriving on the morning of 28 December. "We would assess in the morning and, in the afternoon, our truck would deliver the tents and family kits." By a stroke of luck, the ICRC warehouse at Banda Aceh was spared, although its stock was rapidly exhausted. The non-governmental organization (NGO) Care International also arrived on the same day, with chlorine tablets to purify the turbid water and maternity kits for pregnant women.

Those familiar with the terrain, such as the PMI, ICRC (operational in Aceh for three decades), Indonesian NGOs and the handful of international aid workers allowed to stay in the conflict-torn province, had a head start. Having offices in town, the confidence of the population and knowledge of the local language proved to be key factors. Even so, their baseline data were incomplete and fragmented along sectoral lines. For example, Save the Children had data about specific communities on the north coast. The International Organization for Migration (IOM) had conducted a health-care survey in conflict-affected areas just three weeks before the tsunami. And the UN Children's Fund (UNICEF), working with the World Health Organization (WHO), had a good national database on education, schooling and medical issues, which included details on vaccination coverage for children in Aceh. They all agreed that government information was generally outdated.

Within 24 hours of the disaster, Emmy Hafild, an experienced Indonesian activist, established the Civil Society Coalition for Tsunami Victims, bringing together 18 local NGOs. Three days after the tsunami, 30 of her volunteers reached Meulaboh by road, even though most believed this devastated town was only accessible by air. "We immediately started assessing the neighbouring villages, very roughly: how many survived, what the basic needs were. We were the first ones to feed back the information to the authorities in Meulaboh," she recalled.

Neighbouring countries – particularly Malaysia and Singapore – were also quick to respond. Language and culture proved no obstacle to their teams, which swiftly grasped the immediate needs. Yet many international agencies opted to bring in staff from Europe or America, when they could have exploited the regional pool.

International Federation
of Red Cross and Red Crescent Societies

Box 4.2 Red Cross volunteers provide relief

Among the first to respond to the disaster in Banda Aceh were 40 volunteers from the local branch of the PMI (Indonesian Red Cross). Still dazed after surviving the tsunami, and despite losing family members as well as their headquarters, they began to organize evacuations and basic first aid. Their numbers swelled to at least 1,000 across Aceh province, coming from PMI branches all over Indonesia. With an average age of 21, most belonged to specialized *satganas* (volunteer disaster response teams).

In the first two weeks, the *satganas* evacuated more than 1,000 survivors, organized relief camp services for 13,000 people left homeless by the disaster and recovered 20,000 bodies. They made field assessments, distributed thousands of family kits, identified sources of safe drinking water, and comforted the injured, sick and bereaved.

With the support of the ICRC, volunteers helped trace and reunite families, by collecting information on "I am alive" and "I am looking for" forms and posting them in public places, in local newspapers and on the Internet. By the end of April 2005, 3,400 family links had been restored, while over 800 survivors used ICRC satellite phones to make calls to relatives. ∎

"Taking steps in the dark"

In the first few days, agencies had to take key decisions based on very little field information. "We mobilized logistics before any assessment. It was a guesstimate, made after three days, with an assumption of 300,000 IDPs," said the ICRC's head of delegation, Boris Michel. "One has to be quick, take calculated risks. In a situation like this, the logistics must move forward. If we do some nice assessment, it will take a month." The organization found that its initial guesstimate, grounded in years of experience in the region, was correct and enabled a rapid and timely response. Michael Elmquist, head of the UN's Office for the Coordination of Humanitarian Affairs (OCHA) in Indonesia, concurred. "Fortunately, our initial expectations proved right," he said.

Priorities were quickly identified: clean water, food and basic shelter for the tens of thousands of people left homeless. In the immediate aftermath of the disaster, medical needs were not immense; there were overwhelming fatalities, but relatively few injured. Searching the rubble was fruitless, as no one could have escaped drowning. In Banda Aceh, OCHA called meetings on a tennis court where the handful of actors present sat on the ground and exchanged information verbally. Communications remained problematic, both within Banda Aceh and with Jakarta. Even the satellite telephones brought in from the capital were not reliable. "Slowly, inefficiently, using mostly SMS [short message service], the information started flowing," recalled one witness.

The situation on the west coast, which bore the brunt of the tsunami, remained the big unknown. More than 700 km of road were affected and over 100 bridges swept away. Not to mention the islands. Whole communities were cut off from the world. How many survivors were there, where exactly were they, what did they need? "The only thing we could guess was there were hundreds of thousands of displaced. For the rest, we were taking steps in the dark," remembered Robin Davies, head of the country office of AusAID, the Australian government's overseas aid programme.

Many organizations admitted they were overwhelmed and lacked the time to undertake detailed assessments or consultations with affected people during the first weeks. According to Ole Hauge, the International Federation's head of delegation in Indonesia, "The field assessment and coordination team was made up of six to seven people. It should have been much bigger. Some of them were busy with operational issues; they had no time for a proper assessment."

As usual in the aftermath of disaster, water, food and shelter were high on the list of survivors' initial needs. But what international agencies didn't realize was that the Indonesians themselves would be able to cover these needs, at least in a basic way. The myth of disaster victims dependent on external aid to survive was one of several that agencies did not do enough to suppress (see Box 4.3). Furthermore, as we shall see later, the needs of vulnerable groups, particularly women, were not sufficiently prioritized in agencies' guesswork.

Military play prominent role

Logistics soon emerged as the key problem. With roads, bridges and ports destroyed, the best solution was delivering aid by air. Few commercial aircraft were available. So, in response to an appeal from the head of the Indonesian army, which had just a handful of its own air assets, military planes and helicopters began to arrive within a few days from neighbouring countries, such as Singapore, Malaysia, Australia and New Zealand. A week after the tsunami, the United States aircraft carrier *Abraham Lincoln* anchored off Banda Aceh with 12 Seahawk helicopters on board.

Helicopters touched down and took off from Banda Aceh, like restless ballet dancers, loaded with food and water. The Indonesian army designated each day's destinations. IOM's Kristin Dadey, one of the few civilians on these first flights, recalled, "Every single village along the coast had disappeared; all you could see were house foundations. Suddenly a group of people appeared, walking towards a bridge they didn't know had been destroyed. Coming from nowhere, going nowhere. When they saw us, they would rush desperately. In the beginning, it was impossible to land, we could have killed people." So supplies were thrown from a height of two metres until Indonesian soldiers could cordon off landing areas.

"We could only do very basic assessments: rough numbers of people, whether they could cook rice, whether they needed water, where to find the injured," commented

Box 4.3 **Three myths – among many**

MYTH: Survivors are 'victims' dependent on external aid. With their history of recurrent conflict, including the last 30 years of insurrection, the Acehnese have developed what one observer calls "a long-term insularity in survival mechanisms". But rather than talk of local resilience, including the strength of extended families and the Islamic community, most media opted for the usual angle: painting a picture of hopeless catastrophe and loss. Images of camps for displaced people predominated, whereas most survivors found shelter with host families. Of 67 BBC reports on Aceh during the two months following the tsunami, for example, self-reliance was scarcely mentioned more than three times (and without ever being the main subject). Only Indonesian media emphasized the courage and solidarity of the Acehnese.

MYTH: Hordes of abandoned orphans. The pervasive perception that thousands of orphans were dependent on international aid was spread, wittingly or not, by a number of agencies. On 15 February, Reuters, citing Indonesian government and UNICEF figures, reported: "Up to 10,000 Aceh children seek parents after tsunami." The reality is more complex. Firstly, the numbers: given their physical weakness, a far greater proportion of children were carried off by the waves than adults. UNICEF estimated children comprised half the victims, whereas before the tsunami only one in three inhabitants were children. "We have more orphaned parents than orphaned children," pointed out UNICEF's Shannon Strother. Secondly, their status: by late February, only 60 children had been identified as 'unaccompanied minors', i.e., left without support from any adult they knew before the disaster. All other orphans, between 6,000 and 10,000 according to UNICEF, were in "some kind of foster situation". Their extended family, their neighbours or their friends had taken them in. The challenge facing humanitarian organizations was to ensure these children were monitored within their 'foster' family.

MYTH: Dead bodies spread infection. Faced with tens of thousands of corpses in the streets of Banda Aceh, both the media and the authorities argued that bodies should be buried swiftly to avoid spreading disease. The Indonesian Ministry of Health initially asked WHO to import very expensive body bags to isolate the bodies. "We keep advocating every time the opportunity arises, but there is still confusion in the media and in the general public," sighs Dr. Vijay Kyaw Win at WHO's office in Jakarta. WHO has published several works, most recently *Management of Dead Bodies in Disaster Situations* (2004), which drive home the message familiar to all experts: "the body of a person killed as a result of a disaster does not pose a risk for infection". Only if the corpses were carrying germs endemic to the region might there be a possible risk, and even then, mainly if drinking water were contaminated. In the vast majority of cases, germs die a few hours after their host. In Aceh, there were many mass graves, another practice outlawed by WHO as a "violation of the human rights of the surviving family members". Not to mention the endless administrative complications that their descendants are likely to face in the absence of a death certificate. By the end of January, there were reports of some Aceh communities reopening mass graves to give victims a decent, religious burial. ■

Dadey. Local inhabitants were taken on helicopters, since some villagers didn't speak the national language, *bahasa Indonesia*. Because of the huge number of places to reach and the small number of helicopters, pilots couldn't land for long in one place, but would carry out rapid on-the-spot assessments, leave instructions with survivors and return the next day to deliver aid and collect the injured.

Collaboration between Indonesian and foreign troops was "amazing", according to Dadey and many others. But it was less so between the military and civilians. "In an operation like this one, the military are ready to do everything if the rationale is explained to them," said OCHA's Josef Reiterer. But that was the problem. Initially, there were no 'interpreters', no civil–military coordination experts, from either the military or the civilian side. As a result, some of the military failed to understand why they should take aid workers on board their helicopters to carry out evaluations. Frustration was intense. Claudia Hudspeth from UNICEF said, "We kept begging for information on what they had seen during their sorties but, for one whole week, this proved useless." A timely deployment of the right civil–military liaison people would certainly have helped.

Despite these reservations, most agree that, in the words of Jesper Holmer Lund (OCHA), "without the military, this would have been a major crisis". Especially as they were managing the three air supply hubs at Jakarta, Medan (Sumatra's main city) and Banda Aceh. When the civil–military advisers did arrive, they ensured aid workers had a greater say in planning the military's response.

Convoys also arrived overland at Banda Aceh, but they took time, particularly as it was the rainy season. Within a few days, the airports were clogged by vital deliveries, as well as by undesirable ones: clothes (often ill-suited for a highly conservative Muslim population), rice expensively supplied by one Asian government despite being produced locally, ambulances no one needed. Aceh saw a repeat performance of the same mistakes occurring at every disaster. Rather than trying to find out what was really needed, some donors actually made an already difficult operation even more complicated.

To prevent congestion at Medan, the ICRC organized its own shipments of aid by air and sea from Singapore to the east and west coasts of Aceh, and then by lorry to affected areas. The organization avoided using military assets, but stationed a delegate at the civil–military 'combined coordination centre' in Thailand, to interact with the military and promote understanding for the Red Cross Red Crescent Movement's neutral and independent humanitarian action.

Reality better than expected

"It has been standard practice in such sudden-onset disasters for organizations to rely predominantly on very basic secondary information, like media reports," remarked

Hisham Khogali of the International Federation in Geneva. This particularly applied to the tsunami, the most media-saturated disaster since 11 September 2001. As ever more dramatic stories of human suffering in Aceh hit the headlines, more and more aid organizations poured in, expecting the worst.

The reality gap could be quite startling. On 4 January, UNICEF's Shannon Strother arrived at Meulaboh, dubbed 'ground zero' of the tsunami by the media, "with lots of assumptions". What she found was quite different. "I had certainly never seen that level of destruction. But survivors were being well cared for," she said. The army and the authorities had already provided basic shelter and food for 30,000 people left homeless – quite an achievement just nine days after the destruction of half the city. The Spanish Red Cross was handling drinking water. Médecins sans Frontières (MSF) and a few others took charge of providing treatment at the hospital, which had survived the tsunami intact.

As a result, a scramble for beneficiaries began. Agencies were now arriving en masse, driven by the media (making up for the earlier dearth of information) and unprecedented worldwide generosity. "When the word came out that a new group of displaced had been found, there was a mad dash to get there first," said Peter Pearce of the International Federation. Some agencies, "on shopping expeditions" as one disillusioned observer put it, jealously guarded their information to make sure of their 'niche'. By mid-January, the 'humanitarian space' had become just too small for all these actors.

Many new arrivals were surprisingly ignorant of any coordination hubs, whether those of the authorities, the UN or the PMI. At Meulaboh, in his improvised office, Putu Suryawan, dispatched from Bali to replace the chairman of the local branch of the Red Cross who died in the tsunami, confirmed: "There are even some Red Cross Red Crescent Societies [from other countries] which don't take the trouble to come and see me. I learn of their presence in the town from other sources."

Cash and competition undermine coordination

In such a context, coordination became a "challenge", as the OCHA staff at Banda Aceh put it. Daily coordination meetings rose from an initial seven participants to some 160. But not everyone participated: out of at least 200 agencies known to have been in the province on 24 January, only 46 had submitted reports to OCHA. Yet this was hardly a bureaucratic exercise. Without knowing who was doing what, and where, some communities were inevitably overwhelmed with aid, while others were neglected.

Although the number of beneficiaries was not huge (compared to food crises in Africa or seasonal floods in Asia), they were scattered over a wide area, difficult to reach, and often on the move. Continuously updating information with the joint input of all actors could have made a big difference. Some joint assessments took place, for example, the inter-agency rapid health assessment coordinated by WHO. But they were rare.

OCHA ended up lowering its ambitions from coordination to 'information sharing', with varying degrees of success (see Box 4.4). For some, OCHA found itself in an impossible situation. "They were given the responsibility without the authority," said Peter Pearce. The structure chosen by the UN – a 'deputy humanitarian coordinator' – placed too much reliance on the goodwill of the actors and failed to unite all the UN agencies, let alone other organizations.

Many of the large agencies coordinated, but not all. The ICRC attended OCHA's coordination meetings in Banda Aceh, but would not be coordinated *by* them. "It is of paramount importance to share operational information to avoid redundancy of action or gaps in the humanitarian response, as well as to convey it to our local partner, the PMI," said Marcus Dolder, deputy head of ICRC's Jakarta delegation, "but in order to preserve our independence, we cannot be coordinated by others."

MSF's James Lorenz admitted to not taking part in OCHA's meetings. "There are just too many people there," he said, "and it becomes a vicious circle: the more disorganized it is, the less people go. We write weekly updates on what we are doing and give them to the authorities."

It was generally felt that coordination meetings addressing a specific sector worked better. But not always: of the 120 agencies invited by WHO and the Ministry of Health to discuss strategic issues at the end of January, only 15 took the trouble to attend.

Language proved another problem. The Indonesian NGOs rarely had the staff required to attend OCHA meetings held in English. Foreign agencies did not always have staff available for government meetings, held in Indonesian. Operational information, as well as coordination, inevitably suffered as a result.

Alan Vernon, of the UN's Office of the High Commissioner for Refugees (UNHCR), captured the coordination conundrum: "We have four different structures: the military airlift operation, the government's own big efforts, the community's efforts and the agencies' work. The problem is they all run in parallel to each other. There is simply no structure to bring them together."

However, at the root of the problems with coordination and sharing information was one key factor: too much money. "Everybody got instantly overfunded, and not through the traditional channels, which are the International Federation and the UN," argued the IOM's Bill Hyde. The figures are staggering: one major international NGO had US$ 40 million to spend in Aceh, in 2005 alone. Nearly everyone could

Box 4.4 HIC: staying on top of the picture as it changes

To meet agencies' thirst for information in complex emergencies, OCHA created the Humanitarian Information Centre (HIC) concept in 1999. From being a simple mailbox system in Kosovo, HIC has developed into an ambitious instrument, with web sites for specific crises and products including thematic maps and directories detailing 'who does what where'. Web sites also display any relevant information that HIC staff can find: assessments, situation reports (sitreps), meeting schedules, etc.

Determined to be operational rapidly, two staff reached Banda Aceh with laptops on 3 January 2005 and started producing basic maps of the region. A week later, the 'HIC in a box' arrived, containing computer and office equipment. Global positioning systems (GPS) were distributed to agencies, enabling HIC to create the first map of spontaneous settlements for displaced people. "This was the fastest we ever deployed," said Kathleen Miner, HIC manager at Banda Aceh.

But the technology couldn't keep up: Internet connectivity was very slow. The HIC web site was not operational until 20 January. "Technology has made us dependent," noted Jesper Holmer Lund of OCHA. "We have to accept that, during the first phase of an emergency, we cannot be on the Internet. We have to use the SMS, the e-mail, satellite phones, whatever works."

Another problem is that the HIC could only supply its users with what it received from them since it initially lacked the staff to gather information proactively. "The challenge is how much you stay on top of the picture as it changes," says Miner. Particularly when homeless people keep moving and agencies' projects develop haphazardly. UN coordination meetings echoed the same refrain: "Please let the UN know what information you have, please share your assessments." The site even put up a standard assessments form, but the response was poor. "I hardly have time to share information with my own people. I would not take time to share it with the HIC," said the press officer of a major international NGO bluntly.

An evaluation of HIC just before the tsunami stated, "The HIC's contribution... can be meaningful only when organizations subscribe to a common approach and devote the necessary resources to support it." The report added, "HICs have not been able to provide a quick and dirty analysis of the 'needs and gaps' at the beginning of a response." Hence one of its key recommendations: "Donors should renew their attempts to get agencies to routinely share information with HICs." Kathleen Miner is a firm believer in training. "You cannot teach basic reporting in a disaster," she said, mentioning a few workshops on 'best practices in humanitarian information' held since 2002. "I would like to see more of these."

However, Hisham Khogali of the International Federation argued that: "An organization needs to get a return on the investment in order to share information. Incentives for information sharing and coordination can be very diverse, including funding, being assigned sectoral lead, enhancing your own information and analysis, reducing duplication of efforts, sharing resources and responsibility, and being able to influence others." In January, with agencies overfunded and competing for space, incentives for sharing information were few. But by March, when the HIC requested input for a 'who is going to do what where' database, 170 local and international NGOs replied, fearing that if they didn't, the government could ask them to leave. ∎

hire a helicopter or boats, make their own needs assessments and distribution arrangements, and 'fly the flag'. The classic situation, in which NGOs queue up to become implementing partners of the UN, was reversed. "Everybody was all of a sudden a player on an equal footing. Instead of being a facilitator, the UN became an obstacle," said another observer.

The over-abundance of supply also had positive effects. Basic needs had largely been covered by the end of January, even in remote locations. The much-feared outbreak of epidemics had not occurred. But, as in many major disasters, some aid efforts were duplicated and resources wasted. "Depending on how you look at it," remarked one UN officer, "you can say this has been the best-funded emergency in the world – or the most expensive humanitarian response in history."

Reaching the most vulnerable

By late January, the aid effort was in full swing: the International Federation and PMI had between them reached over 70,000 people with relief. The UN's World Food Programme alone was feeding 330,000 people. In addition to the humanitarians, 3,000 foreign military personnel from 11 countries were still involved in the relief effort on the ground – not counting troops based offshore.

Acehnese women survey the damage in the tsunami-hit Indonesian provincial city of Banda Aceh, 7 February 2005. Women's priorities must become an integral part of aid agencies' assessments and operations.

© REUTERS/ Beawiharta, courtesy www.alertnet.org

International Federation of Red Cross and Red Crescent Societies

Yet this massive response included some questionable organizations (see Box 4.5) and still missed some of the most vulnerable people. During the first few weeks, communities on the east coast of Aceh were far less covered than those on the west

Box 4.5 "The world's largest unregulated industry"

In their yellow T-shirts printed with 'Scientology' in bold black letters, the groups of young Australians are difficult to miss. The badge they sport – 'trauma care' – sends shivers down the spines of many observers. "Do you realize that these people are providing so-called psychological support to traumatized children? And no one can stop them!" exclaims a UN worker. "One cannot claim to be a doctor or an engineer without proper qualifications. Why should it be any different for humanitarian aid workers, given the impact they have on people's lives?"

Among the plethora of organizations and individuals invading Aceh with their good intentions, not all provide the professional guarantees required. Frédéric Pennard, from Médecins du Monde (MdM), cites an incident in a village near Banda Aceh. When MdM arrived with measles vaccines provided by UNICEF and WHO, some children had just been vaccinated by an unknown NGO which left no record of its activities. "We couldn't tell any more who had been vaccinated and who hadn't." By the end of January, this kind of incident (far from isolated) led Oxfam to call on "governments in the tsunami-hit region to work with the UN to introduce immediately a system of accreditation for international agencies to ensure the work they are doing matches their experience".

Non Rawung, director of Indonesian NGO Obor Berkat, agrees. Furious at 'disaster tourists' taking the places of doctors she was flying in from Jakarta, she told the government, "You should have a list of professional NGOs and give them priority!" But

how sort the good from the bad, without international standards? "In the absence of a regulatory framework, it is difficult to determine the capacity and professionalism of organizations," says Bo Asplund, UN humanitarian coordinator in Indonesia. Ethical standards already exist (such as the *Code of Conduct for the International Red Cross and Red Crescent Movement and NGOs in Disaster Response*, which has been signed by over 300 organizations), but they are voluntary, not regulatory. "Why shouldn't there be an Institute of Chartered Humanitarian Workers?" suggests OCHA's Oliver Lacey-Hall.

In the meantime, he and others argued that governments must stop funding NGOs who refuse to work within the agreed coordination structure. Some donors have already started. AusAID (Australia's governmental aid agency) introduced strict quality criteria in 2001 and saw its partner NGOs drop from 120 to 50. But in a disaster such as Aceh's, with so much direct public funding, government filters may not be enough.

Some humanitarians don't believe regulation is possible or desirable. Steve Gwynne-Vaughan, of CARE, believes the 'come and go's', as they are sometimes known, have a role to play: "Of course these smaller NGOs do not coordinate with others. But they are a lot faster; they get in there when everybody else is still talking about it. In a situation of conflict, like here, they have their advantages. You can stop CARE, we play by the rules, but you can't stop them. The desire to help leaks through every hole..." ■

coast, which, because of the scale of destruction and logistical challenges, quickly attracted the most media attention and aid. The government had asked the UN to concentrate its efforts in the west, partly because of the needs and partly because of ongoing military operations in the east. However, none of the agencies that took the initiative to work in eastern areas was prevented from doing so.

"The east coast has always been much poorer than the west, and we are dealing with at least 150,000 displaced there," said Tom Alcedo of Save the Children Fund-US (SCF-US). That compared with an estimated 125,000 people displaced on the west coast and 130,000 in Banda Aceh. SCF-US, which was active in Aceh before the tsunami, worked with its local partners to provide the authorities with the first figures on displaced people in the east. The ICRC also targeted people in the north-east. Their long experience in the province prevented both these organizations from launching a media-driven operation.

Meanwhile, although at least half of Aceh's 400,000 IDPs found a roof with host families, very few of these families received any aid from international agencies in the first month. "This city is literally full of displaced people, but you hardly see them," noted UNHCR's Vernon. "Without doubt, we haven't yet adequately supported the host families," he added, referring not only to UNHCR but other actors as well. His agency found one house sheltering 42 IDPs.

Nurul Aida was one of the lucky ones. She took refuge with her husband and her only surviving child in her grandmother's home, in the village of Samsuar, on the edge of Banda Aceh. "We have received a few clothes and some food four times since the tsunami, from the government and from the PKS," she said, referring to an Islamic party whose members brought relief to survivors within hours and subsequently sent in 1,000 volunteers from across the country.

At the end of January, the authorities were surveying this hidden, scattered population, whose presence was beginning to burden host families and the social services. International agencies, which concentrated on official camps and spontaneous settlements, had scarcely begun to assess their needs. So this impressive example of communal self-reliance reaped few rewards for either the thousands of homeless or their generous hosts.

More generally, five weeks after the tsunami, virtually all agencies admitted they had failed to identify vulnerable categories apart from unaccompanied children. "In a wonderful world, we would partner with the government and the NGOs and do a nice vulnerability assessment," said Claudia Hudspeth at UNICEF's office in Banda Aceh, with an exhausted smile. "But for the first weeks, we were working under such conditions that there was simply no space for any strategic thinking. This will change from now on."

International Federation of Red Cross and Red Crescent Societies

More midwives needed

The highly 'visible' and emotionally charged health sector attracted the greatest concentrations of agencies. Three weeks after the tsunami, the WHO-led joint assessment found 22 health NGOs in one area on the west coast. As with Kosovo in 1999, there was a mismatch between supply and demand, described by the WHO as "an oversupply of temporary tertiary care facilities and medical staff".

Ten international field hospitals were set up in Banda Aceh alone, none of which worked at full capacity – although getting them there used up vital airlifting capacity. Then on 7 February, the *Mercy*, an American hospital ship with 1,000 beds, arrived at Banda Aceh, by which time some of the field hospitals had already been packed up. "By providing free treatment, they risk destroying the local infrastructure," commented one Swiss doctor, "whereas what is really needed at present is to rebuild the health centres washed away by the tsunami."

Consequently, there was an oversupply of surgeons. Their expertise was clearly useful in early January, when hundreds of injured – seriously infected from untreated wounds – poured into the hospitals. But as relatively few survivors were injured, supply quickly outstripped demand. One UN witness in Meulaboh saw "20 surgeons competing for a single patient", towards the end of January. MSF, however, drew their conclusions from the very first assessments. "We were expecting a huge number of injured, and we actually found most people were dead," said James Lorenz, "so, we shifted our focus to water and sanitation, in order to avoid epidemics."

By contrast, midwives and nurses were in short supply. "There remains a significant dearth of providers who can give maternal and child care," noted WHO's inter-agency assessment team in mid-January. Since the tsunami, they said, women on the west coast had to give birth without medical assistance, "an unacceptable risk to the reproductive health of women".

Women suffer disproportionately

Bernard Coquelin, representative of the UN Population Fund (UNFPA) in Jakarta, made the obvious but apparently overlooked point that "women don't stop giving birth because there's been a disaster". His agency immediately sent doctors and obstetric equipment to Aceh. Additionally, in this very traditionalist region, women prefer to be cared for by female medical staff. The Indonesian NGO Obor Berkat was well aware of this and 60 per cent of its medical teams were women. In Lamno (western Aceh), however, the commander of a team of 18 military doctors, despite being from a Muslim country, declared himself unable to understand the need to bring female doctors.

In emergencies, gender issues tend to be "postponed until later, under the tyranny of the urgent", remarked Ines Smyth of Oxfam. Her agency, however, sent a gender adviser in the second week and swiftly forged links with local women's organizations. "In communities, in the very early stages, women asked for underwear, head scarves and sanitary protection," said Smyth. Out of sight of men, they also asked for the contraceptive pill. One Acehnese woman spoke for many when she told Karuna Anbarasan, senior gender adviser with UNHCR, "We don't want to have more children with things as they are."

Both Oxfam and UNHCR strove to organize women's committees to help with aid distribution, reconstruction and getting schools restarted, although in this highly patriarchal society, such systems were slow to emerge. Oxfam, meanwhile, made an effort to include women in cash-for-work programmes.

Women and children, weaker and less able to swim, died in far greater numbers than men. According to WHO, "Most IDPs on the west coast are male and in some villages no child under 5 and only a small percentage of women survived the tsunami." So the camps for homeless people were full of widowers, raising fears of sexual violence. According to Smyth and Anbarasan, it is crucial to have women in assessment teams, otherwise certain issues – from appropriate aid to complaints about sexual harassment – will not emerge.

Working through local structures

International organizations could have made fuller and more systematic use of national agencies. Of course, Indonesian NGOs – practically forbidden until the democratization of the country in 1998 – often have limited capacity. But many would echo the criticism voiced by local activist Emmy Hafild, who had to fight for days before finding funding (Dutch) for her activities in Aceh. "So many of these foreigners didn't think about tapping the potential of the local civil society," she lamented (see Box 4.6). Instead, international agencies weakened Indonesian NGOs by luring local staff away with higher salaries. In Aceh, this criticism was constantly voiced. But it remains an unresolved dilemma for international agencies seeking to tap into local knowledge quickly in the aftermath of disaster.

For their needs assessments and aid distribution, most international agencies went through village heads, known in Aceh as the *lurah*. Re-created in displaced communities and rapidly replaced if killed, these leaders know everyone within their community. Agencies also operated through the *camat* (head of sub-district), the *panglima laut* (an elected representative of local fishing skippers) and the *Muhammadiyah*, the second-largest Muslim association of Indonesia, with branches at local level. These hierarchical structures were known by agencies previously active in Indonesia, and very quickly identified by newcomers.

Box 4.6 Consultation captures resilience of Aceh's survivors

"There were 5,000 of us. Now there are 400," says 40-year-old Wirman, one of the survivors of Kaju, a boat-building community 200 metres from the sea. Despite the death toll, he wants to return, to rebuild his home where it was before. Is he aware that the authorities aim to ban any reconstruction along a 2-km strip by the sea and that, in any case, the tsunami destroyed the building in Banda Aceh containing the property titles? He sweeps all objections aside. "Gotong-royong," he says proudly, using the Indonesian term for 'community self-help'. "If the authorities don't help us, we'll fend for ourselves." Inside the tent, men and women nod in approval. In the meantime, they are willing to move to the barracks the government is building a few hundred metres away, but "for no more than a few months". Have they been told what to expect? "No, we have just seen them building these barracks."

By early February, no official information had reached displaced people on their future, despite the fact that relocation to the barracks was due to start ten days later. True, the authorities were still drawing up their plans. Nevertheless, remarks Amanda Melville of UNICEF, "The lack of information on basic issues like relocation is extremely stressful for these already traumatized people."

Other people left homeless have already taken matters into their own hands. In Lampulo kampong (village), the boats flung onto the rooftops by the fury of the tsunami still rest there, while enormous bulldozers clear away the ruins. The deafening noise and dust do not deter the village head, Jusuf Zakaria, an elderly man impeccably turned out with a carefully trimmed moustache. He has set up his headquarters in a hotel, with a group of young assistants, and is methodically organizing the return of the kampong's survivors (one-third of its 6,322 inhabitants). The survey form which Zakaria himself devised impresses the UNHCR officer visiting that day. The community has already received supplies from the Islamic Student Association and the Indonesian Red Cross. Only water is lacking: "If some international organization builds toilets and drills a new well, my people will come back," he says.

"Relocation is not the only option," says Emmy Hafild, chair of a coalition of 18 Indonesian NGOs planning a reconstruction project at Nagan Raya, close to Meulaboh on the west coast. The inhabitants were consulted on how to protect the coast in the event of a tsunami "and they came up with great ideas", says Hafild. People suggested building a road perpendicular to the coast (at present, the road runs parallel), to enable them to run inland. They noticed the local river had slowed down the wave, and suggested digging it deeper. Many survived by climbing coconut trees, which weathered the tsunami, so they suggested planting more. Villagers also suggested building platforms on top of mosques for refuge. At least 90 per cent of mosques remained intact, sheltering many survivors, because they were solidly built. As one Indonesian observer puts it, when you build a mosque, "you don't cheat God". ■

However, village or district heads couldn't necessarily be relied on to put the needs of the most vulnerable – including women – first. As SCF's Tirana Hassan put it, "Camp or village leaders are men." So, more professional agencies identified alternative pre-existing structures, for example *Tuha 4*, which is a village-level advisory board comprising the imam and the head of the village, but also their wives and youth representatives. Some agencies created new structures, such as women and children committees. But, even by late February, organizations acknowledged that these alternative structures had not been sufficiently employed.

One Swiss NGO opted to fund the People's Crisis Centre, a group of young Acehnese previously working on human rights, to distribute emergency goods to 7,000 displaced people. Unlike the usual system of providing aid to the head of the community, they went from door to door every week. This approach reduced the risk of aid being misused and ensured regular contact with local people – an important way of providing psychological support to those traumatized by recent events and knowing nothing of what the future held.

Conclusions and recommendations

Six weeks into the relief operation, agencies still lacked precise data about internally displaced people. The obstacles to information gathering were particularly numerous in Aceh. The geographic scale of the disaster created huge logistical constraints: settlements along hundreds of kilometres of coast were devastated and cut off from the outside world. During the initial response, and despite the great number of agencies involved, relief players were overstretched: time was in short supply to reach all survivors as fast as possible. Detailed assessments and gathering feedback were sacrificed in favour of delivering material aid.

The ongoing insurgency put agencies off exploring some affected areas or raising protection issues. Rivalries between agencies, competing to spend unprecedented budgets, did not encourage information sharing. Language was an additional barrier, with some people in remoter locations, especially women, speaking only Acehnese. Traditional local power structures and top-down approaches by aid organizations led to the needs of women and other vulnerable groups (with the exception of unaccompanied children) being poorly assessed.

The enormous international response to the tsunami in Aceh succeeded, in its own chaotic way, in getting aid to most of the survivors and preventing further deaths from hunger or disease. Yet, the duplication of effort and competition for profile and beneficiaries give pause for thought. Can it be right, just because donors have given so generously, for certain agencies to fly their own flag rather than work alongside others? Does every NGO or individual brimming with good intentions have to rush in, when they may lack the expertise required? It is difficult to regulate a profession which, by its very nature, is the expression of human solidarity. But the governments of disaster-struck countries don't always have the means to decide which agencies to let in. The debate should continue on how best to accredit and coordinate organizations, without at the same time stifling the creativity and generosity of civil societies.

These issues are not easy to deal with. Some recommendations follow – made by expert observers and aimed at international aid organizations – for improving information sharing and coordination during emergencies:

- **Dedicate more staff to assessments** and consultations with affected people at the very outset of a disaster, so that relief workers can concentrate on relief. More local and regional staff should be included in assessment teams.
- **Appoint an information coordinator in the field** to promote well-informed decision-making during hectic and exhausting relief operations. The UN's Humanitarian Information Centres could train more people in reporting and information sharing.
- **Promote joint sectoral assessments** by agreeing that specific organizations coordinate sector-wide, inter-agency assessments based on accepted criteria, providing vital baseline data for all operational agencies.
- **Deploy enough civil–military liaison staff** from the outset of the disaster, if military aid is likely to play a large role in relief, so that mutual information needs can be shared and misunderstandings ironed out.
- **Work with local NGOs**, rather than poaching their staff, to avoid misunderstanding local issues and weakening local structures. These can be swiftly identified in the first days of a disaster.
- **Work through alternative local groups** from the outset to avoid perpetuating existing power structures that may lead to unfair aid distribution.
- **Prioritize the needs of women**, particularly in patriarchal societies and where there is a risk of sexual violence. Women's issues must become an integral part of agencies' assessments and activities, instead of being, in the words of Ines Smyth, "something strange and additional".

Iolanda Jaquemet, an independent journalist presently based in Jakarta, Indonesia, was principal contributor to this chapter and Boxes 4.1, 4.3, 4.4, 4.5 and 4.6. The International Federation and the ICRC provided the information in Box 4.2.

Sources and further information

Houghton, Rachel. *Tsunami Emergency. Lessons from Previous Disasters.* London: ALNAP (Active Learning Network for Accountability and Performance in Humanitarian Action), 2005. Available at http://www.alnap.org/lessons_tsunami.htm

International Federation. *Recovery Assessment Team Report – Indonesia.* Geneva: International Federation, 2005.

Pan American Health Organization. *Management of Dead Bodies in Disaster Situations.* 2004. Available at http://www.paho.org/english/dd/ped/ManejoCadaveres.htm

Sphere Project. *Joint Quality and Accountability Initiative. Assessment and Scoping Report, Aceh, Indonesia.* 4–13 February 2005.

Sida, Lewis and Szpak, Chris. *An Evaluation of Humanitarian Information Centers, including Case Studies of HICs for Iraq, Afghanistan and Liberia.* USAID Office of US Foreign Disaster Assistance (USAID/OFDA) and the UK Department for International Development (DFID), 2004.

World Bank. *Indonesia: preliminary notes on reconstruction – The December 26, 2004 natural disaster.* Working paper. January 2005. Available at http://www-wds.worldbank.org

World Health Organization. *Inter-Agency Rapid Health Assessment. West Aceh, Indonesia.* 13–19 January 2005. Available at http://www.who.int/hac/crises/international/asia_tsunami/final_report/en/index.html

International Federation of Red Cross and Red Crescent Societies

Web sites

Asia-Pacific area network **http://www.apan-info.net**

Center of Excellence in disaster management and humanitarian assistance
http://www.coe-dmha.org/tsunami.htm

Humanitarian Information Centre for Sumatra
http://www.humanitarianinfo.org/sumatra

International Committee of the Red Cross **http://www.icrc.org**

International Federation **http://www.ifrc.org**

ReliefWeb **http://www.reliefweb.int**

Reuters AlertNet **http://www.alertnet.org**

World Health Organization, Indonesia **http://www.who.or.id**

International Federation
of Red Cross and Red Crescent Societies

Sharing information for tsunami recovery in South Asia

"I don't want to see another cooking pot – I have as many as I will ever need. I want to know where my family is going to be living in one month's time!" Parvita, a widow from Villapurum district, in south India's Tamil Nadu state, sums up what many of her fellow survivors across the region feel, three weeks after the tsunami shattered so many lives: they want clear, hard facts about their future.

Emergencies are confusing, chaotic, fast-changing environments where rumour often plays a more powerful role than fact. Aid agencies focus mostly on the 'hardware' side of a response – rice, pumps, trucks – but neglect the invisible components. In the case of the tsunami, for example, using public information campaigns to dispel fears of further waves and rumours of poisonous flesh-eating fish. Or letting people know what official assistance they are entitled to receive and when, so they can plan for the future.

While governments and international agencies were swift to start installing a high-tech early warning system for Indian Ocean tsunamis, what about the more low-tech information needs of disaster survivors? Was the catastrophic failure to communicate the threat of the oncoming tsunami followed by an equal failure to communicate with affected communities striving to recover? What were the obstacles to capturing and sharing information? Who was left out and what were the implications? What could governments and international organizations learn from how civil society groups shared information and coordinated their action?

This chapter addresses these questions from the perspectives of affected communities across the South Asian region. In Part 1, **Anna Jefferys** analyses the flow of information in the months after the tsunami hit Tamil Nadu. She finds that local civil society groups proved more effective than some international organizations in sharing information, capturing the needs of the most vulnerable and campaigning to put local priorities on the recovery agenda. In Part 2, **Vijay Simha** asks why accurate information was in such short supply in India's Andaman and Nicobar Islands. What impact did restrictions on journalists and aid workers have on disaster survivors?

In Part 3, **Kumudini Samuel** and **Sepali Kottegoda** report on how disaster responders failed to capture the specific needs and priorities of women in the aftermath of the disaster in Sri Lanka. They find, however, that a number of women's

Photo opposite page: Despite an overwhelming humanitarian response civil society groups in Sri Lanka voiced concern that the needs of women were being overlooked.

Yoshi Shimizu/ International Federation

groups have embraced a range of different media to communicate their needs and rights to the wider world. Finally, in Part 4, **Lena Eskeland** identifies the role of communication in the psychological recovery of affected people in Sri Lanka. She finds that dispelling myths, encouraging community discussions and listening to other people's stories are vital tools in nurturing the process of mental healing.

Part 1: Civil society communicates local priorities in Tamil Nadu

The walls of water that laid waste to 1,000 kilometres of coastline in south-east India on 26 December 2004 destroyed buildings, boats and vehicles in 376 coastal and inland villages across 13 districts of Tamil Nadu. The waves' destructive energy swept up to 4 km inland.

Across India, 1 million people were affected. By April the toll of missing and dead had risen to over 16,000 people. The vast majority of victims were children, who had trouble escaping, and women killed on the beaches as they waited for their husbands to return from fishing, or while looking after their children. Hundreds of thousands of people lost all their possessions.

The Indian government led the humanitarian response, with support from over 400 local, national and international non-governmental organizations (NGOs), human rights groups, religious organizations and United Nations (UN) agencies – plus hundreds of private foundations and individuals.

This disaster posed a unique set of communications challenges. The tsunami struck a long, narrow strip of coastline, making communication from one end to the other very difficult. It took weeks for NGOs to undertake even cursory rapid assessments all along the coast. Many humanitarian organizations based themselves in Chennai (Madras), 1,000 km from the southernmost affected areas. Language barriers hampered the work of both national NGOs from north India and international agencies. One international NGO office comprised 12 staff, none of whom spoke Tamil – not even the driver.

The enormous scale of national and international interest in the disaster, flooding the area with material goods and money, complicated the flow of information. The sheer number of actors involved led agencies to compete for space, which encouraged them to conceal rather than share information. Rumour and confusion spread over what needed to be done first and how. The government insisted on controlling the disaster response, leaving relief organizations bewildered about where they fitted in. And, as always, some agencies were less keen to coordinate than others, hampering the smooth flow of information.

International Federation
of Red Cross and Red Crescent Societies

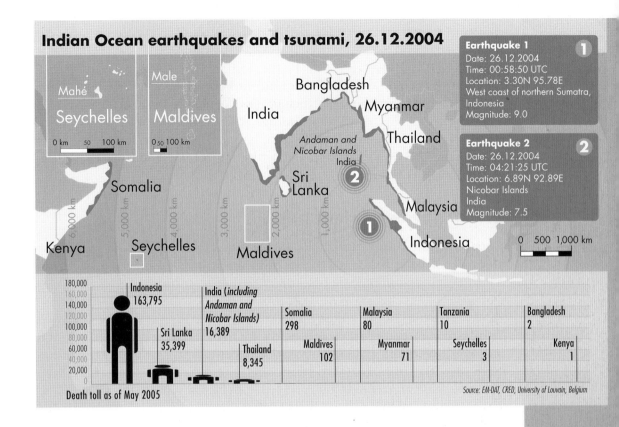

Indian Ocean earthquakes and tsunami, 26.12.2004

Earthquake 1
Date: 26.12.2004
Time: 00:58:50 UTC
Location: 3.30N 95.78E
West coast of northern Sumatra, Indonesia
Magnitude: 9.0

Earthquake 2
Date: 26.12.2004
Time: 04:21:25 UTC
Location: 6.89N 92.89E
Nicobar Islands
India
Magnitude: 7.5

Indonesia 163,795	India (including Andaman and Nicobar Islands) 16,389
Sri Lanka 35,399	Somalia 298
Thailand 8,345	Maldives 102
Malaysia 80	Myanmar 71
Tanzania 10	Seychelles 3
Bangladesh 2	Kenya 1

Death toll as of May 2005

Source: EM-DAT, CRED, University of Louvain, Belgium

Indian government takes control

The Indian government, well practised in dealing with large-scale emergencies, launched a swift and decisive response. Initially, it shunned external aid, calling on international organizations to focus elsewhere in the region. The government delivered relief supplies and water, prevented the spread of disease, reconnected electricity and built temporary housing along the coastline. Families received cash payments for deceased family members, compensation to replace boats and nets, and relief packages of food and material goods. Meanwhile, the Indian Red Cross Society fielded 3,000 volunteers and, in close coordination with the government, delivered aid to half a million affected people.

Many praised both the federal and state governments' emergency responses, despite what was often described as their patriarchal attitude to the intervention and to information sharing. "The government likes to decree, and in many cases it makes the right decisions," said a spokesperson from the 6,000-member South Indian Federation of Fishermen Societies (SIFFS), "but officials do not consult as widely as they could."

For those with access to technology, the clarity and accessibility of information was good. State-level recovery policies were regularly posted on the Tamil Nadu government's web site, alongside facts and figures about the response, who was affected and where.

However, this information did not extend to village level. Those with the least information were, unsurprisingly, marginalized groups, such as *dalits* (low caste 'untouchables'). "The absence of knowledge as to when they receive compensation leads to high levels of anxiety," said Silke Pietzsch, food security and nutrition adviser with Oxfam. "Many of them are taking out loans to survive or to repair equipment, which means they risk sinking further into debt."

Glut of goodwill brings risks

During the first chaotic weeks, the unprecedented media profile of the disaster provoked a flood of NGOs and private citizens to respond – with considerable, but sometimes misguided, goodwill (see Box 5.1).

"There is a glut of money, a glut of goodwill," said Raju Rajagopal of the Bhoomika Trust, a coordination network with experience from the Gujarat earthquake. "You can't stop people from wanting to get involved, but now we have to take the time to make sure the relief doesn't destroy communities." For instance, said Babu Matthews, head of ActionAid International in India, "In some cases, in the rush to provide people with boats, those involved in the boat-building industry were being done out of a job."

"The need to carve up the pie quickly meant that many groups undertook rapid assessments that overlooked some of the complexities of the communities they were assessing," continued Matthews. Donations of too many boats, for example, could encourage recipients to sell them and upgrade to trawlers and mechanized boats, which may lead to dangerous levels of over-fishing.

The Asian Development Bank's recovery report of March 2005 called for more rapid environmental assessments and argued that "actions related to reconstruction and recovery should seek to ensure that the sustainability of coastal and marine ecosystems is not compromised".

The real fears lay with newly formed organizations that lacked the experience to understand the longer-term risks posed by inappropriate rehabilitation. However, more experienced Indian and international NGOs discussed potential pitfalls. Most carried out rehabilitation assessments in consultation with local people and established feedback mechanisms to measure the impact of their programmes.

There were exceptions: the lack of appropriate psychosocial support, for example. "All of the NGOs have been talking non-stop about psychosocial counselling," said

International Federation of Red Cross and Red Crescent Societies

Box 5.1 Used clothes clog up response

One of the most enduring images of tsunami relief operations in south India is the mounds of used clothes blanketing the countryside and clogging city streets. Collected by well-wishers from around the country, and often trucked thousands of kilometres, it shows that it is not just foreigners who can misjudge what is needed.

Fisher families, depicted both nationally and internationally as the poorest of the poor, are actually a relatively prosperous and proud community. Even in such dire circumstances, they would not accept second-hand clothes.

However, in the days after the disaster, middle-class individuals, local community groups and even major companies from northern India put massive efforts into collecting the clothes. And as the waves affected only a narrow coastal strip, the devastated villages were accessible for innumerable well-meaning members of the public offering such assistance.

Their fleets of private vehicles only added to the traffic chaos and the drivers, whether in frustration or through a lack of proper instructions, often simply dumped donations on the roadside. The mounds, including heavy sweaters at the start of a south Indian summer, became such an impediment that municipal workers were diverted from the relief effort to gather them up. In Nagapattinam alone, there were enough clothes to fill a large warehouse.

"Instead of looking at the demand from the field, people sent the supplies they had," says Dr. J. Radhakrishnan, Nagapattinam's top administrator. As well as blocking roads, wasting workers' time and taking up storage space, the unwanted clothing proved a hazard to local livestock which tried to eat it.

Other well-meaning but not well-thought-out aid included shipments of wheat (when rice is the staple of the south) and cooked food (often not to local tastes and delivered in the wrong amounts) which became a health hazard when dumped.

Radhakrishnan is clear that communication is essential: "We spoke in the national and international press about what we needed and just as importantly what we didn't need – emphasizing that materials should be needs based not supply based." His administration worked closely with the Nagapattinam NGO coordination cell, which offered information on needs as well as maps and registration facilities for newcomers.

In Chennai, Raju Rajagopal of the Bhoomika Trust, a local group that concentrated on coordinating aid operations, agrees that communication of what is *not* needed is vital. Within days, Bhoomika had issued a bulletin to their ever-expanding e-mail distribution list (which included government officials, humanitarian agencies and Indians abroad) saying that used clothing was "a waste of time".

This time, that is. Rajagopal emphasizes that needs are different in every case and that assessments must be flexible: "In the next disaster, people may be freezing to death and happy to wear them. There are no hard and fast rules."

He was pleased to see that some lessons did appear to have been learned and says there was not a lot of dumping of medicines, as seen after the Gujarat earthquake. And some good may yet come from the piles of clothes: a local community group is planning to train women in stitching the cast-offs and selling the final results – as quilts. ∎

Gouthami of Christian Aid, "but in spite of this, no one was simply listening to people vent their grief, fear and frustration – that is what they really wanted."

Most international and national NGOs worked through local partners, enabling them to reach the most vulnerable. But there was a risk that local partners would design responses according to their own social hierarchies. One answer, said Guy Clarke of Oxfam Australia, "is to second staff into local, community-based NGOs, who have worked in these villages for years", to help boost accountability.

Civil society shares information

As emergency relief morphed into rehabilitation, confusion arose over the government's longer-term policy. "Officials state what they intend to do but give no indication of when they'll do it," said Babu Matthews.

These problems are common during disaster and apply equally to NGOs. One observer of the tsunami response commented: "There are huge discrepancies between what is reported – in terms of type of intervention, process, numbers of people reached – and what organizations actually do. After a while, you don't know what to believe."

However, in Tamil Nadu, there was no risk that people would quietly accept such confusion. The state has produced some powerful community-based civil society networks giving voice to different groups, including fishing and agricultural unions, human rights groups, religious organizations and networks representing *dalits* and women.

Some of the most active in galvanizing communities into action after the tsunami included SIFFS (representing fishermen), SNEHA (representing women) and the Bhoomika Trust. These state-level groups set up local networks along the coast to share information, discuss key needs of communities and advocate on priority issues – such as village reconstruction or compensation packages – at the highest levels of government. Other groups, for example the Auroville tsunami rehabilitation coordination network, pushed government to accept their designs for permanent housing.

The most effective of these local networks was the Nagapattinam NGO coordination cell. Over 7,000 people in Nagapattinam district alone were killed by the tsunami and nearly 200,000 were affected. SIFFS, SNEHA and Bhoomika set up the cell three days after the tsunami, and 400 NGOs (local, national and international) registered with it.

The cell's main aims were to ensure that affected people's real needs were communicated to disaster responders and to help agencies avoid duplication. Their

International Federation
of Red Cross and Red Crescent Societies

approach was simple: appoint volunteers to liaise with village 'focal points' each day, to identify gaps in the response and capture people's needs and priorities. This information was communicated through the cell's office each evening to the district collector (chief administrator), and informed the government's response.

The cell's volunteers also informed NGOs of the gaps in aid – such as the lack of children's clothes, women's underwear, adequate latrines or basic medicines – at special meetings held to coordinate different aid sectors. This local information-gathering system covered 100 villages in Nagapattinam district.

Following the relief phase, the cell became a resource centre, galvanizing advocacy, liaising between government and NGOs, and posting information such as assessments, policies and case studies on its web site. "There is no formal advocacy route for these people to get their voices across," said local activist Aftab Mohamed, "but because the Nagapattinam administration is fairly responsive, the system we set up seems to work."

Mohamed attributed this success to the detailed knowledge which groups such as SIFFS and SNEHA have of local communities, combined with the experience people gained from the Gujarat earthquake – where coordination cells had even more weight, as the government and UN also participated. Such experience and leadership were lacking elsewhere along the coast and information sharing suffered as a result.

Local networks channel anger into advocacy

"People seem to be going through the usual phases of recovery: shock and denial, frustration and anger, then recovery," said Oxfam's Silke Pietzsch, in late March. "They are in the anger phase now, and it is very powerful!"

Several networks tried to channel this anger and voice the concerns of disaster-affected people. The Tsunami Relief and Rehabilitation Committee (TRRC), SIFFS and Bhoomika rallied civil society groups to help shape the government's policies on the quality of temporary housing and reconstruction of permanent housing.

The government initially established a coastal regulation zone, banning all new housing within 500 metres of the shore. However, due partly to extensive pressure from civil society networks, the new shelter guidelines of 2 April stated that rebuilding could take place either 5 metres above the ground or 500 metres from the sea – a marked change in policy. Local groups continued pushing to protect the beach so that it was not open to takeover by private sector developers.

According to Vibeh Kanata, head of SIFFS: "While the government doesn't engage in substantial consultation with local populations, it does, however, have an open door policy, with village groups free to launch petitions, to schedule meetings with their local representatives, while high-level government officials regularly attend community meetings to address questions."

For some people, however, the government didn't open the door wide enough. In March, one local advocacy network took the concerns of 5,000 tsunami survivors to a Supreme Court hearing. "The state wasn't responding to people's requests for information regarding their entitlements," said Babu Matthews.

Widows testified anxiously in court that they would be entitled to nothing because male members of their extended family still survived. A coir (coconut fibre) producer asserted his right to compensation because, unnoticed by officials, he too had been put out of business by the tsunami. News of the hearing resonated up and down the coast. However, its use will be proved only if the government responds to these concerns.

Capturing the needs of the neglected

The court case raised a difficult issue central to many emergencies: who defines whether people are affected by disaster or not – and how? The answer determines whose needs and priorities are met. The Tamil Nadu government's definition of those 'affected' by the tsunami initially included all who had lost a tangible asset – a relative, a house, a boat or other possessions. This overlooked those who had lost their livelihood.

The focus of the emergency response was on coastal fishermen and their families, since they are the dominant income group in the area. But what about others involved, more invisibly, in the fishing community? The women who dried and sold fish? *Dalit* groups who packaged and transported it? *Idli* sellers who provided rice cakes for returning fishermen? Basket-weavers, net-repairers and boat-carpenters?

Inland fishing communities also suffered, as well as sharecroppers and farm labourers – around 80 per cent of whom are *dalit*. And what about salt-panners, many of whom lost their entire stock and had to take out loans to start again?

Sonya Le Jeune, livelihoods adviser for Save the Children, analysed the needs of many such 'invisible' groups. Her report noted that harvests might have been destroyed for two to five seasons, "yet no systematic loan scheme is being planned" for agriculturalists. Father Yesumarian, from the Dalit Human Rights Group, said: "People coming in from the outside couldn't see past the destroyed boats and nets to the other groups. However, the whole economy of the region was destroyed, not just fishing."

The problem lay mainly in how information was gathered. According to Gouthami of Christian Aid, "There is a heavy data bias towards men in information collected." This is partly due to convenience: "Many go to the village council for information, all of whose members are male." Assessors may have undervalued women's economic contribution to the fishing industry – repairing nets, selling fish and dry fishing – because it is traditionally seen as support work.

When Le Jeune talked to groups of women in one fishing village in Cuddlore district in February, they said it was the first time anyone had asked for their opinion, while the village's men had been quizzed by numerous groups.

Omitting women's needs in the long-term response would have serious implications, particularly for widows (and their children) who risk sinking into dangerous levels of debt. According to Jesu Rethinam of SNEHA, "Widows whose husbands are still classified as 'missing' rather than 'dead' are not yet entitled to any compensation, leaving them very vulnerable."

Meanwhile, wealthier fishermen stood to gain more than their poorer neighbours. Only registered boats could be considered for official compensation – overlooking poorer fishermen, who often bought boats second-hand and didn't have to register them officially. "The big boat-owners with ten, 12 motor-boats will get money," complained S. Thomas, a fisherman in Nagapattinam, "and I, who made my own boat, will get nothing!"

By late April 2005, the state was still trying to identify the real number of fishermen who had lost boats. Speaking to the BBC, one local charity coordinator said: "The problem is that many people who did not own boats have staked a claim to the new ones being given out."

Caste acted as a barrier to obtaining both information and aid. "*Dalits* living in the hamlet next to the fishing village of Uyyalikuppam have claimed bias in the aid distribution, complaining fishermen were stopping aid coming to them," said Father Yesumarian. The fishermen in question denied this, claiming *dalits* exaggerated levels of need. Others cited examples of communities who were forced to 'share' their aid with more powerful neighbours.

"Fisherfolk *Panchayats* [village councils] are powerful – at first they only gave out information about fishermen to assessors, not other groups," said Gouthami. Certainly SIFFS, the fishermen's federation, provided strong leadership, mobilizing communities to strike when they weren't receiving adequate compensation.

Babu Matthews, who has been working in the region for decades, remarked: "In these calamities you just have to assume that the marginalized – be they scheduled castes [*dalits*], the disabled or others – are going to be left out and you must plan your response around reversing this." His method was to approach these groups directly, never through intermediaries, when gathering information.

"At first, the bulk of the attention was on those who were 'visibly' affected," said Silke Pietzsch. Despite the presence of hundreds of NGOs, not all gaps were filled, especially inland. The *dalits* of Shanmuganagar, Cuddlore district, for example, lost houses and people to the tsunami, but had still received no aid three months later.

Realizing how the lack of structured, unbiased information sharing hampered the overall response, four international organizations (Oxfam, Save the Children, Christian Aid and the UN Development Programme) began jointly setting up an information management centre in Chennai. After much negotiation with the government, their proposal was approved in April 2005.

Their aim is to capture village-level information from districts along the coast, outline future research and response plans, and feed information back to villagers through a series of 'information kiosks', each run by a village representative.

While these information kiosks could bridge an important gap, have other, simpler communications tools, such as community radio, been overlooked (see Box 5.2)? The kiosks pose a number of challenges. They should be linked; too often information goes one way, from beneficiaries to donors and government, but is not shared between communities. And agencies should ensure they don't over-bureaucratize the process. The lesson from Nagapattinam is that simple is best.

Democratic communication key to recovery

The scale of the tsunami's impact in south India, plus the vast distances involved and the hundreds of organizations responding, greatly complicated communication channels. On the whole, international NGOs were much slower to coordinate and share information than national NGOs and civil society networks. In the scramble to assess needs, many marginalized people missed out. And poorly conceived rehabilitation plans risked disrupting communities further and damaging the environment.

Gathering and sharing the right information during disasters can save lives and livelihoods. Some key lessons and recommendations arising from Tamil Nadu's post-tsunami experience are as follows:

- **Share needs assessments.** Agencies should recognize the need to coordinate immediately with the host government and each other, by undertaking inter-agency assessments wherever possible. This would relieve the burden on communities constantly having to answer the same questions; reduce the likelihood of inflating expectations; and provide a catalyst to share information about potential responses.
- **Strengthen information links with local networks.** Chennai-based NGO discussions were not always grounded in local realities and often relied on anecdotal evidence to guide planning. Stronger links should be forged between

Box 5.2 Promoting dialogue through radio in Sri Lanka

A small radio is making a big noise at a camp of tsunami survivors crowded into temporary tin huts in Ampara, eastern Sri Lanka. It is mid-February 2005. Puspa Rani bought the red plastic radio using compensation she received for the death of her daughter. As she and her neighbours do their chores, they listen to reports of former US presidents Clinton and Bush Sr visiting to review relief efforts. She has few other possessions – two plastic mats, a chair and a bucket. The radio is their only connection to the outside world.

Up the coast in Batticaloa, the Danish Red Cross's Karen Helene Mourier Havrehed says: "At one camp I was told, 'now we have food and we have cookers, we need information'. They were asking for newspapers and televisions." Havrehed thinks television may pacify rather than empower, but she is keen on distributing radios. "We know here that access to information is very hard from official sources. It is important to provide access to mass media."

Quality matters, as well as access. Mass media can spread ill-informed speculation. One Sri Lankan station rebroadcast an incorrect tsunami warning at the end of December. Tales of a bracelet found in a fish's stomach circulated widely and may have put people off eating seafood.

Sunanda Deshapriya of the local NGO Free Media Movement, fears relief efforts will fade from the front pages. "The people's voices are not reflected unless there is an agitation to cover. They do not track projects over a period of time or run investigative stories." His NGO trained 20 provincial reporters, with the aim of tracking relief projects over the next year.

Local media played a vital role after the disaster. "There were no other communica-

tions; telephones were down, the mail was down," says Neel Weeratunga, head of the southern regional service of the Sri Lanka Broadcasting Corporation (SLBC). "Crowds came in here wanting us to convey messages to their relatives, giving letters to put on air."

For the first ten days, the station's music programming was transformed into a public message board. With few resources they still do what they can. One programme, broadcast live from a relief camp, featured a reporter simply handing a mobile phone to fishermen who vented their frustration at not returning to sea.

Christian Quick of Internews, an international media development NGO, says such outlets prove invaluable, as shock and apathy turn to frustration at the speed of rehabilitation. "It's a two-way mechanism. Going into the camps helps the government by letting them know the needs. And it helps stabilize things by giving people a voice. They know that people like them are getting heard."

Quick, who began assessing information needs ten days after the tsunami, says international organizations can provide a 'buffer' for state-employed journalists who fear criticizing the government, and can support private stations that lack journalistic capacity. Internews subsequently trained two mobile teams to produce tsunami-related reports for local broadcast (see Chapter 7, Box 7.6).

Humanitarians are recognizing the vital importance of information after disasters, says Quick. "Media development is entering the vocabulary in the development world a lot more now as a natural component of humanitarian assistance. Information needs are being seen as part of human rights." ■

local networks and state-level forums. This doesn't require complex technology, just setting up simple information-sharing structures appropriate for people living in technology-free villages.

- **Plan assessments that address the whole community,** not just selected households within it. As a Bhoomika Trust report put it: "The desire to give must not overtake the ability of the community to absorb aid. The social costs of adding massive assets to one section of a community without assessing the impacts are enormous."

- **Consult regularly with affected people.** While rapid assessments are inevitable during the emergency phase, agencies must subsequently take the time to plan in-depth assessments based on meaningful consultation with affected communities. Only in this way can responses address the innumerable ways that different people have been affected by the crisis.

- **Adopt a more holistic approach.** Agencies could benefit from expert analysis of how communities can protect themselves from future disasters. Mangrove swamps, for example, act as a natural buffer against large waves. Restoration of Tamil Nadu's damaged mangroves – within a framework of integrated coastal management – should form part of post-tsunami rehabilitation.

Dispelling myths, tracing lost relatives and informing people about resettlement plans can greatly reduce the psychological trauma felt by survivors.

Yoshi Shimizu/
International Federation

International Federation
of Red Cross and Red Crescent Societies

- **Support democratic communication.** This disaster presents an opportunity for international organizations to support civil society groups campaigning to put the priorities of the most vulnerable at the top of the recovery agenda. Rehabilitation efforts must be designed to expand, not shrink, the opportunities available to marginalized communities. Otherwise, interventions risk entrenching existing inequalities by, for example, shifting people off their land, blocking their access to resources and making them more dependent on 'loan-sharks'. Fostering democratic communication channels that enable information to flow transparently in all directions is fundamental to ensuring this will not happen.

Part 2: Andaman and Nicobar Islands – accurate information in short supply

Fifteen hundred kilometres off the Indian mainland lie the Nicobars – a collection of islands and rocky outcrops that extend New Delhi's sphere of influence well into South-East Asia. However, their strategically significant location near Indonesia and Thailand also placed them – and the Andaman Islands to their north – in the direct path of the 26 December tsunami.

"I think 20,000 people died here," said Manoranjan Bhakta, member of parliament for Andaman and Nicobar, in early February 2005. SEEDS, an Indian NGO which reached the islands two days after the disaster, put the figure at around 15,000. The official toll in late January stood at 1,927 people dead and 5,555 missing. Why was it so hard to get accurate information on what happened in the Andaman and Nicobar Islands, and what impact did this have on tsunami survivors?

Counting the dead was enormously complicated by the sheer scale of the disaster and the geography involved. The Andamans and Nicobars comprise several hundred islands, just over 30 of which are inhabited, scattered across 800 kilometres of ocean. The 6-metre-high tsunami swept many people out to sea and engulfed entire islands such as Katchal, just a metre above sea level: 87 per cent of Katchal's 5,312 people were listed as missing or dead.

"Where could they have gone? There's only the sea or the land here. They are either alive or they are dead," said Bhakta. According to Sameer Acharya, a long-time resident of the Andamans' capital Port Blair and head of the Society for Andaman and Nicobar Ecology, "The 2001 census figures will tell you there were 356,152 people in Andaman and Nicobar Islands. In reality, there were close to 450,000 people when the tsunami struck. How come there were so many? Where did they come from? How did they settle here?" he asks.

"Some of the non-tribal people were living here illegally," said Bhakta, speaking to Reuters news agency in late February. They had originally come over as labourers for public works contracts but stayed on, often settling near the coast. Military officers admitted to Reuters that the official death toll on Car Nicobar island did not include settlers.

At the end of March, the figure of missing across the archipelago was reduced to 2,700 and 3,000 'missing' were recorded as dead, bringing the final toll nearer to 5,000 lives lost. But as long as victims remained missing, their next of kin could not claim official compensation, worth around US$ 2,300 per dead family member.

Meanwhile, international aid organizations had great difficulty accessing the islands to make independent assessments of the needs and priorities of survivors. India's prime minister announced that his country didn't need foreign assistance with disaster relief and, according to an official statement dated 1 January 2005, 90 army engineers, nine navy ships, five coast guard ships and two merchant ships were dispatched to aid the stricken islands. The Andaman administration kept international and mainland Indian NGOs at arm's length for the first fortnight – not a problem faced by humanitarians seeking to respond in the Maldives, another Indian Ocean archipelago swamped by the tsunami (see Box 5.3).

Even before the disaster, access to the islands was very controlled. The administration and tribal councils argued that contact between the archipelago's indigenous tribes and outsiders should be limited. Organizations could only receive permits to visit 'tribal islands' after receiving an invitation letter from the tribal councils. Yet most of these tribes lived in the Andamans. It was the Nicobar Islands – home to sensitive military bases – which were hardest hit by the tsunami.

In mid-January there were 71 registered NGOs in Port Blair, waiting to be allowed access to other islands. "It was only after 15 days that I was able to get to Nicobar," said Manas Ranjan of ActionAid. Oxfam had to wait until early February for its tribal invitation and permit. "Valuable time has been lost because of this delay," said Shaheen Niloufer, the head of Oxfam's operations in eastern India, adding that it was "accelerating the miseries of the poor people". According to Manoranjan Bhakta, even a month after the disaster, relief had not reached Katchal, the worst-affected island. "There is no transparency," he said. News filtered through from survivors, who arrived in Port Blair from remoter islands and described conditions as desperate.

Access to the islands was restricted for journalists. Private Indian television networks, plus the government-run Doordarshan channel, were able to report on the disaster from the day it struck, but only under the supervision of the defence forces. "As media attention grew, the administration was under huge pressure to let in NGOs and INGOs [international NGOs] to respond to the affected men, women and children of the islands," said Sahba Chauhan, Oxfam's communications manager.

Box 5.3 Information flows smoothly after rough ride in the Maldives

Although just over 100 people perished in the Maldives, the scattered atoll nation was hammered by the tsunami, which affected two-thirds of its 300,000 inhabitants and left 80 islands badly damaged or uninhabitable. For a nation spread across 868 kilometres of ocean, the disaster presented a nightmare scenario. Yet the relief operation in the crucial first weeks ran relatively smoothly.

Key to this success was the National Security Service (NSS), the government agency mandated for emergency response, the equivalent to the civil defence in other countries. Meanwhile the capital, Male, was the sole conduit for information sharing and aid distribution, forcing external actors to go through the government.

Detailed information was scarce in the early hours of the emergency, according to Lieutenant Colonel Ahmed Shahid of the NSS. The cell phone network, on which the islands are now heavily reliant, was down and there was little data coming in about damage and casualties. Within hours, the government decided to despatch relief supplies before assessing needs. Shahid conceded there was an element of 'hit and hope' in the initial response: "It was a blanket effort to get relief items out, based on little information. If we had had to wait, it may have been too late." Within a week, telecommunications on all islands were re-established and the picture became much clearer.

Compared to the influx of at least 100 international NGOs in Sri Lanka, the arrivals hall at Male airport was hardly overloaded with foreign aid agencies. There was already a UN presence and they were joined by just six major international organizations in the weeks following the disaster.

The consensus was that the information flow from the government to international agencies was quick and, most importantly, accurate. "The Maldives government was very well organized and it had quickly established an emergency control centre. They looked after NGOs and the media well and they were quick off the mark getting information out," said Mark Evans of Oxfam. Qasim Zahid, representing the International Federation, said the information flow was nearly 'real time' and could be acted on with confidence. "What information they had they were sharing with us. They were very open," he said.

According to Evans, local government also played a key role: "Island and atoll chiefs got under way with their own assessments before external organizations arrived. This proved to be very helpful." Shahid said the government was aware how vital quick, reliable information was: "We gave them [NGOs] whatever we had. We knew that if they were to be able to give us assistance, they needed information. We were also aware that we were the only initial sources of information and transport."

The lack of foreigners overcrowding the response also helped improve information sharing and coordination, according to Qasim Zahid. "There were a small number of NGOs and those that were here were very experienced. There was no competition for resources, while the coordination meetings were some of the most fruitful I've attended. At such meetings in other operations, I've experienced everyone talking but no one listening," he said. Mark Evans concurred: "I have seen waves of competing organizations in previous disasters. It was much easier working in the Maldives." ■

Slowly, controls over access to the islands were eased. In March, Oxfam said they were able to work with the local administration. Tony Vaux, visiting the islands in early April to evaluate international aid responses to the disaster, said: "The remarkable point is that India has opened up at all. The government has shown surprising flexibility in allowing NGOs to operate. Their attitudes have changed."

Part 3: Sri Lankan women's groups use media to lobby for rights

In a few fateful hours on the morning of 26 December 2004, the savage power of the tsunami cut a swathe of destruction that spanned 12 of Sri Lanka's districts, from Point Pedro in the north to Galle in the south and Negambo in the west. It claimed more than 35,000 lives, destroyed or damaged over 100,000 homes and left half a million people homeless.

More women than men lost their lives in the disaster – almost 50 per cent more in some areas. In the eastern district of Ampara, for example, 3,972 women died compared to 2,124 men. For most women, learning to swim or climb a tree was culturally taboo and so, as killer waves up to 10 metres high engulfed them, they couldn't save themselves in the way men could. Women were more likely to spend a few critical minutes gathering their children before fleeing – a delay that often proved fatal. Their traditional clothes, such as sarees and long skirts, made running or swimming in water almost impossible. Many women, whose clothes were ripped off by the waves, were too ashamed to run and remained crouching in the water when the next waves hit. In Ampara, a large number of young, unmarried women died in their homes, reluctant to leave unaccompanied by a male relative.

The immediate relief operations were largely 'gender blind'. Few organizations considered providing women with sanitary needs, underwear or culturally appropriate clothing. The needs of pregnant and lactating mothers were not sufficiently catered for. Many of the welfare centres for homeless people lacked spaces for women to change in private, dispose of sanitary towels, breastfeed their babies, wash or bathe. Women were not usually included in camp management. They couldn't determine how space was allocated or how relief items were distributed. If allowed to participate at all, they were generally relegated to the stereotyped tasks of cooking and cleaning. As camps overflowed, women became nervous at being forced to share living space with so many unknown men.

For its part, the International Federation distributed sanitary pads and created special rooms in their emergency health centres for women who were pregnant or breastfeeding. Ten days after the disaster, a spokesman for the United Nations Population Fund (UNFPA) said: "Women's special needs need to be addressed from the outset." UNFPA

International Federation of Red Cross and Red Crescent Societies

made US$ 3 million available to provide the most basic maternity and hygiene support for women throughout the region. However, as late as 8 March – International Women's Day – Lucita Lazo, the director for South-East Asia of the United Nations Fund for Women (UNIFEM), said: "We need to move from gender blindness to gender sensitivity in helping the tsunami victims." Ongoing gender concerns prompted the International Federation to launch a survey of the issue in May 2005.

Meanwhile, very few women-specific concerns featured in Sri Lanka's newspapers or radio and television discussions. Media interest in women focused on victim stories – some, at best, raising awareness of how the tsunami affected men and women differently. As sporadic reports of sexual harassment began to appear in the press, five women's networks formed the Coalition for Assisting Tsunami Affected Women (CATAW). They issued a press briefing on 1 January calling for an inclusive, gender-sensitive approach to disaster management. The briefing highlighted reports of rape and physical abuse of women and girls during unsupervised rescue operations and in temporary shelters.

This led to a spate of sensationalist reporting by the press, radio and television, with complete disregard for the social and cultural sensitivities that surround such incidents. It served, however, to give sexual violence some visibility and prevented denial. CATAW followed up its briefing with a fact-finding mission. The publicity this raised prompted the state to respond by sending police and soldiers to guard camps and issue guidelines for access and behaviour within camp premises. It also resulted in capturing the attention of agencies such as UNIFEM and UNFPA, which consulted with women's networks to put in place mechanisms to assess gender-based risk and provide protection for women.

Local women's groups and those working on gender concerns found innovative means of accessing the media to create awareness and acceptance of gender equality in the response to the tsunami. Young Asia Television (YATV) made a series of programmes with tsunami-affected women recounting their own stories and proposing solutions to help them rebuild their lives and those of their families and communities.

The Intermediate Technology Development Group produced a video entitled *Facing Disasters, Making Decisions – Gender Dimensions in Disaster Management* to persuade government and NGO officials to address the specific needs of women. The Sri Lankan organization Women and Media Collective aims to enable women directly affected by the tsunami and women working in affected areas to articulate their concerns publicly through feature programmes on radio and television. The collective is teaming up with YATV to provide women with audiovisual equipment to record recovery programmes in their communities.

Women's groups have tried to shift the focus of post-tsunami work towards a rights-based approach. On 24 March, the Women and Media Collective placed an advertisement in the mainstream press reiterating that tsunami-affected communities are not mere victims but citizens with rights. This unique public appeal, to "let women's voices be heard", emphasized women's rights to be informed, be consulted and participate in decision-making. Noting that "women are key in the process of sustainable reconstruction and rehabilitation", they demanded that all reconstruction planning be gender sensitive. They demanded equitable provision of basic needs such as food, energy, water and sanitation in all resettlement sites and called on the authorities to:

- "Prevent violence and harassment of women in temporary shelters and resettlement camps.
- Consult women regarding plans for their relocation and their homes.
- Ensure that there is no discrimination against women in terms of land allocation and ownership as well as in terms of grants for house-building.
- Support women with livelihood assistance in both traditional and non traditional areas that include skill-training and capacity building.
- Ensure that provision of sustained psycho-social support and reproductive health services are an integral part of reconstruction plans."

CATAW continued lobbying through locally-based women's organizations, which in turn networked with local government and NGOs. As international NGOs proliferated, women's groups from Batticaloa district formed the Women's Coalition for Disaster Management (WCDM), bringing together women from international NGOs and communities in an innovative structure of information sharing, decision-making and common activity. The WCDM engaged with local task forces dealing with tsunami assistance, conducted a gender watch and campaigned on a range of issues.

As with most areas of policy in Sri Lanka, women affected by the tsunami had very little, if any, voice in the plans being formulated to determine their recovery and future. However, women's coalitions in Sri Lanka continued to lobby at all levels to put their concerns – on displacement, relocation, land rights, shelter, housing, protection, livelihoods and, above all, women's inclusion in decision-making – on the agenda.

Their efforts may have borne fruit in late April 2005, when the Sri Lankan government approved a proposal made by the Women's Empowerment and Social Welfare minister to ensure gender equality and adequate female representation in all relief and rehabilitation mechanisms. Women's groups welcomed this proposal and called for it to be translated into effective action as soon as possible.

Part 4: Communication crucial for mental recovery in Sri Lanka

The Indian Ocean tsunami of December 2004 not only caused unprecedented physical damage, but created deep psychological scars in the minds of many survivors.

Marygilda is a 34-year-old single mother from Jaffna, in the north of Sri Lanka. During the country's long-lasting conflict, she had to flee to Point Pedro, the island's northernmost tip. Then the tsunami destroyed her home and belongings, forcing her to move again. Now she lives in a tented camp for 'displaced people'.

"When the tsunami came, I was unable to grab my children and all four were washed away. They were saved miraculously, but my eldest daughter and my mother were admitted to hospital," she explains, with a tired look on her face. After the tsunami, her children suffered from sleeping problems and are still afraid of the sea.

According to experts, almost all people affected by a major disaster will experience some kind of adverse psychological reaction, due to their traumatic first-hand experiences, loss of loved ones, being forced from their homes, financial difficulties, loss of livelihood or feelings of guilt. Most recover naturally, but between 5 and 10 per cent may develop long-term psychological problems, requiring professional help.

In Sri Lanka, however, some tsunami-affected districts had no functioning referral services and only one or two psychiatrists to cover large areas. So how could aid organizations help survivors recover psychologically? What kinds of information and communication were most valuable?

Helping them get in touch with their family was a vital first step (see Box 5.4). "Right after the disaster it is important to give psychological first aid. We talk to people, try to keep people alive, remind them to eat, sleep – but we don't try to cure anything," said Kohila Mahendravajad, a trainer counsellor from the Sri Lankan NGO Shanthiham that worked with the Danish Red Cross psychosocial support programme in Jaffna. "Then gradually we can help them start processing their experiences, and identify individuals with serious problems that need to be treated."

The Danish Red Cross built on its experience supporting conflict-affected people in Jaffna to help tsunami survivors in other districts of Sri Lanka. "We see the same psychosocial problems after the tsunami as we saw after the conflict. But there is a higher sense of guilt and grief after the tsunami," said Karin Eriksen, who had worked on the Jaffna programme for the previous two years. "Many feel guilty because they ask themselves: why did I go to the market and leave the children alone? Or they blame others: why didn't you hold on better to our daughter? In war, there is a more physical thing to blame it on. It is difficult to blame it on the sea, also because the sea is what brings many of these families their daily income."

Some experts argued that dispelling myths and spreading accurate information about the nature of the disaster and its consequences contributed to people's mental

Box 5.4 Restoring family links by satphone and Internet

Immediately after the tsunami disaster, the International Committee of the Red Cross (ICRC) – in cooperation with National Red Cross Societies – deployed mobile family links teams to help reunite survivors with their relatives. In Aceh, the teams were active in all affected districts and helped restore family links in 3,400 cases, mainly via satellite phone. They registered almost 19,000 survivors and 25,000 missing people. Lists of both were put on a special web site (http://www.familylinks.icrc.org), printed in booklets and on posters distributed through ICRC and local Red Cross networks, as well as being published in newspapers, allowing people to scan for the names of their loved ones. The tracing teams registered 46 unaccompanied children throughout the province and were able to reunite 34 children with their parents or other close family members.

In Sri Lanka, 12 mobile teams visited over 300 welfare centres and enabled more than 1,700 people to make satellite and mobile telephone calls – the majority to relatives overseas. The teams collected 417 "I am alive" messages that were posted on the ICRC web site and published in the Sri Lankan media. Over 50 particularly vulnerable people were actively traced and contact with their families was restored through Red Cross messages. With the speedy restoration of normal communication channels in Sri Lanka, tsunami-related tracing activities were scaled back within the first few weeks. But in March, the ICRC started distributing mail kits, consisting of stamps, envelopes, paper and pens to allow families to stay in touch with relatives and, at the same time, express their feelings about the ordeal they lived through. ∎

recovery. "It is very important to provide people with accurate information. This can help the person cope with the disaster and understand that it is not his or her fault," said Sylvaine Courbière of the Belgian Red Cross.

In a training workshop run by the Belgian Red Cross in Sri Lanka's Kalutara district, the facilitator asked participants what a tsunami was and what their communities understood about this phenomenon. It emerged that some affected people believed the disaster was caused by something wrong that they did, and that the tsunami came as a punishment. During the discussion, the facilitator drew a sketch on the whiteboard showing circles of waves spreading out from the earthquake's epicentre until they hit Sri Lanka's beaches.

"There is a major phobia in people that there may be another conflict or another tsunami," said Kohila Mahendravajad. "It is important to explain that this is unlikely to happen, or, if it happens, what should we do. It is also important to provide information about the disaster, and problems caused by the disaster. People have to understand the effects and symptoms of traumatic events, and in what way they can come out of the problem," she argued.

International Federation
of Red Cross and Red Crescent Societies

Another local NGO, Plan Sri Lanka, initiated a campaign to help schoolchildren cope with the grief and devastation caused by the disaster. As a part of this, they placed advertisements in the newspaper, explaining what tsunamis are and emphasizing that although they are terrible, they are very rare. "So we don't need to be afraid of the sea," concluded the ad, "the beach is still a great place to play."

For other experts, these facts were less important than ensuring people heard the stories of others who had gone through similar experiences. One Sri Lankan NGO used videotaped case studies from India to show how other affected people were coping.

The American Red Cross followed a similar strategy, training psychosocial volunteers to tell stories or use theatre and pantomime. Affected people were encouraged to tell their story through radio, TV or newspapers. "This way we can have an impact on thousands of people who wouldn't be reached otherwise," said the American Red Cross's Joseph O. Prewitt Diaz, a Puerto Rican psychiatrist with 30 years' experience.

Through these methods, common psychological problems experienced by disaster-affected people were communicated. Then, the communities were asked if they had gone through similar experiences and advice was provided on how to recover. Prewitt Diaz argued that although external experts like himself may be useful for training personnel, the core of a good psychosocial programme is community participation. His team developed flipcharts and other communication tools to ensure that the whole community was involved in discussions and decision-making. "There is a need for all communication to survivors to be rooted in cultural practices of the target country, linguistically appropriate and technically sound," he emphasized.

Kohila Mahendravajad, from the Sri Lankan NGO Shanthiham, cautioned that there are disadvantages with one-way communication methods. "Here there is a stigma related to mental problems; we have to make sure that the information is not misunderstood," she said.

In recent years, Prewitt Diaz and his team have trained around 10,000 Red Cross 'crisis intervention technicians' in India, Nepal and Myanmar. Following the tsunami, they trained teachers and counsellors in Sri Lanka, the Maldives and Indonesia. However, their activities didn't focus only on talking and counselling, but on helping people to become operational again. So information and communication are just the beginning. Encouraging people to eat together, continue daily life or start work are some of the simple techniques that may speed up the process of mental healing.

"We help get women's groups or community kitchens together, get children to paint chairs in the classroom, or men to pick up debris," said Prewitt Diaz. "The objective is that people become actively involved in their own well-being. This way the victim becomes a victor."

Main contributors to this chapter were Anna Jefferys, a freelance journalist who works on humanitarian communications, policy and advocacy issues for Save the Children UK; Vijay Simha, a senior writer for the weekly newspaper Tehelka, *based in New Delhi, India, who visited the Andaman Islands three times this year to report on the tsunami; Kumudini Samuel and Sepali Kottegoda, women's rights activists and co-directors of the Sri Lankan NGO Women and Media Collective; and Lena Eskeland, the International Federation's information delegate for tsunami-related activities in South Asia. Boxes 5.1 and 5.2 were contributed by Joanna Nathan, a New Delhi-based independent journalist. John Tulloch, regional reporting officer for the International Federation's South Asia delegation, contributed Box 5.3. The International Committee of the Red Cross contributed Box 5.4.*

Sources and further information

Asian Development Bank, United Nations and World Bank. *India: Post Tsunami Recovery Program, Preliminary Damage and Needs Assessment.* New Delhi, 8 March 2005.

Coalition for Assisting Tsunami Affected Women (CATAW). *Fact Finding Report: Visit to Galle and Ambalangoda: Information Gathering on Incidents of Violence Against Women Reported in Areas Affected by the Tsunami.* January 2005.

CATAW. *Women's Groups Appeal for an Inclusive Framework for Disaster Response.* Press release. 1 January 2005.

CATAW. *Memorandum to the Members of TAFREN: Representation in Decision Making Bodies on Shelter and Land Rights for Women in the Post Tsunami Resettlement Process.* 26 March 2005.

CATAW and Women's Coalition for Disaster Management (WCDM). *Integrating Gender Concerns in Post Tsunami Relief Operations, Statement to UNIFEM.* 13 May 2005.

Oxfam. *The tsunami's impact on women.* Oxford: Oxfam, 2005. Available at http://www.oxfam.org.uk/what_we_do/issues/conflict_disasters/bn_tsunami_women.htm

Social Scientists Association. *Polity.* Vol.2, No.3, 2005.

WCDM. *Memorandum to the Batticaloa District Disaster Operational Committee: Concerns of Displaced Women's Welfare and Rights.* 12 January 2005.

WCDM. *Memorandum to Her Excellency the President: Concerns of Displaced Women's Welfare and Rights.* 25 April 2005.

Women and Media Collective. *Options.* Vol. 36, No. 1, 2005. Colombo.

Web sites

Andaman and Nicobar Islands official tsunami web site
  http://tsunamiandaman.tn.nic.in
Bhoomika Trust coordination forum **http://www.tsunami-india.org**
Centre of Excellence in Disaster Management and Humanitarian Assistance,
  Hawaii, USA **http://coe-dmha.org/tsunami.htm**
International Federation **http://www.ifrc.org**
Maldives National Disaster Management Centre **http://www.tsunamimaldives.mv**
Oxfam International **http://www.oxfam.org**
Save the Children UK **http://www.savethechildren.org.uk**
South Indian Federation of Fishermen's Societies (SIFFS) **http://www.siffs.org**
SIFFS tsunami web site **http://www.tsunami2004-india.org**
Sri Lanka government's 'Task Force for Rebuilding the Nation' (TAFREN)
  http://www.tafren.gov.lk
Sri Lanka government's Department of Census and Statistics
  http://www.statistics.gov.lk
Tamil Nadu government's tsunami web site:
  http://www.tn.gov.in/tsunami/relief_rehabilitation.htm
Tehelka **http://www.tehelka.com**
The Hindu **http://www.hinduonnet.com**
Tsunami Relief and Rehabilitation Committee **http://www.trrcindia.org**
UN news centre **http://www.un.org/apps/news**
UN Office for the Coordination of Humanitarian Affairs **http://ochaonline.un.org**
United States' National Tsunami Mitigation Program
  http://www.pmel.noaa.gov/tsunami-hazard
Women's Coalition Batticaloa
  http://www.womenscoalitionbatticaloa.blogspot.com
World Health Organization
  http://www.who.int/hac/crises/international/asia_tsunami/en

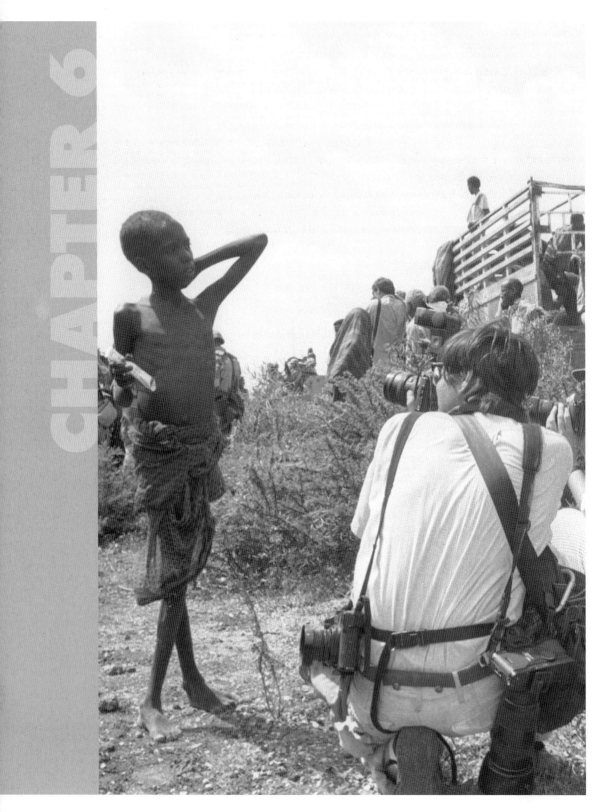

International Federation
of Red Cross and Red Crescent Societies

Humanitarian media coverage in the digital age

The year 2005 opened a week after the Indian Ocean tsunami with relief agencies, for probably the first time in two decades, facing a surplus of funds – exactly the opposite problem to the one they usually contend with.

Media coverage of the 26 December tsunami completely dominated headlines worldwide well into January – much longer than any other disaster in modern history. Only the terrorist attacks of 11 September 2001 were bigger. In the phrase of the writer Martin Amis, both events had the "capacity to astonish". Taking advantage of new lightweight satellite uplink-dishes (from which live pictures are transmitted), 24-hour news channels anchored their output not just from the tsunami countries, but from stricken areas within those countries.

But considering the extraordinary nature of the event – an undersea earthquake that sent massive waves 5,000 kilometres across the entire Indian Ocean at the speed of an airliner, killing over 200,000 people in a matter of hours – the scale of coverage was arguably proportionate, by commercial news criteria. The actual moment of disaster was, crucially, captured close-up on TV through the ever more important medium of amateur video – a key parallel with 11 September. It happened in the middle of the Christmas holiday, when Western newsrooms are always hungry for stories. And it directly involved tens of thousands of tourists from all over the world.

After the tsunami came the metaphorical tidal wave of donations, itself unprecedented and arguably disproportionate, in terms of global humanitarian criteria. On 3 January, France's Médecins sans Frontières (MSF) stunned the humanitarian world when it became the first charity to close its overflowing tsunami appeal, triggering "overdue debate about the links between media coverage of crises and the extent of charitable giving", according to Katrin Bennhold in the *International Herald Tribune*.

Three months later, that debate seemed no nearer solution. An audience of aid workers and journalists, invited by the Reuters Foundation in London to discuss whether the tsunami would divert donor money and media attention from the world's 'hidden disasters', was split down the middle. Some argued editors had been persuaded that "humanitarian news is profitable", as AlertNet's Ruth Gidley put it, but others were scared the tsunami had "pushed other disasters completely off the map".

Photo opposite page: Somalia 1992: famine and civil war triggered an ill-fated Western intervention, accompanied by an influx of journalists. Media interest in Africa ebbs and flows, but it is driven by the demands of the commercial news cycle, not humanitarian criteria.

© Paul Lowe/ Panos Pictures

While most aid agencies crave publicity, they equally bemoan what they see as selective and stereotyped media coverage of the world's crises. Underlying their desire for more widespread, analytical reporting are two assumptions: that this will generate more money for disaster relief (at least from the public); and that it may help focus the attention of the world's decision-makers on humanitarian issues.

This chapter analyses the sometimes turbulent, sometimes cosy relationship between Western news journalists and aid workers. How do they view each other? Why do some humanitarian stories make the news and not others? Can too much media attention be a bad thing? Above all, in the digital age, how can aid organizations promote media coverage that is more proportionate to human suffering?

In many respects, the prevailing winds in the media sphere actually favour humanitarian agencies, but only a few seem equipped to recognize and take advantage of this.

Commercial priorities shape news criteria

Humanitarians sometimes talk as if journalists plotted to cover some crises and not others out of sheer awkwardness. This is not so.

Few of its practitioners would claim that the brand of information called 'news' is a science. But it does conform to patterns. News judgement involving international affairs reflects established criteria. The most obvious, but often overlooked, criterion is simple novelty – news must be new. Another, rarely proclaimed, criterion for many European news organizations is a historic colonial tie. The Portuguese media, other things being equal, are more interested in Angola than Uganda; vice versa for the British media, which in turn are less interested in Chad than the French media.

And in a world in which relatively minor disasters occur almost daily, editors routinely sort stories with the crude question: "How many dead?" One might add this negative criterion: stories that are baffling get less attention. Disasters that are unusual yet explicable and cause a significant amount of death, injury or destruction in accessible places that the audience is believed to care about get covered.

It is journalists' responsibility to quantify and characterize a crisis, to ask exactly the questions about it that an operational non-governmental organization (NGO) might prefer not to answer: "Is Darfur genocide or not?" Journalists are interested in drama and controversy; they will investigate culpability; they need to know what's being done to help, but they are not concerned with the minutiae of relief operations.

News organizations are overwhelmingly commercial or commercially minded. They are dynamic and encumbered with minimal bureaucracy. While they might be politically tinged, they do not engage in advocacy. They have a clear purpose: to cover the news.

International Federation of Red Cross and Red Crescent Societies

In recent years, however, the commercial imperative has sharpened the journalists' purpose: to get *ratings*. "The broadcast news business has radically changed in the past ten years," argues one Geneva-based independent journalist specialized in humanitarian affairs. "Today, it is part news and part entertainment. News organizations are no longer sustained by reputation and prestige alone. In Europe and especially the United States, most are driven by the economic realities of being part of a large media company. Sales and marketing have become as important as the newsroom." Have humanitarians fully grasped this shift in television news towards 'infotainment'?

Judged in this light, it is understandable that sudden, dramatic disasters like volcanoes, tsunamis, earthquakes and big industrial accidents are intensely newsworthy. Whereas, even after the Indian Ocean disaster, it is harder to imagine lifting into any kind of media prominence the long-drawn-out crises that are difficult even to describe succinctly, let alone film: the chronic conflicts, infectious diseases, drought, river erosion and economic collapse which claim more lives but receive far less airtime.

Congo eruption eclipses conflict

It is now half a decade since the then United States secretary of state Madeleine Albright popularized the description of the conflict in the Democratic Republic of the Congo (DRC) as "Africa's first world war". The phrase was apt, precisely the kind of ammunition an interested producer going into a news-budget meeting might be glad of.

BBC special correspondent Fergal Keane has worked hard to keep the DRC within press radar cover, but admits, "The failure of the international media to highlight the tragedy of the DRC is one of the worst sins of omission in media history. We cannot say NGOs didn't tell us. We were all aware that millions had died and millions more were uprooted."

In one dimension, at least, DRC perfectly fits the bill as a major international news story: the death toll.

Few groups have tried harder to bring the running tragedy of Africa's 'first world war' and the humanitarian catastrophe it has spawned to public attention than the International Rescue Committee (IRC). In a series of mortality surveys, the IRC has attempted to convince international opinion that the conflict is by far the world's deadliest, and has argued that the general level of attention, coverage and outrage is far below what it should be. IRC's December 2004 survey found that 3.8 million people had died in the DRC since the conflict began in 1998 and that, on average, 31,000 continued to die every month, almost all from the by-products of war: preventable disease and malnutrition.

Sebastian Taylor, director of IRC's London office, thought he detected a breakthrough in the coverage following the publication of their survey. "Hidden war that claims 1,000 lives a day", read a front-page headline in one of Europe's leading daily newspapers. According to Taylor, "Our press offices in New York, London and Budapest reported a great deal of interest from both national media and the international wire services."

News is often a numbers game. "NGOs need to supply journalists with good data, based on solid fieldwork," Taylor emphasizes. But to maintain a news story takes more than just numbers.

"The obstacles to reporting Congo's war are well known," says Andrew Harding, formerly the BBC's East Africa correspondent. "The huge distances, the random and sporadic nature of the fighting and the complexities of the politics all conspired to keep it out of the headlines." Keane agrees: "Congo is seen as too dangerous, remote and mystifying by many in the mainstream media."

Harding believes he made more headway when the conflict converged around specific locations like Bunia in 2003, or when he and other reporters concentrated on issues like child soldiers or rape. "But the struggle," he adds, "was in trying to sustain real momentum."

The DRC provides a good example of the distinction the media make between highly visible, sudden-onset natural disasters and chronic, hidden crises. The Nyiragongo volcano, which erupted in January 2002, prompted one of the biggest influxes of journalists into the country but killed fewer than 100 people.

Andrew Harding got to Nyiragongo very quickly after the BBC allowed him to charter a plane from Nairobi. He remembers later "sharing the frustration of an MSF-Spain doctor who begged journalists covering the eruption not to ignore the far greater suffering of civilians displaced by the conflict. In four years in Africa, I certainly did more reports about the conflict than the volcano, but nothing ever captured the headlines quite like the eruption."

Decline in humanitarian coverage may be a myth

The last few years have seen numerous aid organizations and institutions analysing crises such as the DRC's, which are often said to have been forgotten by the world's media and humanitarian responders. Since 1998, MSF has published online its 'top ten' most under-reported humanitarian stories of the year (see Box 6.1). According to media monitors quoted by MSF, these ten stories together accounted for just one minute of more than 14,000 minutes of nightly news broadcasting by the notoriously parochial 'big three' US networks during 2004.

International Federation
of Red Cross and Red Crescent Societies

Box 6.1 MSF's 'top ten' most under-reported crises in 2004

Each year since 1998, the international humanitarian organization Médecins sans Frontières (MSF) has published its 'top ten' most under-reported humanitarian stories of the year. For 2004, the list was as follows:

- Tuberculosis (TB) deaths
- Conflict in Chechnya
- Conflict in Colombia
- Conflict in the Democratic Republic of the Congo
- Conflict in northern Uganda
- Democratic People's Republic of Korea (DPRK) crisis
- Somalia crisis
- Liberia crisis
- Hunger and disease in Ethiopia
- Burundi's health care user-fees.

According to MSF, the online media-tracking journal *The Tyndall Report* found the ten stories highlighted by MSF accounted for just one minute out of the 14,561 minutes on the three major US television networks' nightly newscasts – compared to 130 minutes devoted to the prosecution of American lifestyle guru Martha Stewart.

With war in Iraq dominating international reporting, MSF found that only Chechnya received any coverage at all, while TB and the humanitarian concerns in DPRK and Colombia were briefly referred to during reports on other topics. "Once more, DPRK was in the spotlight all year, yet the nightmarish situation for most North Koreans was almost totally ignored," said Nicolas de Torrente, MSF-USA's executive director.

"The outpouring of support for people in South Asia shows the kind of positive impact media coverage can have on efforts to bring relief to people in crisis," said de Torrente. "Why can't it extend to those trapped by wars or dying by the millions from a disease like TB?"

MSF's exercise illustrates how mainstream US media coverage is dominated by political, commercial, human-interest or novelty criteria. By publishing this list, MSF is in effect calling for commercial news values to be reordered to give greater weight to humanitarian criteria. ■

However, not everyone agrees humanitarian coverage is declining. Nik Gowing, a BBC journalist who has written on the role of the media in humanitarian emergencies, bluntly told a 2002 conference on hidden emergencies in Copenhagen, "It is a self-perpetuating myth that increasingly there is less media coverage of humanitarian emergencies."

And in 2004, Professor Steve Ross of Columbia University's Graduate School of Journalism published a major study of the "dynamics of media coverage of humanitarian relief", commissioned by Reuters AlertNet and the San Francisco-based Fritz Institute. In probably the largest survey of its kind ever carried out, Ross interviewed the media relations personnel of 54 humanitarian relief organizations (almost half of them in Europe) and nearly 300 international journalists (one-third from outside North America).

The results are revealing. According to the report: "By a three-to-one margin, journalists say that coverage of humanitarian aid operations is up, conflicting somewhat with NGO press officers' belief that coverage is static or actually declining, especially for chronic problems such as AIDS in Africa."

This is despite, on the part of NGOs, inadequate "press relations training" and the "lack of an ethic for publicly sharing information (and perhaps glory) with peer organizations". The report also criticizes aid agencies for not clearly distinguishing between marketing and press relations and failing to take full advantage of Internet-based tools. In other words, NGOs appear to get more coverage than they deserve.

This is an exceedingly difficult area to generalize about, but Ross also offers data: "A look at coverage in English-speaking publications worldwide, tracked by NEXIS, suggests the journalists are right. The number of articles mentioning AIDS in Africa, for instance, jumped steadily from 3,607 in 1998 to 15,349 in 2002 and 19,375 (after President Bush's announced AIDS initiative) in 2003."

The conventional wisdom among NGOs, according to Ross, is that journalists are "ignorant of chronic problems caused by poverty and disease". This, too, seems to be false when tested scientifically. Journalist respondents answering specific questions and in open-ended comments displayed "a good grasp of chronic problems such as poverty and AIDS".

Ross reserves some criticism for journalists. A lack of specialist knowledge about humanitarian issues and sources, tight budgets, impatience and 'crisis fatigue' are the main issues that "limit strategies for improving coverage".

News or current affairs?

The problem with generalizing about 'the media' is that this term covers everything from a popular tabloid newspaper with little interest in anything foreign to a heavyweight current affairs radio show, to commercial TV news, not to mention web sites, advertising and cinema.

But possibly the most important distinction, which organizations like MSF may not take sufficiently into account, is that between 'news' and 'current affairs'. Seven of their ten most 'under-reported' stories are civil conflicts or their aftermath; the other three are health emergencies. All are chronic and diffuse, changing little from day to day. The news format virtually precludes them, but that should not mean the door to current affairs is closed.

Crises that fail to make headline TV news may nevertheless feature prominently as current affairs stories on the web sites of news organizations. For example, web site

International Federation
of Red Cross and Red Crescent Societies

searches on the same day in late March 2005 on 'northern Uganda' (one of MSF's ten stories) produced the following document results:

News media	
■ BBC News	219
■ *Daily Telegraph*	34
■ *Christian Science Monitor*	30
■ CNN	18

Humanitarian agencies	
■ International Committee of the Red Cross	21
■ Oxfam	10
■ Merlin	4
■ Save the Children UK	2

This simple experiment may not necessarily indicate, as it appears to, that NGOs pay less attention to 'forgotten' disasters than the media. But at the very least, it seems to support one of Professor Ross's principal criticisms of humanitarian agencies: "the potential of Internet technologies has barely begun to be exploited" by NGOs.

Furthermore, most journalists would probably agree that *issues* generate stories. So if disasters are associated with a global issue, as all climate-related events have been for some years now, then coverage of them is likely to be more intense and sustained.

The recent succession of catastrophes in the developed world that were indisputably climatic, if not individually attributable to climate change – such as the European floods in 2002 and heatwave in 2003, and 2004's record-breaking Caribbean hurricane season – have galvanized the media to be far more responsive to 'natural' disasters.

Agencies with a brief to address climate change and climatic disaster are now pushing at an open media door, according to Martin Hiller, who runs communications for the climate change programme at WWF International in Gland, Switzerland. "Two new components have been added – the possibility that it could all get much worse and the existence of culprits, in the form of you and me and the cars we drive, or the politicians who won't sign up to Kyoto, or coal-fired power stations," he says.

Scares and culprits are the stuff of headlines.

Focusing media attention on disasters

So what can aid agencies do to increase the visibility of 'hidden' crises? It is no good simply complaining that journalists under-report these stories and leave it at that. Humanitarians – and especially professional humanitarian communicators – have to work harder (see Box 6.2).

Box 6.2 **Tricks of the trade: how to 'sell' forgotten emergencies**

If suffering makes for a good news story, northern Uganda should be a clear favourite for the front page. A cult-like rebel group abducts 25,000 children, forcing them to commit horrifying atrocities and serve as sex slaves and soldiers. Nearly 2 million people are driven from their homes into squalid camps. And all in a country hailed as Africa's development success story.

But northern Uganda's 18-year conflict rarely gets mentioned, let alone on the front pages. For aid agencies trying to raise funds and awareness, that's endlessly frustrating.

Contrast the Indian Ocean tsunami. The media blitz that followed prompted unprecedented generosity from private individuals, and governments raced to catch up. According to Oxfam, the international community had stumped up US$ 500 per person affected by the tsunami by the end of February 2005. The grand total for each person touched by Uganda's war was just 50 US cents.

Fund-raising aside, many aid workers despair at what they see as editors' pigheadedness in ignoring some of the most gripping human-interest stories out there.

According to analysis of 200 English-language newspapers worldwide commissioned by AlertNet, a humanitarian news web site run by Reuters Foundation, the tsunami generated more column inches in six weeks than the world's top ten 'forgotten' emergencies combined over the previous year.

Those ten emergencies, chosen in an AlertNet poll of more than 100 humanitarian experts, were epic in scale. They included wars in the Democratic Republic of the Congo, Uganda, Sudan and West Africa that have killed millions. They spotlighted suffering in Colombia, Chechnya, Nepal and Haiti, along with the global AIDS pandemic and the scourge of other infectious diseases like malaria and tuberculosis.

"The fact is that news is about things that are new," Andrew Gilligan, a prominent British journalist, told a debate on media coverage of emergencies organized by Reuters Foundation. "People dying in Africa is not new, but people being swept out to sea, killed in five minutes from a big wave that came up the beach, that is new."

Crises that aren't new can still make news. Aid agencies can do a lot to boost the media visibility of long-term, complex emergencies through creative communications. It's not rocket science. It essentially means thinking like a journalist.

Through daily interaction with NGOs, AlertNet has experience of what does and doesn't work. An AlertNet-commissioned study of NGO media relations carried out by the Columbia School of Journalism and sponsored by the Fritz Foundation, *Toward New Understandings: Journalists & Humanitarian Relief Coverage,* also provides useful insights. Here are some practical tips:

■ **Invest in media relations.** It's a straightforward business decision. If aid agencies want greater coverage of forgotten emergencies, they need to invest in communications training and expertise, down to the local level. This is a key finding of the Fritz report. Big organizations like UNICEF, Oxfam and Médecins sans Frontières have formidable communications teams, and it shows in their media exposure. But it doesn't always come down to resources. It may be as simple as hiring former journalists to do the job. "You've got to have journalistic impulses, which is not something you get overnight, that nose for a story," says Helen Palmer, Oxfam's global media officer.

- **Keep up a dialogue with the media.** Most journalists are not specialists in humanitarian issues. They are overworked, overstressed and often overwhelmed by the sheer volume of information competing for limited news space. Aid agencies can help by taking on a quasi-education role, entering into constructive dialogue about emergencies. The time to do this is not 15 minutes before deadline. It's an ongoing process.

  Some NGOs have made a point of sitting down regularly with commissioning editors and other 'gatekeepers' at news organizations. "It is trying to work closely, it is talking, it is discussing the issues," says Graham Wood, head of policy at Ockenden International.

  The Fritz report shows that journalists are hungry for background material such as crisis profiles and fact sheets to help them get a grip on complex emergencies. NGOs can provide this on their web sites, along with up-to-date contact details of experts for interviews.

- **Put a number on it.** Darfur hit the headlines when the UN put the number of people affected at a million. The DRC made the news when the IRC released a mortality study with the jaw-dropping figure of 3.8 million dead since 1998. Ditto Colombia after estimates that violence had displaced almost 3 million.

  It may seem a cynical way to drum up attention, but such numbers give journalists pegs to hang their stories on. And they answer the question that so often haunts long-term emergencies: "Why write about this today?" They also capture the public imagination, going some way towards quantifying the unimaginable.

  A well-crafted superlative can do the same. UN relief coordinator Jan Egeland gave reporters something to write about in March 2005 by saying the toll in the DRC over the past six years amounted to "one tsunami every six months". He added: "In terms of human lives lost... this is the greatest humanitarian crisis in the world today."

- **Bring in the big names.** It's controversial, but enlisting the help of celebrities can work. Call it the 'Diana effect'. The press follows the famous face and ends up reporting on the cause.

  Oxfam thrust northern Uganda into the spotlight by taking British actress Helen Mirren there late last year. The agency followed up with an event in which TV news personality Jon Snow interviewed her about her experiences. Mirren's fame also got her an audience with British Foreign Secretary Jack Straw, who agreed to make a public statement on the crisis.

- **Make it visual.** Nothing sells a story like a good picture. In disaster zones where access is difficult, aid agencies may have the only photos available. Strong images from the DRC and northern Uganda are always worth their weight in gold. The International Federation has attracted global coverage in Sudan and elsewhere by distributing photos over the Reuters picture wire.

- **Be creative and proactive.** Tell the bigger story through the eyes of individuals. Follow the news agenda closely and find ways to fit what you're doing into it. If you're dealing with local press, look for local angles. A key barrier to crisis coverage identified by the Fritz report was the cost and logistical difficulty of sending journalists to crisis zones. So if your budget allows, consider organizing trips for reporters.

- **Finally, never give up.** In this game, persistence really does pay off. ■

According to AlertNet editor Mark Jones, NGOs need to put more emphasis on training. "There is a serious lack of real media skills in NGO press departments," he argues. But the reality is more complicated. Many NGOs do employ people with solid media skills, but they are often not the ones calling the shots, even about communications. A quick glance at most NGO press-release archives, for example, suggests that many press releases are issued for internal departmental or political, rather than solid editorial, reasons. Journalists have limited interest in press releases anyway – and the more they receive the less interested they become.

The hard graft of cultivating relationships with editors, writers and producers is a hundred times more important. Sifting through press releases is often the most junior job in a newsroom, sometimes not even an editorial function at all. Reporters are far more interested in *sources*.

Targeting the right journalists is important. The best chance of getting forgotten disasters like drought and locust swarms in Africa onto the airwaves and into newspapers might be via the environment correspondent rather than the news desk.

Speed is another key factor. When sudden disaster strikes, modern media organizations can move equipment and personnel within minutes. No paperwork changes hands internally, no 'mission orders' – common in the humanitarian world – have to be filled out. While Professor Ross's journalist interviewees told him the biggest single barrier to expanding coverage of humanitarian issues is cost, the second largest is "lack of timely response [to the media] from groups at the scene".

Humanitarian communicators must face the question: what slows us down? The honest answer, in even relatively dynamic organizations, is bureaucracy. According to Greg Barrow, a spokesman for the UN's World Food Programme, "The key is to make sure that when the story is 'hot', organizations extract the maximum amount of publicity for the cause of the afflicted." This means a permanent state of high readiness. After being taken by surprise two years running by major disasters that broke over Christmas, some agencies have begun to wonder whether they can go on basing their operations on Western business hours.

Above all, says Ross, aid organizations have to raise their game when it comes to using digital communications technology. For example, they should promote existing sources such as ReliefWeb; make multimedia products – photos, video and audio – available to journalists who do not have the budget for field trips; use long-established tools such as LISTSERVS and newsgroups; and enable journalists interested in humanitarian coverage to get information online "without becoming saturated with press releases and individual pleas for coverage from NGOs".

Digital technology helps in Darfur

Conflict, famine and humanitarian crisis in Sudan have been cited twice by MSF as an under-reported disaster in the last seven years. Some media commentators and NGOs initially characterized the limited coverage of Darfur as a press failure. Carroll Bogert of Human Rights Watch wrote an article in the *Los Angeles Times* in April 2004 entitled 'Another Africa Calamity – Will Media Slumber On?' in which she argued: "The international media don't send reporters to cover genocides, it seems. They cover genocide anniversaries."

The readers' representative for the *San Francisco Chronicle,* Dick Rogers, wrote as late as November 2004 in his own paper, "One lesson of Rwanda, site of another African genocide, is that much of the world was allowed to look away. Newspapers, this one included, should apply that lesson in Sudan."

Esther Mujawayo, a survivor of the Rwandan genocide who lost her husband, parents and more than 200 other members of her extended family, believes the Western media have to share the moral responsibility with Western governments. "If the media had told it straight – called what was happening 'genocide' in good time," she said, "things might have been different."

However, Darfur in 2003–2004 reinforces the danger of generalizing about 'the media'. To assert that journalists ignored it en masse does an injustice to reporters like Emily Wax of the *Washington Post,* who spent three weeks living rough in rebel territory and then walked back to the Chad border when her car broke down irretrievably. Or the Al Jazeera television network, whose correspondent was jailed by the authorities in Khartoum for covering Darfur. Bogert, interviewed in March 2005, said she "would not write the same article today", but nevertheless, "using the Bosnian war as a coverage yardstick, Darfur still does not measure up".

The images that did emerge, from a desert killing field the size of France, were inconclusive. There was no massacre aftermath video on the scale of the Nyarabuye church in Rwanda. The International Commission of Inquiry, asked to determine whether or not genocide had occurred, worded its January 2005 report cautiously.

According to Oxfam's Khartoum spokesman, Adrian McIntyre, in February 2005, "The harassment, the beatings, the robbery, the rape, the murder continues on a daily basis, and unfortunately it continues well below the radar screen of the international media and of the international diplomatic machine."

Mujawayo, who now works as a psychotherapist with refugees in Germany, sounds a warning: "By the time we're absolutely sure what's happening in Darfur is genocide, it will be too late."

The relative shortage of television coverage, due to poor access as much as lack of interest, belied the ease with which video can now be fed from the middle of nowhere. An obscure technology called 'store-and-forward' (digital compression) – proved during the Iraq war of 2003 – has revolutionized TV news coverage from remote areas. For many years the holy grail of broadcast engineering, it allows high-quality video to be sent on a narrow-band satellite phone call from anywhere. The trek back to what used to be called the 'feedpoint' (from where TV pictures were relayed, usually located in a major city) is history.

Store-and-forward kits the size of laptops greatly facilitated what television coverage there was from Darfur. Andrew Harding was one of the first Western TV correspondents into the area last year. He thinks store-and-forward might represent a breakthrough for mainstream African coverage. "For TV news," he says, "there is a grey zone of stories which aren't seen as quite big enough to warrant the expense of sending in a satellite dish, but nonetheless deserve to be covered. Store-and-forward can fill the gap."

NGO press officers trying to organize 'facilities' (visits) for TV crews to remote areas can take advantage of this. For bringing hidden crises to light, television is the key medium.

Raising the media profile of chronic, ongoing disasters such as the crisis in Darfur is a major challenge for aid organizations. Cultivating relationships with journalists and feeding them accurate, timely information on the suffering is far more effective than issuing press releases on humanitarian activities.

© Olav A. Saltbones/ Norwegian Red Cross

International Federation
of Red Cross and Red Crescent Societies

Saturation coverage brings its own risks

Too much TV coverage can bring its own dilemmas for humanitarians. And this was never more starkly evident than after the Indian Ocean tsunami. An agile '24/7' media, whose digital technology can project the full emotional impact of sudden disaster into living rooms within hours, fuels not only public funding but also the demand for instant action. This often prompts international agencies to launch high-profile, 'quick-impact' interventions, or risk being written up for dithering by reporters unconcerned with the finer points of needs assessment and disaster policy.

According to a diplomatically worded report by Oxfam in January 2005, "The influx of money [after the tsunami] meant that there are too many organizations working without the appropriate experience, competencies and skills... A lack of consultation has meant that some of the aid delivered is not what is most needed."

One conclusion could be that aid organizations should base their responses on the observed needs of affected people rather than on the cash and resources available. Journalists would be entitled to ask – but rarely do – why the humanitarian community has to relearn this lesson over and over again. The answer is that the media have to take some of the blame. For example, specially chartered Ilyushin-76 transport aircraft roaring into the air get on the evening news, almost no matter what is in the back, whereas up-country assessment missions don't, even if they only take a few days to produce results.

Another ironic but potentially dangerous result of the high-profile media coverage of the tsunami was the prospect that aid organizations raised more money than they could usefully spend. *The Times* of London reported that British charities had "admitted" they would "struggle to spend the vast sums of money" – the equivalent of nearly US$ 750 million. However, they felt "saying so publicly", according to the newspaper, "would result in a belief that they did not need donations in the future".

MSF-France raised 4 million euros (around US$ 5 million) for the tsunami in the first week of its appeal – six times the sum it had managed to gather for Darfur over a two months period in 2004, for what was then one of its biggest-ever operations. Their tsunami appeal closed on 3 January, causing near-consternation in the humanitarian community. No service-providing humanitarian organization can spend more than a certain amount of money both quickly and wisely, and public contributions cannot easily be given back. MSF were not just honest; they were smart, too.

Oxfam closed its tsunami appeal in late January, a month before the UK's Disasters Emergency Committee (DEC) of which it is a part. With public generosity and concern still far from exhausted, other organizations, including the International Federation, also called a halt. The International Red Cross and Red Crescent Movement, with its network of local branches and volunteers in all countries, is far better placed than most organizations to develop credible projects on which to spend money. But amid saturation media coverage, some organizations let fund-raising run far beyond what they knew they were equipped to spend.

Meanwhile, aid experts expressed concern about media companies, especially newspapers, running tsunami appeals on behalf of specific NGOs, on whose work they might then find it difficult to report objectively. Stephan Oberreit, communications director at MSF-France, believes that during the tsunami, the media "crossed the line" from being reporters to being actors. "That is not their role," he asserts.

Holding agencies to account

In their desire for the media to report the world's humanitarian crises in greater depth, aid organizations run the risk of exposing their own operations to the critical eye of correspondents. Or do they?

Professor Ross describes the relationship between journalists and humanitarians as "symbiotic". Coincidentally, this is exactly the word veteran BBC correspondent Michael Buerk uses in his autobiography, published in 2004, when talking about the help he received from Oxfam in bringing the 1984 Ethiopian famine to light (see Box 6.3).

The two professional communities need each other, even depend on each other. So when news and humanitarian organizations are trying to placate the same domestic audience, does this symbiotic relationship ever get too cosy? In the breaking international emergency scenario, it is rarely in the interests of either side to question what the other is doing. When journalists and aid workers trade profile for angles, do the facts get squeezed?

The American writer David Rieff returns again and again to this point in his 2002 book, *A Bed for the Night: Humanitarianism in Crisis*: "…in relations between relief workers and the media," he says, "it has never been entirely clear who was exploiting whom." He believes NGOs have been "hoisted onto a plinth" by an "adoring media".

This may be changing. According to Ross's survey, "By a four-to-one margin, journalists say criticism and skepticism in the press about relief organizations has increased." Why? He finds that "for reasons of inertia and marketing" most NGO web sites do not provide links to web sites of other NGOs operating in the same areas. "Few things annoy journalists more," he says, "or are more likely to raise their suspicions about NGO motives."

International Federation
of Red Cross and Red Crescent Societies

A decade ago, Lindsey Hilsum, international editor of the UK's Channel 4 News and a seasoned observer of humanitarian relief operations, wrote: "The only form of [NGO] accountability is through the press, but criticising aid agencies seems to be taboo." Interviewed this year for the *World Disasters Report,* she says the Western media do now "to some extent" hold aid agencies to account "especially on issues such as the diversion or inefficient use of funds". But she points out that the world of aid has become very complex and specialized and many reporters "simply don't understand it".

Hilsum is surely not alone in believing that "the most important thing is that journalists and the general public in countries where aid agencies operate should hold to account both their governments and the NGOs. Imagine if Sudanese journalists had reported from Darfur on what was happening. That really would be progress."

Stephan Oberreit, however, argues that the world cannot look to journalists to enforce international NGO accountability. "The media provide information and analysis about humanitarian action, and the quality and pertinence of aid, among many things," he says. "But policing NGOs isn't their primary role."

Much of the debate around humanitarian accountability has centred on the question of aid sent, with the best intentions, into war zones actually perpetuating conflict by leaking into the hands of combatants. But what of natural disaster? John Twigg, of University College London's Benfield Hazard Research Centre, calls on journalists to avoid easy answers and engage with the difficult questions around disaster response. "Media treatment of disasters is stereotyped," he argues. "Relief is either heroic or failed – there is nothing in between."

As an expatriate development worker resident in Sri Lanka observes, "In emergencies which hit the headlines, the NGO community are given plenty of free airtime, and unless it's a politically sensitive environment or a conflict zone, they are rarely challenged. Someone needs to ask whether it was really necessary to airfreight bottled water into the tsunami zone from Europe. And why were various agencies still sending high-tech reverse-osmosis water treatment units into Sri Lanka a month after the wave struck? In the first week or so, there was a need for clean water in bigger towns and camps for the displaced, but could it not have been met locally?"

Year after year, the *World Disasters Report* has shown how inexpensive, low-tech and local preparedness and capacity building produce better disaster response and save more lives than expensive, media-friendly interventions from abroad. And the ten-year-old *Code of Conduct for the International Red Cross and Red Crescent Movement and NGOs in Disaster Response* calls on its 300-plus signatories to "build disaster response on local capacities".

Box 6.3 Ethiopia 1984: 'biblical famine' or man-made disaster?

"Dawn, and as the sun breaks through the piercing chill of night on the plain outside Korem it lights up a biblical famine, now, in the 20th century. This place, say workers here, is the closest thing to hell on earth...."

Michael Buerk, BBC News, 24 October 1984

No country has been at the epicentre of a more fierce debate about aid and the publicity axis between humanitarian agencies and the media than Ethiopia.

The 20th anniversary of the 1984 famine saw no resolution, with people still divided over whether to emphasize Ethiopia's progress or continuing vulnerability, and what role overseas aid should play, if any.

Michael Buerk, the BBC correspondent whose famous 1984 report jolted the world into action and led to Band Aid, also published his autobiography last year. Buerk, who has been criticized for 'oversimplifying' Ethiopia, is highly critical of the UN in his book and says that "television launched the biggest emergency rescue operation in history".

The *World Disasters Report* invited two people from opposing sides of the argument to comment.

Daniel Wolf

(First Circle Films, writer of *The Hunger Business*, Channel 4, 2000)

The UN Emergency Office for Ethiopia ran the famine relief operation in Ethiopia. Its first head was Kurt Jansson, who published a revealing memoir in 1987, *The Ethiopian Famine*. In it, he wrote: "My overall impression of Chairman Mengistu was one of intelligence, quiet dignity, reserve and great courtesy."

Mengistu was responsible for the 'Red Terror' of the late 1970s, in which tens of thousands of suspected opponents of his regime were mur-

dered. By the mid-1980s, he was using famine as a weapon of war, causing the deaths of many more of his citizens.

Jansson's comment reveals an extraordinary lack of judgement, but he was not alone in seeing without understanding.

Michael Buerk's BBC news report, on 24 October 1984, converted a political famine into a natural disaster. The aid operation followed suit, excluding criticism of the Ethiopian government's use of famine as a military tactic, and largely ignoring evidence of violations of human rights, sometimes taking place before their eyes. One such was the forcible resettlement programme, which cost an estimated 100,000 lives.

A UN food monitor I have interviewed, who was stationed in Wollo at the time, reported to Jansson that food aid was being diverted *away* from the epicentre of the famine, probably to put pressure on starving local people to agree to resettlement.

It was an implicit axiom of the Ethiopian aid operation that such facts should not be made public. Nothing should be allowed to endanger the flow of aid.

As Bob Geldof put it in an interview with me for *The Hunger Business*: "If one person was helped, one, it's worth it." This myopic view is a large part of the problem. If the cost of helping one person is the death of thousands of others, then it is a bad bargain.

The Ethiopian aid operation was one-sided, not just in that it favoured the government over the rebels, but in that, in effect, it sided with the government over the victims. Aid became a central part of the government's military strategy. It was manipulated to shore up government control over disputed territory, to lure people from rebel-held areas, to maintain vulnerable garrisons and to keep open threatened roads. Attempting to alleviate the famine, we were aiding the very people who had done most to cause it.

A handful of agencies, Oxfam among them, did try to help the starving in the rebel-held areas, where about half of the famine-stricken were living and dying, but most ignored them; 90 per cent of the aid went through government hands.

As a tougher approach to Mengistu was never tried, nobody knows what the result would have been. But until aid agencies recognize the full consequences of their activities, they will continue to mislead the public and themselves.

Hugh Goyder

(Ethiopia Country Director, Oxfam, 1982–1986)

Daniel Wolf is right to point out the naivety of Kurt Jansson's remarks about Mengistu, but wrong to extend his argument into a wider conspiracy theory about the response of the West to the Ethiopian famine in 1984.

The global context of 1984 was very different from the current one. The West was probably even less interested in Africa than it is in 2005, but it was especially reluctant to engage with Mengistu's Soviet-backed regime in Ethiopia.

There is a difference between what was publicized at the time and the reality on the ground. Of course, Michael Buerk's historic BBC news broadcast on the 'biblical famine' could not analyse the political context behind the famine. But it did succeed in its intention, which was to mobilize an enormous international response, including inspiring Bob Geldof to start Band Aid and mobilizing a huge public reaction, which forced the British government to commit the Royal Air Force.

While much of the publicity that followed Buerk's broadcast was indeed simplistic and showed endless food distributions to starving Ethiopians, there was considerable debate going on behind the scenes.

Oxfam, in common with other relief agencies, used much of the millions of pounds it received as a result of the hugely successful international appeal to channel cash and food through the Eritrean and Tigrayan People's Liberation Fronts. Given the rugged terrain and the continuing civil war, this got far less media exposure than the similar relief operation on the government side.

In order to operate in any country, whether Sudan in 2005 or Ethiopia in 1984, aid agencies have to either cooperate to a minimal extent with brutal regimes or leave.

There was much internal debate in Oxfam and other relief agencies both about the extent of cooperation and how much they should be publicly critical about the Mengistu regime. The broad consensus was that it was better to remain in Ethiopia, provided we were still able to get relief supplies through and monitor their distribution.

One exception to this consensus was MSF, which decided to speak out strongly against the Ethiopian government's resettlement policy and had to withdraw.

It is naive to suggest that if more relief agencies had followed MSF's example, Mengistu would have suspended resettlement. On the contrary, he still had considerable Soviet backing, and away from Western eyes resettlement would probably have continued at a much faster pace and with an even higher death toll.

The famine also covered a huge area of Ethiopia and the civil war at that time was mainly in Tigray and Eritrea. In the rest of the country, a conventional relief operation was both possible and essential. ■

The Code also requires agencies to ensure their publicity represents disaster victims as dignified humans rather than fearful, hopeless objects (see Box 6.4). But inevitably, the code is self-policing.

Why don't journalists report in more depth on the issues of efficiency and integrity that often arise during sudden-onset emergencies? Oxfam veteran and author Tony Vaux suggests a reason in his 2001 book, *The Selfish Altruist*: "The media generally allow aid agencies to get away with any sort of response on the premise that public confidence should not be undermined by criticism."

Exciting times

This chapter began by saying that some media trends actually favour the humanitarian community, such as the growing prominence of the climate-change issue and the technical advances in video newsgathering.

There is also the gradual rise of Africa as a geopolitical question: witness President Bush's initiative on AIDS and Prime Minister Blair's Commission for Africa, even if the DRC, northern Uganda and other crises continue to languish in the shadows. Other trends which may encourage greater humanitarian coverage include the posited link between poverty and terrorism; an ever more globalized culture, with the growth of peer-to-peer media like blogging, messaging, texting, Internet telephony and soon, it's expected, peer-to-peer video; and the approach of the 2015 Millennium Development Goals.

If the conflicts in Afghanistan and Iraq were the first wars to have been thoroughly dissected by countless thousands of Internet bloggers, the tsunami was the first natural disaster. Indeed, there is one humanitarian activity in which blogs are a vital ingredient: tracing lost people.

But these developments will only help the humanitarian cause if NGOs can position themselves to take advantage of them: to get onto a media timeline and think in terms of minutes instead of days; to shift control of all-important web sites from information technology (IT) professionals to communicators; to cultivate specialist correspondents tracking the new 'catastrophism'; to develop solid media skills or give the in-house communicators who already possess them control over their own budgets and a greater say in what goes out; to issue fewer press releases and hold more press conferences; to offer more field-based observations and fewer opinions; and, perhaps most important of all, to generate better content.

In an age when it is perfectly possible to post 'broadcastable' (as opposed to thumbnail) video on the web and in a country in which 'e-commerce' and broadband access are surging, not one of the UK's 12 major charities offers even downloadable magazine-quality still photos on its web site. Public sector charities must catch up with the private sector in Internet technology if they want to influence the news agenda.

In dramatic contrast to what Professor Ross finds about the humanitarian sector, digital technology and the Internet have transformed the media, including newspapers, in recent years. Broadcast engineering, for example, has almost become a branch of IT. Newspapers with online editions are closer to being real-time outlets than television news was in the pre-24-hour era. And by the end of 2005, 70 per cent of US homes are expected to have broadband connections.

Over the past two decades, after the Internet, the most important change to the way disasters (as well as everything else) are reported is the advent of real-time, 24-hour news. Stories are no longer reported just by reporters, but, as anyone who has ever worked in 'rolling' news will attest, by anybody with relevant expertise who can be found at short notice. This has vastly increased the market for humanitarian testimony, and it is increasing again with the arrival of non-Anglophone networks such as Al Jazeera, Al Arabiya and 'CNN à la française' (the nickname for the new French international news channel due to be launched in 2006).

Meanwhile, the cost of next-generation, high-definition cameras – intended mainly for the domestic market, but which produce fully broadcastable video – has fallen to only a few thousand dollars. Add another US$ 5,000 for an edit deck and accessories, and an NGO is also a production company.

Christian Aid, for example, which has a fully-fledged film unit at its London headquarters, pursues a deliberate strategy of "bypassing the mainstream TV channels by putting streamed video on our web site", according to executive producer Isabel Morgan.

In the meantime, NGOs can reach audiences just by being a bit quicker off the mark than TV companies. "We often hand out material we've shot ourselves," says Morgan, meaning raw footage – not video news releases, "and in the run-up to the war in Afghanistan, we got Christian Aid coverage of people affected by the drought there on to all the major news channels."

These are exciting times for aid agencies. Audiences are still likely to welcome intermediaries to interpret and filter the exponentially increasing quantity of information available in all media. But this role can increasingly be played by humanitarians, not just journalists.

However, some fundamentals will remain. The more closely the output of humanitarian communicators resembles journalism or academic research, the more

Box 6.4 **Faith, hope, dignity**

"Charity degrades those who receive it and hardens those who dispense it," warned the 19th-century French writer George Sand.

The giving of alms has always been seen as potentially injurious to the dignity of the beneficiary. And Sand's maxim echoes today. In the 21st century, humanitarian relief that has no developmental component is considered defensible only to ensure physical survival, as a short-term expedient and nothing more.

The 300-plus signatories to the *Code of Conduct for the International Red Cross and Red Crescent Movement and NGOs in Disaster Response* have set themselves the not inconsiderable task, in their publicity material, of recognizing "disaster victims as dignified human beings, not hopeless objects" (Principle 10).

As the International Federation found with the Indian Ocean tsunami, it is extremely difficult to depict the moment of interaction between 'humanitarian' and 'beneficiary' without eroding the dignity of the latter. And if the humanitarians are strapping, healthy Western males towering over frail, traumatized Asian women and children, the end result can be unfortunate. If the beneficiaries are smiling in apparent gratitude, it can be more unfortunate still.

Photographs of aid recipients, which are obviously posed to give maximum prominence to donor logos, do little to enhance human dignity either. It might be said that this is all just perception. But the problem is that in what the Code of Conduct calls "information, publicity and advertising activities", both dignity and its absence are entirely matters of perception.

So how do humanitarians living in a competitive world publicize their actions without insulting the people they try to help? "Charity vaunteth not itself, is not puffed up," says the Bible.

As few humanitarian agencies work in the video medium, and as text is less of an ethical minefield, the issue is most pertinent to stills photography. Few photographers, arguably, have succeeded in capturing the brutality of war and the agony of bereavement more acutely than the legendary Don McCullin, but – in a sometimes almost miraculous way – at the smallest cost to the dignity of his subjects.

McCullin was for most of his career a photojournalist, but later turned his hand to landscape and explicitly humanitarian work, on AIDS in Africa with Christian Aid, for example. What his photographs seem to establish is that it is possible to show suffering, even dying, people, while highlighting their heroism and determination more than their hopelessness.

"It is difficult to associate the word 'dignity' with conditions such as I photograph," McCullin said in an interview in 1987, "yet dignity is what I try to show. I find it most in the people who suffer the most. They seem to marshal the energy of dignity, because they will not surrender, like the Biafran mother with the child at her breast. You cannot imagine a more dignified human being."

The anonymous, lachrymose face of an African child has come to emblematize humanitarianism – and the humanitarian web site in particular. The *World Disasters Report* was criticized for using a version of this image for the cover of its 2003 edition, ironically about ethics in aid. It has become a lazy cliché, suggesting a 'victimhood' and hopelessness that many Africans find offensive.

How can humanitarian publicists do better? Giving the names of beneficiaries would be one way of presenting them less as 'objects' and more as dignified human beings. Showing them using aid rather than just receiving it might be another. A third would be to try, like McCullin, to capture defiance in the face of suffering, rather than just carefully controlled relief events. ∎

Which photo is more injurious to human dignity?

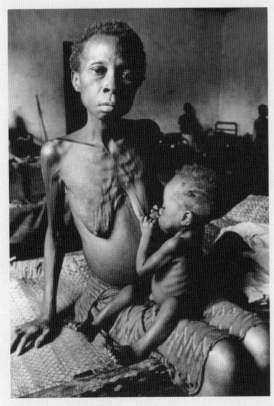

Biafra, Don McCullin, 1970
© Don McCullin/Contact Press Images/NB Pictures

Zambia, Bo Mathisen, 2002
© World Disasters Report 2003/International Federation

notice journalists, and the public, will take of it; the more it resembles institutional public relations, the less notice they will take. Journalists will continue to focus on stories, especially human stories, because that is what their audiences respond to. Humanitarian communicators, ironically, sometimes neglect the importance of 'human interest'. Above all, it is not enough for aid workers to complain about too much of the wrong media coverage or too little of the right coverage. Only by developing a much closer relationship with editors, reporters and the wider public can humanitarians hope to make their messages understood.

Alex Wynter, a former producer and bureau chief in commercial television news, contributed this chapter and Boxes 6.3 and 6.4. He wrote the International Federation's guide to media relations and advocacy, reissued in 2003. Jonathan Walter, editor of the World Disasters Report, *wrote Box 6.1. Tim Large, deputy editor of Reuters' AlertNet, contributed Box 6.2.*

Sources and further information

Bennhold, Katrin. "Charity sets off storm with tsunami aid halt", *International Herald Tribune,* 6 January 2005. Available at http://www.iht.com/articles/2005/01/05/news/assist.html

Bogert, Carroll. "Another Africa Calamity – Will Media Slumber On?", *Los Angeles Times,* 2004. Available at http://hrw.org/english/docs/2004/04/28/sudan8540.htm

Buerk, M. *The Road Taken.* London: Hutchinson, 2004.

Dertouzos, M. *What Will Be.* London: Piatkus, 1997.

De Waal, A. *Humanitarianism Unbound.* London and Kigali: African Rights, 1994.

De Waal, A. *On defining genocide.* London: Index on Censorship, 2005.

Frean, Alexandra and Hoyle, Ben. "Charities struggle to spend cash for tsunami", *The Times,* 14 February 2005. Available at http://www.timesonline.co.uk/article/0,,18690-1483564,00.html

Gourevitch, P. *We wish to inform you that tomorrow we will be killed with our families.* New York: Farrar, Straus & Giroux, 1998.

Gowing, N. *Dispatches from Disaster Zones – The Reporting of Humanitarian Emergencies.* Conference paper, 1998. Available at http://www.usip.org/events/pre2002/gowing.pdf

Hilhorst, D. *A living document? The Code of Conduct of the Red Cross and Red Crescent Movement and NGOs in Disaster Relief.* Research paper. Wageningen University, The Hague, 2004. Available at http://www.pso.nl/asp/documentsite.asp?document=363

International Commission of Inquiry on Darfur. *Report to the United Nations Secretary-General.* Geneva: United Nations, 2005

Kampfner, J. *Blair's Wars.* London: Simon & Schuster, 2003.

Owen, B. *The Internet Challenge to Television.* Cambridge, Massachusetts: Harvard University Press, 1999.

Rieff, D. *A Bed for the Night: Humanitarianism in Crisis*. London: Vintage, 2002.

Rogers, Dick. "Looking away as a tragedy unfolds", *San Francisco Chronicle*, 21 November 2004. Available at http://www.sfgate.com/cgi-bin/article.cgi?file=/chronicle/archive/2004/11/21/EDG549T39S1.DTL

Ross, S. *Toward New Understandings: Journalists & Humanitarian Relief Coverage*. San Francisco: Fritz Institute, 2004. Available at http://www.fritzinstitute.org/resources_HMC.html

Vaux, T. *The Selfish Altruist*. London and Sterling, Virginia: Earthscan, 2001.

Web sites

Africa Confidential **http://www.africa-confidential.com**
American Journalism Review **http://www.ajr.org**
BBC News **http://news.bbc.co.uk**
Christian Aid video output **http://www.christian-aid.org.uk/video/index.htm**
Columbia Journalism Review **http://www.cjr.org**
Global Diffusion of the Internet Project **http://mosaic.unomaha.edu/gdi.html**
Information for Development Program **http://www.infodev.org**
International Federation's guide to media relations
　　http://www.ifrc.org/publicat/commsguide
International Institute of Communications **http://www.iicom.org/index.htm**
International Rescue Committee **http://www.theirc.org/news/index.cfm**
Massachusetts Institute of Technology media lab **http://www.media.mit.edu**
Médecins sans Frontières **http://www.msf.org**
Oxfam UK **http://www.oxfam.org.uk/press/index.htm**
Reuters AlertNet **http://www.alertnet.org**
Swedish government **http://www.sweden.gov.se**
The Advocacy Project **http://www.advocacynet.org**

CHAPTER 7

International Federation
of Red Cross and Red Crescent Societies

Radio in Afghanistan: challenging perceptions, changing behaviour

(District bazaar): Sounds of people shouting. Nek Muhammed intends to search the debris of Jamdad's bombed shop. Rahim tries to stop him and warns him of the dangers of more explosives in the wreckage. But Nek Muhammad doesn't care: "My life is worth nothing if I do not find my son," he declares. Rahim reassures him that Ali Gul (a local ICRC worker) has promised to bring the demining team to check if the area is safe. But Nek Muhammad can't wait. Ali Gul and Zalmay approach. Ali Gul wonders what Nek Muhammad is doing. He replies he is searching for his lost son. Zalmay says he is sorry to hear this, but warns that searching is dangerous. He calls on his team to start carefully removing the debris.

Synopsis of a scene from episode 655 of *New Home New Life* radio soap opera

Despite recent advances in information technology, traditional radio broadcasting remains a vital form of direct, rapid communication with people most at risk from disaster, conflict or disease.

This chapter examines how radio can be used to build disaster awareness, reduce risks and promote reconciliation before, during and after disaster and conflict. It focuses specifically on a BBC soap opera that has been broadcast to Afghans for over a decade. The chapter also describes adaptations of this approach to prepare for hurricanes in the Caribbean, respond to the aftermath of the 1999 earthquake in Colombia, tackle the HIV/AIDS pandemic in Madagascar, build peace in post-war Sierra Leone and spread potentially life-saving information in Nepal and in tsunami-affected areas (see Boxes 7.1–7.6).

One critical question still debated by aid and communications professionals is: Can media alone bring about behavioural and social change, unsupported by complementary activities on the ground? To assume that unsupported media have very limited impact is to suggest that media fail just where they should be strongest, that is, at reaching large numbers of people quickly and cheaply, where alternative means of contact are not immediately possible. However, this chapter presents evidence that radio broadcasts alone, when professionally produced over a long enough period of time, can change the way people behave.

The BBC's radio soap opera, *New Home New Life,* is a long-term initiative that aims to combine good communications and development practice in a complex humanitarian

Photo opposite page: Radio soap opera can communicate life-saving messages about, for example, awareness of landmines and disease

Jessica Barry/ International Federation

Box 7.1 *Radionovelas* promote hurricane preparedness in Central America

Since 2002, before the advent of each hurricane season, dozens of radio stations in Central America have aired four dramas (*radionovelas*) that highlight hurricane preparedness. The project, coordinated by Costa Rican NGO *Voces Nuestras* (Our Voices), is called 'Hurricane season: time for prevention'. Each drama consists of five half-hour instalments, which form part of a multimedia campaign to promote public debate via radio talk shows, written support material, sweat shirts and posters. The stories challenge official inaction and gender stereotypes. They celebrate community mobilization, solidarity and preparedness for hurricanes. Most listeners are housewives and students, because the soaps are broadcast in the morning. The campaign has, in some cases, led to demands for municipal action to reduce risk.

In one story, a young teacher called Julia comes to work in a school at the foot of a hill near the River Piedras Blancas. She can't understand why it is located somewhere so prone to landslides. On closer inspection, she finds that a local landowner and benefactor arranged for the school to be built there, rather than in a more secure location, for political reasons. The story takes place just as a hurricane approaches, threatening the area with torrential rains and landslides. The drama helps listeners reflect on their politicized society, the lack of preparedness and the importance of evacuation plans.

Assessors visited each country to measure the broadcasts' impact. They found that people related the stories to their daily lives and strongly identified with the characters dramatized in the *radionovelas*. Some of the dramas' messages that changed people's behaviour included "boil water", "move far away from the river", "have a torch at hand", "all communities, no matter how small, must be prepared", "help move people to other places" and "don't wait until the last minute to leave". One listener commented: "It's a real pity this programme was not aired before [Hurricane] Mitch, since I would have known better what to do and how to protect my family."

Since the campaign began, people have started to map risk zones in their communities for the first time. Radio stations see the initiative as valuable, too: 46 took part in 2002 and 86 in 2003. After agreeing to air the programmes, they were given guidance on how to make and finance a multimedia campaign, and were put in touch with local disaster relief organizations.

Given the importance of calypso-type songs in the region, the Red Cross Red Crescent and European Union have recently supported the creation and broadcasting of songs about hurricane safety. One of these contains the lyrics: "Try to make your home secure/To avert a disaster/Take care of your family/Try to make them live happy/ Have a household plan/Taught to everyone/Disasters dey deadly/You better be ready." ■

emergency the war in Afghanistan. It has been widely emulated in countries as far apart as Albania, Botswana, Cambodia, Colombia and Rwanda.

New Home New Life represents a pioneering attempt to engage listeners and the humanitarian aid community in a dialogue with each other, through the medium of radio drama. It has been broadcast in two local languages three times weekly without

International Federation
of Red Cross and Red Crescent Societies

interruption since May 1994. During this time, both the BBC and independent agencies have carefully monitored its impact.

But did it succeed in its lofty aim to help 20 million highly vulnerable people survive in a time of war? Were key themes understood, remembered, discussed and acted on? And what can be learned from this case study, so that the media can be used to greater effect to mitigate future disasters and humanitarian emergencies? The story of *New Home New Life* provides some significant pointers to future deployments of the media in conflicts and humanitarian emergencies.

From reporting the news to supporting survival

In the mid-1980s, BBC broadcasters were faced with a set of opportunities, as well as difficulties, in developing 'socially useful' radio programmes, designed to have an 'intended outcome'. In conflict situations such as Afghanistan, impartial radio news programmes from respected broadcasters are themselves socially useful, in that they are often the only reliable means for people to learn about security and political issues on which their lives may depend.

The respected American broadcaster and correspondent during the Second World War, Ed Murrow, explained this succinctly: "To be persuasive we must be believable; to be believable we must be credible; to be credible we must be truthful."

On the positive side, the BBC was perceived by the great majority of Afghans to be fair in its reporting and analysis of the vicious and largely secret war waged during the 1980s by Soviet occupiers and their Afghan allies against the *mujahedin* (holy warriors) and their supporters. In wartime, travel is difficult and dangerous, people are isolated and often afraid, and radio is an all-important source of reliable news and comment.

BBC audience research from the time indicates that Afghans were voracious listeners of every radio station broadcasting in Pashto and Persian languages, particularly the BBC, but also VOA (Voice of America) and other international stations. They listened to the state broadcaster Radio Afghanistan as well – most of them with deep scepticism – although the station aired some socially useful programmes, including a daily one on family life. Many Afghans made real sacrifices to buy batteries and those without radios often listened with their neighbours.

In the 1980s, the BBC had a large, loyal audience both inside Afghanistan and among the 5–6 million Afghan refugees in Pakistan, Iran, the Gulf states and further afield. This was fertile ground for extending programmes from news to socially useful issues and for providing advice on everyday survival from health to mines awareness. The rationale was compelling: in rural areas of Afghanistan, people's lives had been turned

Box 7.2 Positive role modelling after Colombia quake

Inspired in part by the BBC's *New Home New Life* radio drama in Afghanistan, *Los Nuevos Vecinos* (New neighbours) was a radio soap opera developed in Colombia after an earthquake in 1999. Twenty-eight mountain villages were destroyed, 1,000 people died, 8,000 were injured and about 100,000 made homeless. The drama's objective was to help people make sense of the chaos resulting from the disaster and to give them the tools to reconstruct their communities peacefully.

Los Nuevos Vecinos was part of a communication project carried out by the NGO *Viva la Ciudadania* (Long live citizenship). The soap told a story about the living conditions faced by the victims of the earthquake, 16,000 of whom lived in camps and temporary housing. A critical objective was to reduce the level of conflict and misunderstanding over how to cope with the disaster and manage the relief effort. Rumours circulated by the media created false expectations and mistrust between different organizations and the community. In particular, the media's emphasis on the scale of the disaster, rather than on reconstruction efforts, demotivated survivors. To counter this, the soap opera set out to provide affected people with a model of success to restore confidence in the reconstruction process and to defuse potential conflicts.

The story focused on the transformation of a little boy, Isias, who stopped speaking after watching his mother die in the earthquake. The woman who became his guardian, Mile, emerged as a community leader standing up to those, including her own father, who sold food aid corruptly and sought to discredit relief organizations. Storylines included setting up conciliation committees dealing with issues such as shared laundry, cooking facilities and noise control. The people who researched, wrote and acted in the drama were all victims of the earthquake.

Over eight months, 120 episodes of *Los Nuevos Vecinos* were broadcast on three commercial and 14 community radio stations. The soap opera was the second highest rated radio programme between 05:00 and 07:00. It was reinforced by a comic strip of the stories and a live theatre production of the show, which toured affected villages.

The success of the project can be attributed to several factors:

- The relevance of the issues the soap dealt with. In the camps, people said they had come to understand the importance of dialogue for resolving their differences. "Like in *Los Nuevos Vecinos* we have to work together, to rebuild our homes and our lives," said one listener. Others stated that the radio soap opera gave them tools to organize the community and improve their living conditions.

- The participatory process by which it was created and produced. The actors, researchers and technical personnel were all victims of the earthquake. Most of them lived in the camps. The team who created the plot were supported by conflict resolution experts, sociologists, psychologists and other professionals.

- The sound quality: the atmosphere created was realistic; the voices were not those of professional actors, but of community members.

Los Nuevos Vecinos is an example of a creative media project that contributed to social reconstruction, peace building and bringing communities together. It also demonstrates that positive results depend on the partnership between commercial and community media, the community and other organizations. ∎

International Federation
of Red Cross and Red Crescent Societies

upside down. Most schools and health centres had been destroyed, and they had to face the hazards posed by millions of anti-personnel mines scattered from aircraft. Farmers faced new challenges in cultivating crops and keeping their animals alive. The basic services supplied by non-governmental organizations (NGOs) had to be supported by information about coping with the burning issues of everyday life. Radio Afghanistan was not fulfilling these information needs, particularly those related to rural areas and the refugee camps where most people lived.

The biggest problem for the BBC Pashto and Persian services was that they broadcast from London, some 5,000 kilometres away. Programmers who set out to provide useful advice on health, farming and social issues had to research the specific issues with great care, which was difficult at such a distance. The BBC's audience research department was geared almost exclusively to finding out how many people were listening, not what their broadcasting needs were.

Another problem was that effective social communication is participatory and interactive, again made very difficult by the distances and dangers of travel inside the country. There were hardly any phones available to listeners, and cell and satellite phones had yet to be invented. Also, programmes aimed at social change were very new to the BBC, and many people within the corporation were hostile to the concept. It was, they believed, akin to propaganda.

Then there was the cost: programmes aimed at social or behavioural change are comparatively expensive to research and produce. Donors were slow to understand the potential impact of broadcasting socially useful programmes, despite the well-known popularity of the BBC among Afghans. After 18 months, the International Committee of the Red Cross (ICRC), the United Nations Development Programme (UNDP) and the UN Children's Fund (UNICEF) provided sufficient funds to launch *New Home New Life*. All three original donors remained firm supporters of the project over many years.

New Home New Life: tackling serious issues through entertainment

New Home New Life was the most significant BBC radio programme aimed at bringing about social change in Afghanistan. It was produced in the Pakistani city of Peshawar, as Afghan cities were either unsafe or too remote. This allowed participatory research with listeners and recruitment of some of the finest Afghan writers and broadcasters who had fled war-torn Kabul. A total of about 150 staff eventually became involved, including writers, radio producers, educationalists, an evaluation team and 50 part-time actors. For the first time, a soap opera was broadcast in Dari (Afghan Persian) as well as in Pashto, the two major languages of the country.

Box 7.3 **Locally produced radio tackles AIDS in Madagascar**

This is a critical time in the fight against HIV/AIDS in Madagascar, one of the world's poorest countries. Until recently, it was remarkably untouched by the pandemic, but now national prevalence rates are estimated at 1.7 per cent. That still compares very favourably with other sub-Saharan countries: Mozambique is Madagascar's nearest neighbour, just 400 km across the Mozambican channel. Both have a population of around 19 million, but Mozambique recorded a national HIV prevalence of 12.2 per cent and 110,000 HIV-related deaths in 2003, compared with 7,500 in Madagascar.

It is a mystery as to why prevalence rates have not soared in Madagascar, unlike every other country in the region. But the fear is that they will soon. In Mozambique, HIV prevalence among attendees at sexually transmitted disease (STD) clinics shot up from 3 to 19 per cent between 1987 and 1997. STDs are generally a vector for the HIV virus and STDs, apart from HIV/AIDS, are very common in Madagascar. The challenge is to achieve what has failed elsewhere in Africa: raise awareness of the disease and change sexual behaviour among the population, to avoid an explosion in the HIV prevalence rate.

Madagascar's president, Marc Ravalomanana, has underlined the threat of HIV/AIDS by personally overseeing the prevention strategy. An important part of that, in this huge, mountainous country (the fourth largest island in the world), is the use of radio, which is being pioneered by a British NGO, the Andrew Lees Trust (ALT).

ALT has been working in the remote south of the country for the past six years on a participatory rural radio development initiative, *Projet Radio* (Project Radio), which involves 24 local NGO partners and 17 radio stations delivering educational radio programmes to 300,000 people. Around 700 village listening groups have formed, initially as custodians of the wind-up or solar-powered radios which were distributed. Up to 15 people can agree to form a listening group. They must elect someone to take responsibility (a *responsable*) for the radio, preferably a woman who remains in the village most of the time, plus a deputy. *Responsables* are given training in the use and maintenance of radios and told at what times of day the project's programmes are broadcast. They are told the radio is not a gift but part of an exchange process: ALT asks for their participation in focus group research on what sorts of programmes they want to hear and, later, what they think of the programmes. The cost of broadcasts is less than one dollar per listener per campaign.

The ALT approach is unique because, instead of working with broadcasters, it trains local NGO extension workers to research and make radio programmes of interest to their community – anything from using fuel-efficient stoves or protecting tortoises to immunizing children and raising awareness of HIV/AIDS. After three or four training sessions of four days each, most NGO workers can turn out well-researched and creatively produced radio programmes. ALT broadcasts have also been effective in encouraging villagers to apply for small grants available to communities, money that the World Bank feared would not be spent because people didn't know about the scheme's existence.

In December 2003, the executive secretary of the National Aids Committee in Madagascar requested *Projet Radio*'s help in the campaign against HIV/AIDS. A team of two local producers and two journalists was trained by ALT and began researching local information needs on HIV/AIDS. The team carried out focus groups and interviews with 170 villagers and analysed the results to identify specific themes and issues to be addressed in the radio campaign. They then produced 24 programmes over six months, in participation with local listening groups.

Explaining complex medical issues to an illiterate audience is challenging, particularly in a region where the traditional belief is that illnesses are a sign of being possessed by evil spirits. An early *Projet Radio* broadcast on HIV/AIDS used a simple analogy from local farming practice to get across the message that the disease has a rational cause. Traditionally, farmers' fields are protected from browsing or destructive animals by a natural form of fencing made from a local cactus plant (*raketa mena*). The radio programme dramatized a conversation in Antandroy dialect between two women, one of whom explains how insects (representing the HIV virus) can ravage the protective cactus (representing human antibodies or the immune system). As a consequence, local animals (representing opportunistic infections) can then enter the field (representing the human body) and destroy it.

Pre-testing was conducted prior to broadcast, and people were able to identify the key messages that arose out of the programme. During later evaluations, the drama in which this analogy featured was the second-most recalled programme in the Antandroy region. One village listening group commented: "The broadcast helped us a lot, especially when she took an example from our daily lives and she used the cactus, the field and other ene-mies of our culture, and we really appreciated it."

Following feedback and monitoring with 190 listeners and two local health-service providers, the project established that radio was the primary source of information. Results from the main towns were revealing. One of them, Tsihombe, had no working radio station at the time of the campaign. In the other two towns, Ambovombe and Fort Dauphin, over 80 per cent of listeners were aware of HIV/AIDS and could name one method of protection, compared with just 33 per cent in Ambovombe before the broadcasts. In Tsihombe, the results were 42 per cent and 20 per cent respectively. In Fort Dauphin, 75 per cent of respondents could accurately recall two methods of HIV/AIDS transmission, while only 13 per cent of respondents in Tsihombe could do the same. Clearly radio was highly effective in getting the message across. Inquiries about the disease in local hospitals increased and almost half of those inquiring had heard the radio programmes.

The National Aids Committee has asked ALT to participate in the national HIV/AIDS prevention campaign. To date, ALT has provided a radio journalists' training manual in Malagasy language and trained national and regional representatives of the AIDS committee to distribute radios, set up listening groups and produce programmes in participation with rural populations.

Unfortunately, red tape in government and among international aid organizations means that progress has been a lot slower than President Ravalomanana would have wished. And with evidence from elsewhere suggesting that the HIV/AIDS virus spreads rapidly after a 1 per cent prevalence rate has been reached, time is something that may not be on Madagascar's side. ∎

Evaluations of a previous BBC Pashto language drama, *Good Health,* had confirmed that soap opera was a popular and effective genre among Afghans, especially women, whose numbers listening regularly to the Pashto service doubled following its broadcast. The audience soon became used to the multiple storylines, which could focus on specific themes for months on end without boring the audience or appearing to preach at them. This repetition is often essential if key issues are to become accepted and acted on by listeners.

The over-arching reason for *New Home New Life*'s popularity was its mix of fast-moving, well-written storylines and fine acting. It was also the only topical radio drama available to a population that was isolated and starved of entertainment. The skills of Afghanistan's most talented writers and actors were rapidly honed into the genre of soap opera.

Major storylines ranged from the gently romantic saga of the heroine Gulalai, whose health worker activities were a role model for female listeners, to the escapades of the village chief Jabbar Khan and his clowning servant Nazir. The comic scenes struck a chord with the black humour that Afghans found so popular during their dark years of conflict and oppression. The drama also tackled serious issues familiar to listeners, such as living with lawlessness, international humanitarian law, infant and child health, abuse of drugs, protecting livestock from disease, rural livelihoods, deforestation, awareness of mines and unexploded ordnance, education for girls, marrying young girls to much older men, and the practice of trading unmarried women in order to end family or tribal feuds.

Despite the strong pro-women agenda, even the Taliban were avid listeners, caught up in the suspense of what would happen next to their favourite characters. There were public outcries from listeners on a number of occasions, when one popular character was 'killed' by a stray bullet in a feud, for instance, or when another tried to commit suicide rather than be married against her will. This degree of identification with the drama led to a gradual assumption by many listeners that *New Home New Life* was 'owned' by them rather than imposed on them.

Editorial challenges: keeping a balance

New Home New Life was high profile: the scheduling of the programme was prime time. The editorial stance was daring but not reckless. It was not overtly political, but many of its storylines were controversial in those volatile times of civil war, Taliban rule and social upheaval. Girls' education has been consistently championed by the drama, as has women's employment outside the home. Repressive customs such as forced marriages were dramatized. Sterility among males, commonly blamed on women and used as an excuse for taking a second wife, was tackled.

International Federation of Red Cross and Red Crescent Societies

Box 7.4 Multimedia support for sustainable peace in Sierra Leone

Search for Common Ground is an international NGO that specializes in using media to help populations in conflict and post-conflict situations. The NGO's programme in Sierra Leone, Talking Drum Studio (TDS), undertakes a number of activities, to "strengthen communities to participate in building a tolerant, inclusive society for sustainable peace".

These activities include helping local people produce relevant radio programmes, setting up five community radio stations, equipping them and training staff, forging close links with community groups (both strong and weak ones) and creating good working relationships with the chiefs, army and police.

Two years into the project, an evaluation for the UK's Department for International Development (DFID) found evidence that its impact has been considerable:

■ According to the assistant commissioner of police in Freetown, "TDS helps the police in our new community policing role. We have partnership boards all over the country now. Before, we were masters over the people, but now one of the cardinal changes is that we're trying to come closer to people." TDS carries regular personal messages from soldiers to their families, so it is well liked by the army as well.

■ Radio Mankneh runs a popular phone-in programme where local functionaries and government officials are invited to the studio to answer questions such as, "Why haven't the roads been mended?", "Why isn't the market rehabilitated yet?", "Why do patients have to wait so long to be seen at the hospital?" or "Why have all the doctors gone to Freetown?" The evaluation commented that radio has "contributed significantly towards changes in officials' behaviour, if not their attitudes". The evaluation also noted a reduc-

tion in petty corruption – for instance, overcharging for fishing permits or hospital staff demanding unlawful payments – because the correct procedures were better known through radio broadcasts.

■ Rape victims have spoken live on phone-in programmes, something considered very bold in Sierra Leonean society. Ordinary people in towns and villages are now discussing other taboo subjects, such as sex and polygamy, openly. This was unheard of a few years ago.

■ TDS has also had an impact on peace building. According to the evaluation, "The confidence of fleeing residents of Kailahun town following a shooting incident, which left one soldier dead, was quickly restored by Radio Moa through the dissemination of accurate information." Multimedia activities, combining radio, video and community theatre, were found to have "greatly enhanced TDS's role in achieving a sustainable peace. The various peace carnivals linked with live radio broadcasts held around the country have given communities the opportunity to know what is happening in other parts of the country... building a sense of nationalism among a population that has experienced a very brutal conflict."

The evaluation team found that people's attitudes and behaviour did not generally change because of media campaigns alone; they need to be supported by the authorities and community organizations, hence the value of TDS's activities in community mobilization. A second reason is that TDS's definition of peace building is very wide: corruption, participation in community affairs, gender awareness, HIV/AIDS, domestic violence and post-conflict trauma are all legitimate topics if the aim is to reduce violence and the causes of violence. ■

Box 7.5 Red Cross radio captures attention in Nepal

"*Namaste* from the Nepal Red Cross!" At 08:35 every Thursday morning, an estimated 800,000 Red Cross volunteers and staff from all over Nepal glue their ears to a 15-minute humanitarian radio programme. Launched in May 2004, the programme aims to increase people's awareness of Fundamental Principles such as humanity and impartiality, to explain the laws of war and to support special campaigns, such as combating the stigma suffered by people living with HIV/AIDS. The programme reports on the latest Red Cross operations and advises listeners on how they can prepare to respond better during disasters.

Ongoing conflict in Nepal since 1996 has cost around 12,000 lives and displaced some 200,000 people. This, combined with the mountainous terrain, makes it difficult to access remoter parts of the country. But radio has proved an effective means of conveying humanitarian news and advice. The programme is broadcast by the state-owned Radio Nepal, the only station with national reach.

Listeners' clubs have sprung up spontaneously to discuss the issues raised. In the first nine months, the Nepal Red Cross received 500 letters from listeners all over the country. They ask questions, often about the conflict, which are answered on air the following week: "How does international humanitarian law protect us?", "How can we trace people who have disappeared?"

After repeated requests, the programme changed from a fortnightly to a weekly slot. One listener, Gyani Prasad Ojha, from a district in remote western Nepal, wrote: "I had an interest in humanitarian service but did not know what I could do. The Red Cross radio programme has come as an inspiration to me." ■

Despite the sensitivity of the topics, research conducted at the time concluded that *New Home New Life* successfully created a fictional 'space', which allowed taboo social issues to be discussed and questioned within the family – the first stage of shifting social norms.

Maintaining a successful editorial balance was critical. The reform agenda had to be balanced with prevailing values of a patriarchal society, while final scripts had to be carefully edited to avoid indiscretions and unintended ambiguities. The language, moreover, had to be colloquial and easily understood. This was not easy, as both Pashto and Dari are normally written in a more formal style. But the BBC team succeeded.

When the Taliban came to power in 1995, they reportedly debated whether or not to ban radio listening at the same time as banning TV viewing. However, moderate voices prevailed, realizing the enormous resentment that such an edict would cause to a people so devoted to their radios for news and, thanks to *New Home New Life*, entertainment and education.

International Federation
of Red Cross and Red Crescent Societies

On a number of issues, the Taliban even issued edicts prohibiting practices that had been highlighted by the drama. One example was the story of Asghar, a student at a *madrassah* (religious school) who was sent to battle. Following the broadcast, the Taliban swiftly banned the practice of sending young students to the front line or providing *madrassahs* to accommodate soldiers. Whether this edict was always respected is another matter.

Changing behaviour through mass communication

Why was *New Home New Life* so popular and apparently so influential? It is commonly supposed that communications interventions cannot by themselves change behaviour. As the American social psychologist Albert Bandura put it: "Social persuasion alone is not enough to promote adoptive behaviour. To increase receptivity one must also create optimal conditions for learning the new ways, provide the resources and positive incentives for adopting them, and build supports into the social system to sustain them."

In a war zone such as Afghanistan, this created some difficulties. How could mass media interventions be supported by government programmes and incorporated into a social system when there was no meaningful government and little security? The response of the *New Home New Life* team was to make maximum use of radio – two repeats in one week, as well as other channels available to reinforce the key issues of the soap opera. A series of radio educational feature programmes was produced and a cartoon magazine in Dari and Pashto, colourfully produced and using simple language, was distributed through aid organizations. These NGOs, working inside Afghanistan and in the refugee camps of Pakistan, provided additional information, goods and services that formed the basis of the drama's educational content.

The absence of government was a mixed blessing. The major drawback was the lack of nationwide service delivery or any 'positive incentives' to encourage behavioural change. On the other hand, there was a refreshing lack of bureaucracy and a 'can-do' attitude from Pakistani-based NGOs involved in health, education, farming, demining and other activities.

Close collaboration with the NGOs was central to *New Home New Life*. They were invited to monthly consultation meetings so that they could comment on draft storylines and ensure they were culturally appropriate and technically accurate. Listeners were also consulted through regular needs assessment surveys inside Afghanistan and among Afghan refugees.

However, the central test of the usefulness of any communications intervention is whether people are influenced in their behaviour through being exposed to it. There

Box 7.6 Disaster and public information: still an afterthought

Within days of the Indian Ocean tsunami, it was clear that credible information represented a basic, urgent need for victims, as much as emergency food, water, health care and shelter. Many had no means of receiving information other than by word of mouth. Rumour was rampant and survivors remained uninformed about the aid effort, the fate of loved ones or the dangers of contaminated water and open wounds.

Despite proof of the importance of credible humanitarian information during previous catastrophes over the past decade, only a handful of wind-up and transistor radios were distributed in Aceh, Sri Lanka and other tsunami-struck countries. When I visited Aceh in mid-January, none of the hundreds of international aid agencies flocking to the scene appeared to have included radios as part of their basic support.

Ten days after the tsunami, Internews, an international media development NGO, surveyed 100 respondents near Hikkaduwa, down the road from Colombo and one of the most accessible of Sri Lanka's disaster zones. Surveyors found an "absence of trusted media", as both the state and commercial broadcasters were considered to be politically biased. Less than one-third of respondents had access to a radio and barely 3 per cent to television. Moreover, Internews found that "while many humanitarian relief organizations have press and information officers, in the field there is no systematic coordination of public information on the part of the relief effort, or by the government". By early February, Christian Quick of Internews concluded: "Very little has been done to increase information access in Sri Lanka's affected areas subsequent to the disaster."

To fill the gap, Internews set up two mobile radio production units in mid-March, one to cover the south and one the east. Each unit consisted of an international producer/trainer, a technician and a rotating team of four journalists. The mobile units produced 15–20 minutes of tsunami-related reports for broadcast each evening, in Sinhalese and Tamil languages. The programmes aimed to "engage tsunami victims in the national dialogue on the recovery process with intimate accounts and interviews from the affected areas". However, access to radios in affected communities remained an issue: Commercial Radio Australia donated 5,000 radio sets in early February, but they were still languishing in Sri Lankan customs three months later.

Back in Banda Aceh, the UN's Education, Scientific and Cultural Organization (UNESCO) and the Danish-based NGO International Media Support undertook a needs assessment during late January. They found that half of the 30 local radio stations that existed prior to the disaster were seriously damaged or destroyed, including all those in Meulaboh. UNESCO decided that substantial media support was needed and issued an appeal for US$ 600,000.

Such surveys are clearly useful but they take time. So-called 'radios in a suitcase' costing a few thousand dollars can be set up in a few hours to transmit relevant, computer-downloaded programming from major radio networks, whether domestic or international. Specially tailored humanitarian programming can be developed in days, using local journalists, as happened in Kosovo. 'Lifeline media' teams can be trained in advance and ready to deploy with humanitarian organizations to disaster zones within hours. Along with stockpiled mobile radio stations, generators, transmitters and wind-up radio receivers, they could play a vital role in bridging the information gap between aid agencies and the people they seek to help. ∎

International Federation
of Red Cross and Red Crescent Societies

are two main problems in evaluating this. The first is separating what people say they do with the information from what they actually do. The second is isolating the impact of the chosen media intervention from the impacts of other media or interpersonal interventions.

Regarding the latter, Afghanistan at war presented an opportunity. There was so little development communication work going on, and the BBC's popularity was so well documented, that it was possible to attribute impact on key issues to the soap opera. It was, however, more difficult to isolate actual from reported change.

Evidence of reported change

From the many unsolicited examples of behavioural and social change recorded since the BBC first started educational programming in Afghanistan in 1988, several stand out. One is a letter in 1991 from a health worker in Kunar province, where he was undertaking a vaccination campaign:

> ...[U]nfortunately the women of the area were not prepared to be vaccinated by us. The next day, while sitting with elders of the area, we heard a BBC message about the tetanus bacteria... and how important the vaccination programme was... we were happy and surprised to see that the next day the men of the area who had obviously listened to the BBC brought 300 of their women to be vaccinated.

Evidence shows that people can adopt safe behaviour simply after listening to radio programmes carrying humanitarian message

Jessica Barry/
International Federation

CHAPTER 7

This rethink was probably prompted by the interpersonal reinforcement of health workers on hand to answer questions, which supports Bandura's argument that mass media are most effective if backed up by other resources.

An extract from a diary kept by a village woman in a different part of Afghanistan indicates a similar impact five years later:

> 28/11/96: A team of vaccinators came to our village... I asked them if the elders of the families tried to stop them vaccinating people. They replied that a few years back there were some people in families who were against vaccination; they allowed the children to come but not the ladies. Now that they have listened to the drama most people know that they should be vaccinated and they let women go too.

The diary writer went on to describe a conversation with a woman at a wedding ceremony, who confided that she feared the threat that malaria posed to the health of her children:

> I heard from the drama that the disease is caused by mosquitoes. I will try and get nets for the windows and doors and I am sure the children won't get this disease if I can find nets.

The BBC's evaluation team uncovered a similar story in the northern city of Mazar-e-Sharif, though significantly there was no reinforcement by health workers in this case:

> In Mrs Wazir's house in Mazar-e-Sharif, the first thing we noticed was a bright white mosquito net covering the bed... showing us the mosquito net, she said she made it herself with netting cloth because nets are not available in Mazar. She laughed and said the BBC told her to do it.

And the following was recorded by a journalist during Taliban rule in 1998:

> One woman, who gave her name as Imam Jam's wife, said that the example of Gulalai [the female health worker from *New Home New Life*] had persuaded her to let her daughters work outside the house. Her daughter, cradling a 10-day-old baby, said she had even taken off her *burqa* [veil] once or twice. Her mother clicked her tongue in disapproval.

These few extracts indicate the power of credible radio drama characters to model behaviour, which listeners can later recall. The next section examines the more difficult question of whether they act on what they have heard.

Evidence of actual change

From the earliest BBC educational broadcasts, it was clear that Afghans were quick to learn and remember facts from radio programmes. With *New Home New Life,* the BBC introduced a more systematic evaluation process, asking specific questions related to important issues before and after the relevant episodes of the drama, then

International Federation
of Red Cross and Red Crescent Societies

returning two years later to ask the same questions and test people's ability to retain the information.

A sample of 300 respondents was used, taken from a town, a village on the road and a village off the road. The results, shown in Figure 7.1, are indicative only and not representative of the entire population, as the samples were small and not strictly random. But the trends are revealing. The percentages are those who answered correctly, in this case, to questions related to mines awareness.

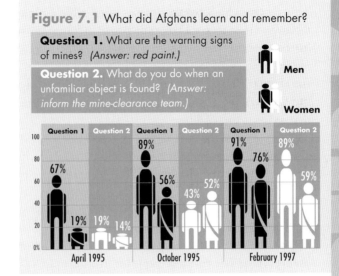

Figure 7.1 What did Afghans learn and remember?

Question 1. What are the warning signs of mines? *(Answer: red paint.)*

Question 2. What do you do when an unfamiliar object is found? *(Answer: inform the mine-clearance team.)*

Men
Women

The general trend is an increase in knowledge and an ability to remember the key points (without reinforcement), plus considerable knowledge retention two years later.

The following example gives us an indication of whether listeners acted on this new knowledge. The data are from a survey commissioned by the United Nations Office for the Coordination of Humanitarian Aid to Afghanistan (UNOCHA) and undertaken by CIET International, an NGO which specializes in impact surveys.

The survey was tasked to assess the most effective way of informing Afghans about the dangers of landmines. Fieldwork inside Afghanistan focused on a random sample of 86 'sentinel' communities, representing 57,000 people from over 9,000 households, including 86 male, 86 child and seven female focus groups, as well as interviews with 471 mine victims.

Along with *New Home New Life*, the efforts of three other organizations involved in community-based mines awareness training were assessed. CIET International's results, published in 1998, showed that the BBC was not only effective in getting the key messages across, but in fact had a strikingly positive impact on mines casualties:

> Considering only those in mine affected areas, a non-listener was twice as likely to be a mine victim after 1994 [when *New Home New Life* started], in comparison with a *New Home* listener (odds ratio 2.01, p<0.05). This encouraging indicator contrasts with the notable absence of evidence of impact on mine events by the three direct [face-to-face] training programmes.

This survey, which was as close to a scientific nationwide sampling as it was possible to have at that time, also found that BBC listeners were more likely to report mines incidents than non-listeners: 23 per cent of listeners said they would not enter a marked minefield or mined building. Meanwhile, 27 per cent recalled the long-running *New Home New Life* story of Jamdad, whose leg was blown off by a landmine. He suffered depression during his months of recovery, but finally found a job, got married and had children.

There were distortions in the survey, particularly in terms of the small number of female respondents. However, of the 50 per cent of household heads who replied that they listened to the BBC, 93 per cent listened to *New Home New Life*. Nearly three-quarters of these listened to the show with their wives and children.

What these examples, and particularly the CIET survey, indicate is that listeners can change behaviour through exposure to mass media alone, contrary to the claims of many researchers. But to achieve this level of impact, programmes have to be well researched, produced and structured, and broadcast at times convenient for the target listeners.

Broadcasters and humanitarians combine forces to save lives

The impact of using media in disaster response and development can be greatly enhanced if it is undertaken in alliance with relevant aid organizations. A striking example of this was in November 1994, when a combination of special announcements and features broadcast on a number of BBC programmes, including a storyline in *New Home New Life,* gave the widest possible publicity to the biggest immunization campaign in Afghanistan for 17 years.

Thanks to this, along with the painstaking efforts of the World Health Organization, UNICEF and local NGOs, which set up the infrastructure for the campaign and negotiated with government and warlords, there was a nationwide ceasefire for one week – the first in Afghanistan for 16 years. Not only were 1 million children and 300,000 women vaccinated, but hostilities were also suspended. It was a revealing example of what can be achieved when an issue benefiting all sides is effectively negotiated during a period of conflict.

This set a precedent, and a number of ceasefire national immunization days (NIDs) were subsequently negotiated, one of them due to take place just as coalition forces were about to invade Afghanistan in October 2001. The aid agencies had pulled out of the country and there was near panic in Kabul because the US-led bombing campaign was expected to start at any time. Yet the NID was scheduled to continue.

International Federation
of Red Cross and Red Crescent Societies

The BBC broadcast a series of announcements after *New Home New Life* along the lines of: "Even if you are on the move, please get your children vaccinated. Emergencies will pass, but if a child catches polio, he or she may have to live with paralysis throughout their life." The NID took place and a large number of children were vaccinated. Later, one woman in Kabul spoke to the BBC and said:

> With a lot of people leaving Kabul, one thought the Americans were coming to wipe Afghanistan off the face of the earth. But when we heard in *New Home New Life* that vaccination was being carried out and when we saw it happening, I suddenly thought: "There is still hope." That is how I got my children vaccinated and I decided to stay put, for which I am happy. Many other people who ran suffered a lot.

Freedom of the airwaves

Radio in wartime can be particularly influential, even if delivery is by short-wave foreign broadcasts. There is generally little competition, so the audience is not fragmented. As a result, if there is a popular programme like *New Home New Life* broadcast over years rather than months, the impact can be considerable.

In peacetime, the trend in many countries, especially in Africa and Latin America, is towards media deregulation. Localization provides many opportunities to fine-tune media interventions to community needs, creating a dialogue between broadcasters and listeners, driving discussion and debate on issues such as HIV/AIDS forward. The downside – in terms of disaster response – is that the audience is fragmented and multiple media outlets need to be mobilized in order to provide early warnings. In addition, expensive, well-researched drama is often not an option, though it was used with conspicuous success after funds were made available following an earthquake in Colombia in 1999 (see Box 7.2).

In post-war Afghanistan, freedom of the media has been enshrined in law and, oiled by generous aid money, about 40 independent community FM radio stations have set up. Whether they will thrive after the short-term funds finish remains to be seen. In Bosnia following the Dayton Peace process, a similar donor-driven quest for independent media failed, because transmitters and studios did not add up to good-quality programmes. People there continued listening to the ethnically polarized stations, because the new stations made mostly boring programmes. Lack of donor funds to train people in production skills – a long-term process – can ultimately lead to failure in encouraging media diversity.

While Afghanistan's independent radio sector has been generously funded, the state broadcaster Radio Afghanistan has received much less help in restructuring itself, although it has benefited from new transmission and television equipment. As with many governmental media organizations, it has too many staff who are badly paid and weakly led. Reforming Radio Afghanistan will almost certainly lead to conflict between donors and the government, and will take time.

For foreign broadcasters such as the BBC, the proliferation of FM radio stations has led to a fragmentation of the audience, although they have responded by building their own networks of FM relay stations. It is likely that *New Home New Life* will never have quite the influence it had in the past, although a recent study (March 2005) by the international media development NGO Internews indicates that it remains the best-known radio programme in the country.

Conclusion: radio's reach remains unrivalled

New Home New Life shows that Afghan listeners can absorb key information from radio drama and, in some instances, act on it without reinforcement from the state or other sources. Nevertheless, the ceasefires to facilitate immunization campaigns show that mass media are more effective when backed by complementary activities on the ground. In a country as large, remote and dangerous as Afghanistan, this support can only be delivered sparingly. So the role of radio, which reaches into the homes of most Afghans, remains essential.

Ultimately, the question remains as to whether the Afghan broadcasting experience is relevant in other conflict and disaster zones. All situations are unique, and the Afghans' trust of the BBC is not replicated everywhere, although it is, for instance, in Somalia where BBC listening figures are also very high. But a convincing case can be made that people with access to radios do respond to 'solutions-orientated' entertainment programmes, particularly those broadcast in their local languages, which reflect their lives and with which they can identify.

Organizations such as Search for Common Ground can point to the positive impact of radio drama on national broadcasters in places such as Burundi and Sierra Leone (see Box 7.4). Radio-based social education projects have mushroomed over the past decade, with the BBC World Service establishing a trust to promote and implement new projects of this kind. With the help of improved satellite delivery systems, deregulation of broadcasting and new digital technology, it seems that the humble transistor radio receiver still has an important part to play in 'socially useful' communication with the poor, the remote and those threatened by conflict or crisis.

What follows are ten lessons for employing radio as a means of communicating vital issues to people at risk:
- **Be credible and entertaining.** Broadcasters can have considerable influence during humanitarian emergencies, if they are credible and produce relevant, socially useful programmes that are entertaining as well as informative.

International Federation
of Red Cross and Red Crescent Societies

- **Ensure access to programmes.** Research whether target listeners have radios, what time is best for them to listen and what radio stations they tune in to. Then negotiate airtime with radio stations.
- **Encourage participation.** Involving the audience in production and feedback increases the influence of radio programmes on behavioural change. Participation may also help traumatized populations to recover more quickly.
- **Quality counts.** Well-produced radio programmes, transmitted in good quality at prime time, can change perceptions and behaviour. While interpersonal contact to reinforce key issues is a great help, the impact of radio soap operas alone is striking.
- **Partner with aid organizations and/or governments.** This is vital in terms of coordinating operations (such as immunizations), verifying the accuracy of information and delivering services (e.g., relief efforts, health, education, mines clearance).
- **Stay close to the crisis.** To keep abreast of fast-changing events, choose appropriate aid agency collaborators and recruit the best local research and production staff.
- **Role modelling** through carefully researched soap opera characters can be a powerful influence on listeners. But it can be expensive and time-consuming, and needs to be thoroughly researched and continuously monitored.
- **Use everyday language.** This is all-important, as people identify not only with what is said but how it's said. In radio, it's important to write for the voice in an accessible way.
- **Structure the information.** Plan carefully to sequence key issues and themes so the audience can absorb them, especially in drama or a long-running series.
- **Stay for the long term.** Successful media interventions are proactive, well-researched and long term.

Gordon Adam is director of Media Support, a Scottish-based NGO and consultancy working in development communications projects in southern Africa and Afghanistan, and former head of the BBC Pashto section. This chapter is adapted from an article he wrote, which will be published in Tufte, Thomas and Hemer, Oscar (eds.), Media, Communication and Social Change – Rethinking Communication for Development, Nordicom, University of Gothenburg. *Adam also contributed Box 7.2, which he wrote in collaboration with Lina Holguin, a Colombian journalist who specializes in media and peace-building work for Oxfam Canada, as well as Boxes 7.3 and 7.4. Fresia Camacho (Voces Nuestras, Costa Rica), Allan Lavell (Latin American Graduate Faculty of Social Sciences, Costa Rica) and Xavier Castellanos (International Federation, Panama) contributed Box 7.1. Box 7.5 was contributed by Khem Aryal (Nepal Red Cross Society information officer) and Box 7.6 by Ed Girardet, a former foreign correspondent and the author of several books on humanitarian, conflict and media issues. He also writes for* National Geographic, *the* International Herald Tribune *and other publications.*

Sources and further information

Adam, Gordon and Harford, Nicola. *Radio and HIV/AIDS: making a difference.* Geneva: UNAIDS, 1999. Available at http://www.unaids.org

Bandura, Albert. *Self-Efficacy in Changing Societies.* Cambridge: Cambridge University Press, 1997.

Bandura, Albert. *Self-Efficacy: The Exercise of Control.* New York: Worth Publishers, 1997.

CIET International. *The 1997 National Mine Awareness Evaluation: final report to UNOCHA.* New York: CIET International, 1998.

Department for International Development (DFID) (UK). *Working with the Media in Conflicts and Other Emergencies.* London: DFID, 2000. Available at http://www.dfid.org

Eknes, Age and Andresen, Lena. *Local Media Support.* Oslo: FAFO, 1999. Available at http://www.fafo.no/engelsk

Everett, Paul; Williams, Tennyson and Myers, Mary. *Evaluation of Search for Common Ground activities in Sierra Leone. Undertaken for Search for Common Ground and DFID.* Washington DC: Search for Common Ground, 2004. Available at http://www.sfcg.org/sfcg/evaluations/sierra2.pdf

Girardet, Edward and Walter, Jonathan. *Afghanistan. Crosslines Essential Field Guide.* Geneva: Crosslines Publications Ltd, 2004 (2nd edition). Available at http://www.crosslinesguides.com

Lynch, Jake. *Reporting the World.* Oxford: Reporting the World, 2002. Available at http://www.reportingtheworld.co.uk

Web sites

Andrew Lees Trust **http://www.andrewleestrust.org.uk**
BBC World Service Trust **http://www.bbc.co.uk/worldservice/trust**
Internews **http://www.internews.org**
Media Support **http://www.mediasupport.org**
Nepal Red Cross Society **http://www.nrcs.org**
Search for Common Ground **http://www.sfcg.org**

CHAPTER 8

  International Federation
of Red Cross and Red Crescent Societies

Disaster data: building a foundation for disaster risk reduction

Disaster data are vital for identifying trends in the impacts of disaster and tracking relationships between development and disaster risk. This chapter offers a brief review of selected international disaster databases. It identifies challenges for the collection, validation and presentation of disaster data, and considers options for improving data for future disaster risk reduction and humanitarian action.

International disaster databases are becoming increasingly useful and important, as their data are being fed into analytical tools to help prioritize international action to reduce disaster risk. Such risk reduction tools include the Disaster Risk Index of the United Nations (UN) Development Programme, the ProVention/World Bank's Natural Disaster Hotspots Analysis, and the Americas Indexing programme (sponsored by the Inter-American Development Bank) which includes a comparative assessment of national disaster risk management performance. Galvanized in part by the Indian Ocean tsunami disaster, international disaster databases are also being used to develop early warning tools.

Four international databases are reviewed in this chapter: EM-DAT, NatCat, Sigma and DesInventar (see Box 8.1).

EM-DAT

The Emergency Disasters Data Base (EM-DAT), managed by the Centre for Research on the Epidemiology of Disasters (CRED), at the Catholic University of Louvain, Belgium, is the most complete, publicly accessible, international database. It produces estimates of human and economic losses from disasters. The database includes relatively small disasters (ten deaths or more) where reliable data exist. Because the main aim of EM-DAT is to support research, an average of four weeks elapses between a disaster event being declared and its being entered into the public record. This allows time for data to be verified.

The contribution of EM-DAT to policy planning is constrained primarily by the lack of systematic and standardized local and national disaster data collection. This is a particular challenge for EM-DAT, which draws from international sources built on local and national data. Aside from weakening the validity of data across the dataset, a particular problem is the lack of spatial specificity found in international reports.

Photo opposite page: Disaster databases pla a vital role in identifyin disaster trends and reducing future risks.

International Federation

Box 8.1 International disaster databases

	EM-DAT	NatCat	Sigma	DesInventar
Web site	www.em-dat.net	www.munichre.com	www.swissre.com	www.desinventar.org
Management	University (CRED)	Private (Munich Re)	Private (Swiss Re)	University/NGO (La Red)
Access	Public	Limited public	Limited public	Public
Audience	Research	Insurance	Insurance	Research
Hazard types	Natural and technological	Natural (hydro-meteorological and geological)	Natural and technological	Natural and technological
Criteria for disaster entry	At least ten deaths, or 100 affected, or state of emergency, or call for international assistance	1980–present: any property damage and person injured or killed. Pre-1980: only 'major' events	At least 20 deaths, or 50 injured, or 2,000 homeless, or insured losses of at least US$ 15.1m (marine), US$ 30.2m (aviation), US$ 37.5m (other) or total loss US$ 74.9m*	Any social loss
Principal data source	Humanitarian agencies, governments, international media	Insurers, international media, supported by site visits	Insurers, international media	Local/national media, agency and government reports
Time for new disaster to enter public database	Four weeks	Around three weeks	An annual loss review published each spring	Around one week to one month
Period covered	1900–present, with good accuracy from 1980	Historical data extends over 2,000 years, but with good accuracy from 1979	1970–present	1970–present
Data fields (not all data are available for every disaster event)**	Mortality, injured, homeless, total people affected, estimated economic losses, country of impact, scale of event	Insured and economic losses, human losses. Geo-referenced to local site of loss. Only large-scale disasters included	Insured losses (primary focus), economic losses, mortality, missing, injured, homeless. Only large-scale disasters included	Mortality, injured, missing, victims, affected, destroyed and affected houses, evacuated, roads/education centres/livestock lost, economic losses. Geo-referenced to local site of loss

* Using 2004 US dollars, monetary values adjusted annually.
** No dataset covers ecological loss.

International Federation
of Red Cross and Red Crescent Societies

Consequently, EM-DAT catalogues events by country, making it difficult to identify sub-national patterns of disaster loss, with changes in international borders complicating historical analysis. For a more detailed analysis of the caveats surrounding EM-DAT's data, see Annex 1, which follows this chapter.

NatCat and Sigma

NatCat and Sigma are databases managed by Munich Re and Swiss Re respectively, two of the world's largest reinsurance companies. Both databases are highly sophisticated systems, geared towards the needs of the global insurance industry.

NatCat has created its own methodology for calculating total economic losses from large-scale disasters (excluding those associated with drought). The direct economic impact of a disaster can be calculated once insured losses are known, based on weighting for the country affected and the natural hazard trigger type. The accuracy of the methodology has been verified by comparison with final loss estimates from the field.

Sigma presents annual information on insured property losses, as well as economic and human losses, from large natural and technological disasters. Sigma uses the disaster event as the basis for each entry, even if it covers multiple countries. This contrasts with the use of categorizations by country in NatCat and EM-DAT.

Both NatCat and Sigma provide limited information on countries with low insurance density. This reduces their data coverage for Africa, Asia and Latin America. In particular, rural areas lack comprehensive data. However, the inclusion of data from sources beyond insurance reports enables the databases to provide some information on these areas.

DesInventar

DesInventar is managed by a regional coalition of academic and non-governmental actors and covers 16 countries in Latin America and the Caribbean, collectively called La Red. Sub-national DesInventar databases also exist for individual states in Brazil, Colombia, India, South Africa and the United States.

DesInventar specializes in local records of disaster loss. It can cover events of national and international significance, but presents them through local loss data. Similar to EM-DAT, DesInventar gathers data on human and economic losses. However, DesInventar's approach to data collection means it tends to record higher numbers of people affected by disaster.

DesInventar's focus on local disasters introduces a number of specific challenges for data quality. The media are a prominent source of information, yet there is no systematic method for media reporting on losses. In addition, the reliability of the media in estimating disaster losses is debatable. One aim of DesInventar is to collect information on secondary impacts and losses to infrastructure, but this information is unevenly reported, even locally. Sometimes DesInventar has to draw on national sources of data and, in these cases, it is very difficult to disaggregate the statistics to determine the local distribution of losses.

Challenges

Disaster data have improved greatly in the last 20 years, but there remain a number of common challenges, as follows:

Defining hazards and distinguishing events

Of all natural hazard types, drought is the deadliest. However, drought and disasters related to it are also the most difficult to study. Problems arise from the lack of a common definition for drought, which is variously defined using meteorological, hydrological or agricultural variables. In each case, there is no common rubric for drawing spatial and temporal limits around drought events. This creates major challenges for the comparative analysis of drought impacts, compounded by the slow-onset nature of drought.

Associated environmental and human factors, such as soil loss, armed conflict or HIV/AIDS, can make it difficult to judge whether drought is a cause, effect or context for reported losses. CRED is working with Columbia University in the United States to refine the way drought is handled in EM-DAT. Moreover, in 2004, CRED started a Complex Emergencies Database, which may help distinguish losses associated with drought within wider emergencies.

When disasters are associated with hazards that impact more than one country, such as the Indian Ocean tsunami or Hurricane Mitch, this can potentially lead to double counting in datasets, when losses are recorded for individual countries and the event as a whole. Careful monitoring of data sources and cross referencing of impact data help to reduce this.

A harder challenge to overcome is the product of disaster 'cascades'. This happens when an initial hazard triggers a secondary event, for example when landslides follow seismic activity or flooding. With no common methodology for the local reporting of disaster losses, impacts might be associated with either event. Again, careful monitoring of data sources and the experience of data analysts help address the problem but cannot eliminate it entirely. The root of the problem lies in accurate and standardized data collection on the ground.

One recent advance is an agreement between agencies to use a common and unique global identifier (GLIDE) number for each event (see Box 8.2).

International Federation of Red Cross and Red Crescent Societies

Standardized and systematic data collection

The absence of standard guidelines for collecting data on local disaster loss is compounded in most countries by an ad hoc system of data collection by local media, government or civil society groups. Local data are collated and fed to international databases by intermediaries. Not only do intermediaries lack a standard set of definitions to organize their data, but they might be tempted to exaggerate or suppress data for professional, political or economic advantage.

Each key indicator of disaster impact faces its own limitations. Mortality is the 'cleanest' indicator of disaster loss. But even here the distinction between deaths and people missing creates uncertainty, with some countries requiring that people be declared dead after they have been missing for 12 months. Wide variation in reports of mortality is common.

For example, after December 2003's earthquake in Bam, Iran, the death toll was put at 43,200 by the UN Office for the Coordination of Humanitarian Affairs (OCHA), 31,884 by the media organization Agence France Presse and 26,796 by the International Federation. More recently, the death toll from the tsunami in India's Andaman and Nicobar Islands has been the subject of much debate (see Chapter 5). Figures for numbers of people affected by disaster are even more open to dispute, since there is no universal definition for what is meant by 'affected'.

However, data are most incomplete for economic losses. Over the past three decades, according to the World Bank, macroeconomic losses were reported for less than 30 per cent of all natural disasters, with least data for developing countries. Scarcity of data is compounded by the lack of a standardized methodology for reporting

CHAPTER 8

Box 8.2 GLIDE: the global identifier number

The GLIDE number aims to simplify the process of tracking reports and data concerned with a particular event, once an accredited agency has identified it as a disaster. CRED, the Food and Agriculture Organization, the International Federation, the International Strategy for Disaster Reduction, La Red, ReliefWeb, the United Nations Development Programme, the United States Office for Disaster Assistance, the World Bank and the World Meteorological Organization all use GLIDE.

GLIDE helps to clarify the global disaster dataset for regular users. For those new to disaster data, knowledge of the aims of database managers helps to explain its use. For humanitarian actors, GLIDE is useful, but can cause complications when a humanitarian crisis is caused by a succession of natural events for which multiple GLIDE numbers exist.

GLIDE cannot be expected to solve long-standing challenges, such as the lack of a common definition for a 'disaster event'. Currently GLIDE numbers can be created for natural events, even when these do not have humanitarian consequences. ■

macroeconomic losses. Generally, only direct losses are reported with no breakdown of losses by sector. With only a few international data sources, verification is difficult.

In Bam, CRED had to choose between macroeconomic loss estimates of US$ 32.7 million from the US Geological Survey and US$ 1 billion from Swiss Re. A possible model for a standard methodology for reporting macroeconomic losses has been developed and applied by the Economic Commission for Latin America and the Caribbean.

At the other end of the scale, livelihood losses are also poorly understood and rarely recorded. This is particularly the case for livelihoods in the informal sector, which in some cases can make up more than 50 per cent of the economic activity of a village or region.

In response to the challenge of data quality, CRED has developed a ranking system to rationalize its choice of data sources. This improves transparency but cannot address the lack of standardized and systematic data collection. In 2003, the *World Disasters Report* (Chapter 7) argued that data quality could be improved by encouraging active rather than passive data collection. Resources do not exist for international database managers to coordinate local collection, but despite this, efforts have been made to build closer links with local data providers. Examples include Munich Re, whose 60 national offices lead impact assessments following major disasters. Meanwhile, the UN's ReliefWeb organizes regional workshops, which bring humanitarian information providers together to discuss best practice in information exchange and management.

Public accessibility of data

The NatCat and Sigma datasets are not fully accessible to the public. Even public database web sites could be more user-friendly. Their presentation reflects the history of disaster data analysis, which has been undertaken largely by in-house technicians or a relatively small number of professionals and organizations. The growing numbers of local, national and international organizations with an interest in disaster data suggest a rethink in access provision may be needed. Costs, however, may be prohibitive: redesigning web sites will be expensive for academic and UN organizations and is unlikely to be seen as cost-effective for the private sector.

Opportunities for progress

In 2003, the *World Disasters Report* proposed a code of conduct for ethical disaster data collection and use. This call reflected a concern that local data should not be used to the detriment of those whom the data describe, nor for commercial, political or military use. This is an understanding that already exists among many practitioners, through informal guidelines. It is hoped that future standardization and systematization of data collection will provide an opportunity for further reviewing the possibility of a shared code of practice.

International Federation
of Red Cross and Red Crescent Societies

Recommendations for governments, data collection organizations (including the International Red Cross and Red Crescent Movement) and international data managers looking to improve disaster data are summarized in Box 8.3.

The greatest need is for the systematic collation and standardized collection of local disaster data. This should include agreed protocols for:

- The start- and end-dates of disasters.
- Geo-referencing disasters.
- Distinguishing between cascading hazards.
- Measuring human impacts.
- Measuring economic impacts (including secondary losses).
- Measuring livelihood losses (particularly in the informal sector).
- Measuring ecological impacts.

For international disaster databases, improved local data collection needs to be supported by greater standardization and transparency amongst intermediaries.

Baseline data on the social, economic and ecological status of areas at risk would enhance the accuracy of disaster loss measurement. Developing baselines goes beyond the capacity of the disaster community, but it is an agenda in which disaster data managers could usefully participate.

The recommendations presented here respond, in part, to the UN's Hyogo Framework for Action 2005-2015, which endorsed the need for more work on disaster data and analysis to feed into disaster risk reduction. In May 2005, two important initiatives were already under way. First, OCHA's Global Disaster Alert System, which aims to provide initial data within 24 hours of an event. This will be useful for humanitarian actors. Secondly, a Global Risk Identification Programme, which is being developed by a consortium of international disaster data managers and users. This aims to improve the comprehensiveness and accuracy of measuring disaster impacts by building on the work of existing disaster databases.

Box 8.3 Recommendations for future action

- Build local and national human resources for systematic disaster impact data collection.
- Standardize methodologies for local disaster data collection, with a focus on measuring total economic losses and incorporating ecological losses.
- Standardize definitions for drought and complex humanitarian emergencies.

- Systematize disaster data information flows between local collectors, intermediary collators and international database managers.
- Support collaboration between international database managers to minimize overlap and encourage the sharing and verification of data.
- Improve public accessibility to basic and summary impact data. ■

Principal contributor to this chapter and boxes was Mark Pelling, Senior Lecturer in the Environment and Development Research Group, Department of Geography, King's College, London.

Sources and further information

Department for International Development (DFID). *Disaster risk reduction: a development concern.* London: DFID, 2004.

Guha-Sapir, D. and Below, R. *The Quality and Accuracy of Disaster Data: A Comparative Analysis of Three Global Datasets.* A report for The ProVention Consortium, 2002.

International Federation. *World Disasters Report.* Geneva: International Federation, 2003.

La Red. *Comparative Analysis of Disaster Databases.* A report for Working Group Three of the International Strategy for Disaster Reduction, 2002.

Pelling, M., *Visions of Risk: A review of international indicators of disaster risk and its management.* UNDP, 2005.

UN International Strategy for Disaster Reduction (ISDR). *Hyogo Framework for Action 2005-2015: Building the Resilience of Nations and Communities to Disasters.* Kobe, Japan: ISDR, 2005.

UN ISDR. *Comparative Analysis of Disaster Databases.* Final Report submitted to Working Group 3, 30 November 2002. Available at http://www.unisdr.org

Wilhite, D.A. 'Drought as a natural hazard: concepts and definitions' in Wilhite D.A. (ed.) *Drought: A Global Assessment.* London: Routledge, 2000.

World Bank. *Expert consultation on collection and validation of economic data related to disasters.* Meeting report, December 2004.

Web sites

Assessment methodologies for disaster losses
http://www.proventionconsortium.org/toolkit.htm
Centre for Research on the Epidemiology of Disasters (CRED) **http://www.cred.be**
EM-DAT (CRED) **http://www.em-dat.net**
Indicators for Disaster Risk Management in the Americas
http://idea.unalmzl.edu.co
ISDR **http://www.unisdr.org**
La Red/DesInventar **http://www.desinventar.org**
Munich Re **http://www.munichre.com**
ProVention/World Bank's Natural Disaster Hotspots Analysis
http://www.proventionconsortium.org/projects/identification.htm
ReliefWeb **http://www.reliefweb.int**
Swiss Re **http://www.swissre.com**
UNDP's Disaster Risk Index
http://www.undp.org/bcpr/disred/english/wedo/rrt/dri.htm

World Disasters Report

Annexes

2005

ANNEX 1

International Federation
of Red Cross and Red Crescent Societies

Disaster data

The death toll from natural and technological disasters during 2004 soared to around 250,000, mainly due to the Indian Ocean tsunami on 26 December. This is substantially higher than the annual average of around 67,000 deaths per year recorded from 1994 to 2003, according to the Centre for Research on the Epidemiology of Disasters (CRED).

Last year, however, the number of people affected by disasters dropped to around 146 million, which is considerably lower than the annual average of 258 million recorded over the previous decade. Floods in Bangladesh, India and China in 2004 affected 110 million people, while the tsunami affected just 2.4 million, according to CRED.

The cost of damage inflicted by disasters last year was estimated at US$ 100–145 billion, depending on which database is used. The German reinsurance company Munich Re, which draws on highly detailed property insurance databases, put a US$ 60 billion price tag on 2004's hurricane season alone.

Official development assistance (ODA) from members of the Development Assistance Committee (DAC) of the Organisation for Economic Co-operation and Development (OECD) grew to US$ 69 billion in 2003 (the latest year for which complete data are available). This equated to an average of 0.25 per cent of all DAC donors' gross national income – well below the United Nations (UN) target of 0.7 per cent.

However, preliminary data show ODA rising further to an estimated US$ 72.2 billion during 2004. In 2003, emergency/distress relief (not including the relief provided by multilateral institutions and non-governmental organizations) grew significantly to US$ 5.87 billion (see Figures 1–5).

EM-DAT: a specialized disaster database

Tables 1–13 on natural and technological disasters and their human impact over the last decade were drawn and documented from CRED's EM-DAT. Established in 1973 as a non-profit institution, CRED is based at the School of Public Health of the Catholic University of Louvain in Belgium and became a World Health Organization (WHO) collaborating centre in 1980. Although CRED's main focus is on public health, the centre also studies the socio-economic and long-term effects of large-scale disasters.

Since 1988, with the sponsorship of the United States Agency for International Development's Office of Foreign Disaster Assistance (OFDA), CRED has maintained

Photo opposite page: Around 4,000 Haitians died during floods and landslides between May and September 2004. While emergency relief and development aid continue to rise, more resources need to be devoted to disaster preparedness and risk reduction.

Marko Kokic/ International Federation

EM-DAT, a worldwide database on disasters. It contains essential core data on the occurrence and effects of 15,000 disasters in the world from 1900 to the present. The database is compiled from various sources, including UN agencies, non-governmental organizations, insurance companies, research institutes and press agencies.

Priority is given to data from UN agencies, followed by OFDA, governments and the International Federation. This prioritization is not a reflection of the quality or value of the data but the recognition that most reporting sources do not cover all disasters or may have political limitations that could affect the figures. The entries are constantly reviewed for redundancies, inconsistencies and the completion of missing data. CRED consolidates and updates data on a daily basis. A further check is made at monthly intervals. Revisions are made annually at the end of the calendar year.

The database's main objectives are to assist humanitarian action at both national and international levels; to rationalize decision-making for disaster preparedness; and to provide an objective basis for vulnerability assessment and priority setting.

Data definitions and methodology

CRED defines a disaster as "a situation or event, which overwhelms local capacity, necessitating a request to national or international level for external assistance (definition considered in EM-DAT); an unforeseen and often sudden event that causes great damage, destruction and human suffering".

For a disaster to be entered into the database, at least one of the following criteria must be fulfilled:
- Ten or more people reported killed
- 100 people reported affected
- Declaration of a state of emergency
- Call for international assistance.

The number of people killed includes persons confirmed as dead and people missing and presumed dead. People affected are those requiring immediate assistance during a period of emergency (i.e., requiring basic survival needs such as food, water, shelter, sanitation and immediate medical assistance). People reported injured or homeless are aggregated with those reported affected to produce a 'total number of people affected'.

The economic impact of a disaster usually consists of direct consequences on the local economy (e.g., damage to infrastructure, crops, housing) and indirect consequences (e.g., loss of revenues, unemployment, market destabilization). In EM-DAT, the registered figure corresponds to the damage value at the moment of the event and usually only to the direct damage, expressed in US dollars (2004 prices).

EM-DAT distinguishes two generic categories for disasters (natural and technological), divided into 15 main categories, themselves covering more than 50 sub-categories. For the production of the tables in this report, natural disasters are split into two specific groups:

- **Hydrometeorological disasters:** avalanches/landslides, droughts/famines, extreme temperatures, floods, forest/scrub fires, windstorms and other disasters, such as insect infestations and wave surges.
- **Geophysical disasters:** earthquakes, tsunamis and volcanic eruptions.

The technological disasters comprise three groups:

- **Industrial accidents:** chemical spills, collapse of industrial infrastructure, explosions, fires, gas leaks, poisoning and radiation.
- **Transport accidents:** by air, rail, road or water means of transport.
- **Miscellaneous accidents:** collapse of, or explosions or fires in, domestic/non-industrial structures.

In Tables 1–13, 'disasters' refer to disasters with a natural and technological trigger only, and do not include wars, conflict-related famines, diseases or epidemics.

The classification of countries as 'high', 'medium' or 'low human development' is based on the 2004 Human Development Index (HDI) of the UN Development Programme. For countries not appearing in the HDI, the World Bank's 2004 'classification of economies' by the countries' level of income is used ('high', 'middle' or 'low').

Caveats

Key problems with disaster data include the lack of standardized collection methodologies and definitions. The original information, collected from a variety of public sources, is not specifically gathered for statistical purposes. So, even when the compilation applies strict definitions for disaster events and parameters, the original suppliers of information may not. Moreover, data aren't always complete for each disaster. The quality of completion may vary according to the type of disaster (for example, the number of people affected by transport accidents is rarely reported) or its country of occurrence.

Data on deaths are usually available because they are an immediate proxy for the severity of the disaster. However, the numbers put forward immediately after a disaster may sometimes need to be seriously revised several months later.

Data on the numbers of people affected by a disaster can provide some of the most potentially useful figures, for planning both disaster preparedness and response, but they are sometimes poorly reported. Moreover, the definition of people affected remains open to interpretation, political or otherwise. Even in the absence of manipulation, data may be extrapolated from old census information, with assumptions being made about percentages of an area's population affected.

Data can also be skewed because of the rationale behind data gathering. Reinsurance companies, for instance, systematically gather data on disaster occurrence in order to assess insurance risk, but with a priority in areas of the world where disaster insurance is widespread. Their data may therefore miss out poor, disaster-affected regions where insurance is unaffordable or unavailable.

For natural disasters over the last decade, data on deaths are missing for one-tenth of reported disasters; data on people affected are missing for one-fifth of disasters; and data on economic damages are missing for 70 per cent of disasters. The figures should therefore be regarded as indicative. Relative changes and trends are more useful to look at than absolute, isolated figures.

Dates can be a source of ambiguity. For example, a declared date for a famine is both necessary and meaningless – a famine does not occur on a single day. In such cases, the date the appropriate body declares an official emergency has been used. Changes in national boundaries cause ambiguities in the data and may make long-term trend analysis more complicated.

Information systems have improved vastly in the last 25 years and statistical data are now more easily available, intensified by an increasing sensitivity to disaster occurrence and consequences. Nevertheless there are still discrepancies. An analysis of the quality and accuracy of disaster data, performed by CRED in 2002, showed that occasionally, for the same disaster, differences of more than 20 per cent may exist between the quantitative data reported by the three major databases – EM-DAT (CRED), NatCat (Munich Re) and Sigma (Swiss Re).

Despite efforts to verify and review data, the quality of disaster databases can only be as good as the reporting system. This, combined with the different aims of the three major disaster databases (risk and economic risk analysis for the reinsurance companies and development agenda for CRED), may explain differences between data provided for the same disasters. However, in spite of these differences, the overall trends indicated by the three databases remain similar.

The lack of systematization and standardization of data collection is a major weakness when it comes to long-term planning. Fortunately, due to increased pressure for accountability from various sources, many donors and development agencies have started giving attention to data collection and its methodologies.

Part of the solution to this data problem lies in retrospective analysis. Data are most often publicly quoted and reported during a disaster event, but it is only long after the event, once the relief operation is over, that estimates of damage and death can be verified. Some data gatherers, like CRED, revisit the data; this accounts for retrospective annual disaster figures changing one, two and sometimes even three years after the event.

Ongoing major changes in EM-DAT

In the past year, some efforts have been made to improve the EM-DAT information available to the public. These changes may not immediately affect the results in some tables (except for people affected by drought/famine in 2004), but will modify some trends in the years to come. The two main areas of changes are:
- **Economic loss/damage figures.** Information gaps and the lack of a single, consistent methodology led CRED to revise its dataset on economic data and consolidate its methodology on economic data entry. These data are being revised from 2000 onwards by creating new fields (direct and indirect damages, analysing information by sectors) and determining an appropriate methodology.
- **Drought/famine figures.** The improvements (in collaboration with the International Research Institute for Climate Prediction) include a review of over 800 historical drought disasters and 80 famines in EM-DAT, with dates and loss figures being reassigned as necessary according to a strict methodology.

US Committee for Refugees

The United States Committee for Refugees (USCR) is the public information and advocacy arm of Immigration and Refugee Services of America, a non-governmental organization. USCR's activities are twofold: it reports on issues affecting refugees, asylum seekers and internally displaced people; and it encourages the public, policy-makers and the international community to respond appropriately and effectively to the needs of uprooted populations.

USCR travels to the scene of refugee emergencies to gather testimony from uprooted people, to assess their needs and to gauge governmental and international response. The committee conducts public briefings to present its findings and recommendations, testifies before the United States Congress, communicates concerns directly to governments and provides first-hand assessments to the media. USCR publishes the annual *World Refugee Survey*, the monthly *Refugee Reports* and issue papers.

The data in Tables 14–16 were provided by USCR. The quality of the data in these tables is affected by the less-than-ideal conditions often associated with flight. Unsettled conditions, the biases of governments and opposition groups, and the need to use population estimates to plan for providing humanitarian assistance can each contribute to inaccurate estimates. The estimates reproduced in these tables are USCR's preliminary year-end figures for 2004.

Table 14 lists refugees and asylum seekers by country of origin, while Table 15 lists the two groups by host country. Refugees are people who are outside their home country and are unable or unwilling to return to that country because they fear persecution or armed conflict. Asylum seekers are people who claim to be refugees; many are awaiting a determination of their refugee status. While not all asylum seekers are refugees, they are nonetheless entitled to certain protections under international refugee law, at least until they are determined not to be refugees. USCR also includes people granted various forms of humanitarian relief if that relief is based on factors related to the UN's definition of a refugee, as distinct from, for example, relief granted because of natural disaster.

Table 16 concerns internally displaced persons (IDPs). Like refugees and asylum seekers, IDPs have fled their homes, but remain in their home country. No universally accepted definition of IDPs exists. USCR generally considers people who are uprooted within their country because of armed conflict or persecution – and thus would be refugees if they were to cross an international border – to be internally displaced. Broader definitions are employed by some agencies, however, who sometimes include people who are uprooted by natural or human-made disasters or other causes not directly related to human rights. IDPs often live in war-torn areas and are neither registered nor counted in any systematic way. Estimates of the size of IDP populations are frequently subject to great margins of error.

In the following tables, some totals may not correspond due to rounding.

Philippe Hoyois, Regina Below and Debarati Guha-Sapir, from the WHO Collaborating Centre for Research on the Epidemiology of Disasters (CRED), Université catholique de Louvain, Brussels, Belgium (http://www.cred.be), prepared the section on natural and technological disasters. For questions regarding this section or data, please contact cred@esp.ucl.ac.be. The US Committee for Refugees (1717 Massachusetts Avenue NW, Suite 200, Washington DC 20036, USA; http://www.refugees.org) prepared the section on refugees, asylum seekers and IDPs. For questions regarding this section or data, please contact uscr@irsa-uscr.org.

Erratum

World Disasters Report 2004

Chapter 8, Table 16. An error occurred in the analysis at the end of the table. The first line should have read: "Approximately 2 million less people were internally displaced at the end of 2003 than at the end of 2002."

International Federation of Red Cross and Red Crescent Societies

Figure 1

ODA net disbursements (US$ million, 2003 prices): 1994–2003

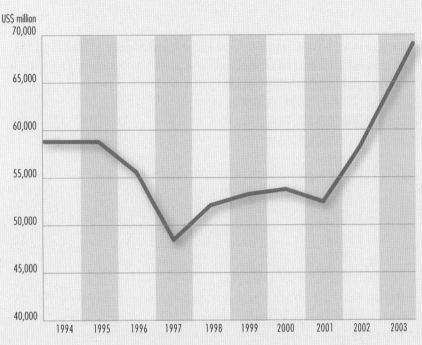

US$ million

Source: OECD DAC: *International Development Statistics*, 2005

ODA from members of OECD's DAC grew to US$ 69 billion in 2003 (the latest year for which complete data are available), an increase, in real terms, of 4.8 per cent compared to 2002.

Preliminary data for 2004 show ODA rising to an estimated US$ 72.2 billion (2003 prices), a probable increase of 4.6 per cent compared to 2003.

In 2003, 42 per cent more aid was given than in 1997, the year with the lowest figure for the decade considered, and 17 per cent more than in 1994.

These figures do not take the following into account: non-DAC donors' development assistance (e.g., from the Republic of Korea and Saudi Arabia); voluntary contributions from the public via non-governmental organizations; and private financial flows from migrants to their countries of origin.

In the future, ODA, based on DAC members' post-Monterrey commitments, should grow to more than US$ 100 billion in 2010, although this is still not enough to ensure the Millennium Development Goals will be met. (Source: *World Bank Global Monitoring Report*, April 2005.)

Figure 2
ODA net disbursements in 2003 (US$ million, 2003 prices)

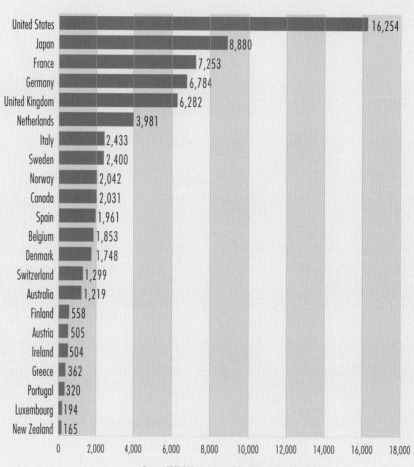

United States	16,254
Japan	8,880
France	7,253
Germany	6,784
United Kingdom	6,282
Netherlands	3,981
Italy	2,433
Sweden	2,400
Norway	2,042
Canada	2,031
Spain	1,961
Belgium	1,853
Denmark	1,748
Switzerland	1,299
Australia	1,219
Finland	558
Austria	505
Ireland	504
Greece	362
Portugal	320
Luxembourg	194
New Zealand	165

Source: OECD DAC: *International Development Statistics, 2005*

The five biggest donors of ODA in 2003 were the United States (24 per cent of all ODA), Japan (13 per cent), France (11 per cent), Germany (10 per cent) and the United Kingdom (9 per cent). Their combined total of US$ 45.4 billion represents two-thirds of all ODA.

If the contributions of the 15 countries forming the European Union during 2003 are aggregated, their ODA amounts to US$ 37.1 billion, representing more than half of all ODA.

International Federation
of Red Cross and Red Crescent Societies

Figure 3

ODA: evolution of DAC contributions (US$ million, 2003 prices)

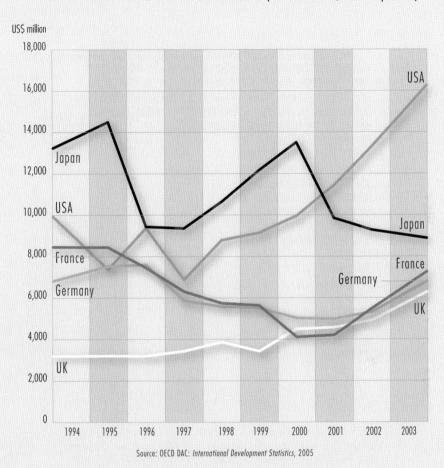

Source: OECD DAC: *International Development Statistics, 2005*

The United States' development assistance more than doubled during 2003, compared to its low point in 1997. European countries' ODA increased by a factor of 1.47 compared to its lowest level in 2000. Japan's ODA in 2003 was its lowest for the decade.

Compared to 2002, the biggest individual increases came from the United States (up US$ 2.96 billion), France (up US$ 1.77 billion), Germany (up US$ 1.46 billion) and the United Kingdom (up US$1.36 billion).

Comparing 2003 with 2002 in real terms and in percentage terms, significant increases in ODA were made by Belgium (40.7 per cent), the United States (20.4 per cent), Switzerland (19.7 per cent) and the United Kingdom (14 per cent).

Figure 4
ODA as percentage of DAC donors' GNI, 2003

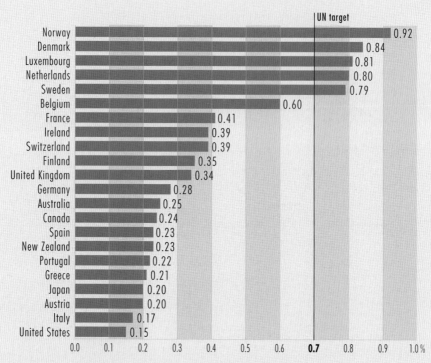

Source: OECD DAC: *International Development Statistics*, 2005

Expressed as a percentage of donor countries' gross national income (GNI), only five countries (Norway, Denmark, Luxembourg, Netherlands and Sweden) exceeded the UN's 0.7 per cent target for ODA during 2003.

Compared to 2002, the proportion of aid as a percentage of GNI in 2003 increased for nine of the 22 OECD countries (Norway, Luxembourg, Belgium, France, Switzerland, United Kingdom, Germany, New Zealand and the United States). This increase was particularly significant in Belgium (a 40 per cent improvement on 2002) and Switzerland (a 22 per cent improvement).

Compared to 2002, the proportion of aid as a percentage of their GNI decreased in 12 countries (Denmark, Netherlands, Sweden, Ireland, Australia, Canada, Spain, Portugal, Greece, Japan, Austria and Italy).

In 2003, ODA as a share of all DAC donors' average GNI was 0.25 per cent. According to the World Bank, this should grow to 0.32 per cent in 2010, based on DAC members' commitments announced after Monterrey, although this is still insufficient to meet the Millennium Development Goals. (Source: *World Bank Global Monitoring Report*, April 2005.)

International Federation
of Red Cross and Red Crescent Societies

Figure 5

Emergency/distress relief by DAC donors in 2003
(US$ million, 2003 prices)

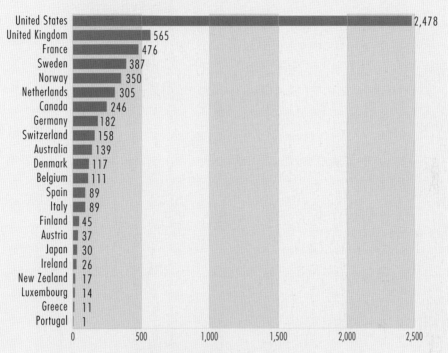

United States	2,478
United Kingdom	565
France	476
Sweden	387
Norway	350
Netherlands	305
Canada	246
Germany	182
Switzerland	158
Australia	139
Denmark	117
Belgium	111
Spain	89
Italy	89
Finland	45
Austria	37
Japan	30
Ireland	26
New Zealand	17
Luxembourg	14
Greece	11
Portugal	1

Source: OECD DAC: *International Development Statistics*, 2005

In 2003, bilateral emergency/distress relief (not including the relief provided by multilateral institutions and non-governmental organizations) grew significantly from US$ 3.87 billion (in 2003 prices) to US$ 5.87 billion, an increase of more than 50 per cent. However, DAC rules allow donors to count the cost of refugees in donor countries as emergency/distress relief (part of ODA) during the first 12 months of their stay.

This increase is largely due to the United States, which raised its 2002 level of relief by over US$ 1 billion (79 per cent) in 2003. The United States remains the biggest donor, accounting for 42 per cent of such relief.

Sharp annual increases of emergency/distress relief were also made by Belgium (nearly four times higher), Spain (nearly three times higher), France and Greece (nearly double), New Zealand and Ireland (up by half), although the amounts concerned are far below those of the United States.

The aggregated emergency/distress relief contributions of the 15 countries forming the European Union during 2003 were US$ 2.5 billion, rising by 40 per cent since 2002.

ANNEX 1

Table 1 Total number of reported disasters,[1] by continent and by year (1995 to 2004)

	1995	1996	1997	1998	1999	2000	2001	2002	2003	2004	Total
Africa	63	58	56	83	144	196	186	201	163	161	1,311
Americas	99	95	102	112	137	147	128	153	119	131	1,223
Asia	177	176	195	209	240	289	295	301	264	313	2,459
Europe	72	55	60	66	78	122	92	111	85	93	834
Oceania	8	17	15	17	15	13	18	18	20	21	162
High human development[2]	128	104	128	126	135	176	145	165	135	131	1,373
Medium human development	237	237	237	274	366	431	402	455	372	456	3,467
Low human development	54	60	63	87	113	160	172	164	144	132	1,149
Total	**419**	**401**	**428**	**487**	**614**	**767**	**719**	**784**	**651**	**719**	**5,989**

Source: EM-DAT, CRED, University of Louvain, Belgium

[1] In Tables 1–13, 'disasters' refer to those with a natural or technological trigger only, and do not include wars, conflict-related famines, diseases or epidemics.
[2] See note on UNDP's Human Development Index country status in the section on data definitions in the introduction to this annex.

With 719 reported disasters, 2004 was the third worst year of the decade, with Asia remaining the most frequently hit continent.

2004 was the worst year of the decade for countries of medium human development (MHD), which accounted for nearly two-thirds of the year's disasters.

The average annual number of disasters reported during 2000–2004 was 55 per cent higher than during 1995–1999.

Over the same period, disasters doubled in countries of low human development (LHD), with the greatest increase in Africa. The increase was 57 per cent in MHD countries and 20 per cent in countries of high human development (HHD).

International Federation
of Red Cross and Red Crescent Societies

Table 2 Total number of people reported killed, by continent and by year (1995 to 2004)

	1995	1996	1997	1998	1999	2000	2001	2002	2003	2004	Total
Africa	2,962	3,484	4,064	7,006	2,688	5,756	4,462	8,272	5,810	4,308	48,812
Americas	2,628	2,541	3,069	21,865	33,989	1,820	3,460	2,285	2,026	8,269	81,952
Asia	75,590	69,706	71,033	82,373	75,890	11,608	29,255	13,358	37,860	236,102	702,775
Europe	3,366	1,204	1,166	1,434	19,448	1,627	2,196	1,699	31,046	1,182	64,368
Oceania	24	111	388	2,227	116	205	9	91	64	35	3,270
High human development¹	8,223	2,170	2,435	3,070	5,420	2,221	2,136	2,115	31,606	1,248	60,644
Medium human development	19,493	17,146	18,157	42,635	70,163	13,272	33,349	15,169	41,743	239,904	511,031
Low human development	56,854	57,730	59,128	69,200	56,548	5,523	3,897	8,421	3,457	8,774	329,502
Total	**84,570**	**77,046**	**79,720**	**114,905**	**132,131**	**21,016**	**39,382**	**25,705**	**76,806**	**249,896**	**901,177**

Source: EM-DAT, CRED, University of Louvain, Belgium

¹ See note on UNDP's Human Development Index country status in the section on data definitions in the introduction to this annex.

The Indian Ocean tsunami in December 2004 left at least 224,495 people dead (end April 2005 figures), accounting for around 90 per cent of the year's death toll.

If the tsunami's reported deaths and missing people are not considered, the number of people who died from disasters during 2004 drops to 25,401 – the second lowest figure of the past decade.

During the decade, seven other large disasters were reported: a famine in the Democratic People's Republic of Korea from 1995–1999 (at least 270,000 deaths); a flood in Venezuela in 1999 (30,000 deaths); a heatwave in Europe in 2003 (29,915 deaths); three earthquakes – one in Iran in 2003 (Bam: 26,796 deaths), one in India in 2001 (Gujarat: 20,005 deaths) and one in Turkey in 1999 (Izmit: 17,127 deaths); and a hurricane in Central America in 1998 (Mitch: 18,791 deaths).

Over the decade, Asia accounted for 78 per cent of the world's disaster deaths.

Table 3 Total number of people reported affected, by continent and by year (1995 to 2004) in thousands

	1995	1996	1997	1998	1999	2000	2001	2002	2003	2004	Total
Africa	9,535	4,282	7,736	10,150	14,362	23,044	18,386	31,736	20,951	9,000	149,183
Americas	1,152	2,380	2,711	16,966	5,008	1,348	11,246	2,046	3,739	4,268	50,864
Asia	225,621	207,163	56,269	315,714	188,605	230,044	141,177	583,216	228,895	131,956	2,308,659
Europe	8,220	30	679	622	6,549	2,907	786	1,205	1,121	524	22,644
Oceania	2,682	652	730	328	151	7	32	41	38	124	4,785
High human development[1]	11,648	2,610	1,946	2,663	5,698	1,058	7,361	2,075	813	887	36,758
Medium human development	219,830	203,207	57,506	334,198	196,443	228,970	142,708	584,874	232,711	139,708	2,340,156
Low human development	15,732	8,690	8,673	6,918	12,534	27,322	21,558	31,294	21,221	5,278	159,220
Total	**247,210**	**214,507**	**68,125**	**343,780**	**214,675**	**257,350**	**171,627**	**618,243**	**254,745**	**145,872**	**2,536,134**

Source: EM-DAT, CRED, University of Louvain, Belgium

[1] See note on UNDP's Human Development Index country status in the section on data definitions in the introduction to this annex.

While December 2004's tsunami affected around 2.4 million people, floods last year affected 69 million people in Bangladesh and India, and nearly 42 million people in China.

On the basis of available data, an average 250 million people per year were affected by disasters over the decade – over 90 per cent of them in Asia.

During the decade, the disasters with the widest impact were the drought that affected 300 million people in India in 2002, and floods in China that affected 180 million people in 2002 and 150 million in 2003.

Disasters during 2000–2004 affected one-third more people than during 1995–1999. Over this period, the numbers of people affected by disasters in countries of low human development doubled, with Africa showing the greatest increase.

International Federation
of Red Cross and Red Crescent Societies

Table 4 Total amount of disaster estimated damage, by continent and by year (1995 to 2004) in millions of US dollars (2004 prices)

	1995	1996	1997	1998	1999	2000	2001	2002	2003	2004	Total
Africa	205	134	22	366	823	164	339	144	5,684	1,480	9,362
Americas	27,702	14,835	11,682	20,094	14,639	3,588	11,090	3,547	14,272	27,891	149,340
Asia	192,918	35,896	30,832	33,169	30,238	18,074	17,160	7,853	17,766	67,395	451,301
Europe	15,695	396	11,408	5,430	40,654	9,070	895	17,081	19,108	2,028	121,765
Oceania	1,585	1,126	291	327	967	553	364	410	617	516	6,756
High human development[1]	207,499	16,344	21,190	18,954	44,331	11,850	11,810	19,484	40,533	76,794	468,789
Medium human development	11,893	32,324	33,026	40,289	42,973	12,745	17,495	9,499	16,553	21,837	238,634
Low human development	18,711	3,719	19	143	17	6,853	542	53	362	679	31,099
Total	**238,104**	**52,387**	**54,235**	**59,386**	**87,321**	**31,448**	**29,848**	**29,036**	**57,447**	**99,310**	**738,523**

Source: EM-DAT, CRED, University of Louvain, Belgium

[1] See note on UNDP's Human Development Index country status in the section on data definitions in the introduction to this annex.

Figures for the cost of damage are notoriously unreliable; they are missing for 84 per cent of reported disasters (for 2004). Methodologies for calculating existing data are not standardized and, depending on where the disaster occurred and who is reporting, estimations vary from zero to billions of dollars.

Last year was the second costliest of the decade after 1995, when direct damage from the Kobe earthquake alone was estimated at almost US$ 163 billion.

The latest estimate of direct damage from the 2004 tsunami (for eight of the 12 countries affected at end April 2005) was nearly US$ 8 billion, making it the second most costly disaster in 2004.

In Japan, the earthquake near Honshu in October 2004 caused an estimated US$ 28 billion of damage and the cumulative losses due to typhoons reached US$ 16.3 billion. In the United States and the Caribbean, Atlantic tropical storms and hurricanes caused at least US$ 26 billion of damage.

The most costly disasters in financial terms are earthquakes and typhoons in Japan; hurricanes, storms and floods in North America; floods and storms in Western Europe; and floods in China.

Table 5 Total number of reported disasters, by type of phenomenon and by year (1995 to 2004)

	1995	1996	1997	1998	1999	2000	2001	2002	2003	2004	Total
Avalanches/landslides	15	24	13	21	15	29	21	19	21	16	194
Droughts/famines	16	8	18	34	30	48	47	41	21	13	276
Earthquakes/tsunamis	25	12	17	18	33	31	25	36	40	42	279
Extreme temperatures	13	5	13	13	8	31	23	15	18	15	154
Floods	95	70	76	88	112	152	159	172	158	128	1,210
Forest/scrub fires	7	5	15	16	22	30	14	22	14	7	152
Volcanic eruptions	5	5	4	4	5	5	6	7	2	5	48
Windstorms	59	63	68	72	86	101	98	112	76	121	856
Other natural disasters[1]	4	1	3	1	2	4	2	0	0	13	30
Subtotal hydro-meteorological disasters	209	176	206	245	275	395	364	381	308	313	2,872
Subtotal geophysical disasters	30	17	21	22	38	36	31	43	42	47	327
Total natural disasters	**239**	**193**	**227**	**267**	**313**	**431**	**395**	**424**	**350**	**360**	**3,199**
Industrial accidents	45	35	35	43	36	50	54	48	46	81	473
Miscellaneous accidents	29	37	30	29	51	47	49	52	44	62	430
Transport accidents	106	136	136	148	214	239	221	260	211	216	1,887
Total technological disasters	**180**	**208**	**201**	**220**	**301**	**336**	**324**	**360**	**301**	**359**	**2790**
Total	**419**	**401**	**428**	**487**	**614**	**767**	**719**	**784**	**651**	**719**	**5,989**

Source: EM-DAT, CRED, University of Louvain, Belgium

[1] Insect infestations and waves/surges.

In 2004, the three most frequent types of disaster were transport accidents (30 per cent), floods (18 per cent) and windstorms (17 per cent). Two-thirds of industrial accidents occurred in China, 70 per cent of them mine accidents. Almost 60 per cent of transport accidents were due to road traffic.

Over the year, 44 per cent of all disasters were hydrometeorological. But the number of geophysical disasters in 2004 was the decade's highest. For the first time in the past decade, windstorms accounted for one-third of natural disasters.

Table 6 Total number of people reported killed, by type of phenomenon and by year (1995 to 2004)

	1995	1996	1997	1998	1999	2000	2001	2002	2003	2004	Total
Avalanches/landslides	1,497	1,129	801	981	351	1,099	692	1,149	700	357	8,756
Droughts/famines	54,000	54,000	54,520	57,875	54,029	370	199	538	9	81	275,621
Earthquakes/tsunamis	7,966	596	3,039	9,599	21,870	204	21,355	1,606	29,617	225,377	321,229
Extreme temperatures	1,730	300	619	3,225	771	922	1,653	3,369	32,403	239	45,231
Floods	8,145	7,309	6,958	9,695	34,366	6,330	4,678	4,354	4,050	6,957	92,842
Forest/scrub fires	29	45	32	109	70	47	33	6	53	14	438
Volcanic eruptions	n.a.	4	53	n.a.	n.a.	n.a.	n.a.	254	n.a.	2	313
Windstorms	3,724	4,380	5,330	24,657	11,899	1,129	1,864	1,093	995	6,513	61,584
Other natural disasters[1]	n.a.	20	400	n.a.	3	1	n.a.	ndr	ndr	27	451
Subtotal hydro-meteorological disasters	69,125	67,183	68,660	96,542	101,489	9,898	9,119	10,509	38,210	14,188	484,923
Subtotal geophysical disasters	7,966	600	3,092	9,599	21,870	204	21,355	1,860	29,617	225,379	321,542
Total natural disasters	**77,091**	**67,783**	**71,752**	**106,141**	**123,359**	**10,102**	**30,474**	**12,369**	**67,827**	**239,567**	**806,465**
Industrial accidents	513	674	1,033	1,942	742	1,743	1,271	1,147	1,101	1,797	11,963
Miscellaneous accidents	1,711	1,159	1,277	748	1,330	1,112	1,783	2,023	1,361	2,115	14,619
Transport accidents	5,255	7,430	5,658	6,074	6,700	8,059	5,854	10,166	6,517	6,417	68,130
Total technological disasters	**7,479**	**9,263**	**7,968**	**8,764**	**8,772**	**10,914**	**8,908**	**13,336**	**8,979**	**10,329**	**94,712**
Total	**84,570**	**77,046**	**79,720**	**114,905**	**132,131**	**21,016**	**39,382**	**25,705**	**76,806**	**249,896**	**901,177**

Source: EM-DAT, CRED, University of Louvain, Belgium

[1] Insect infestations and waves/surges.

Note: n.a. signifies no data available; ndr signifies no disaster reported. For more information, see section on caveats in introductory text.

Unusual catastrophes like December 2004's tsunami, which was responsible for around 90 per cent of all reported disaster deaths in 2004, introduce great variability to the mortality series. But it reminded us that geophysical disasters, while rare compared to floods and windstorms, remain among the deadliest. In 2004, the numbers of deaths caused by the three most frequent disasters (transport accidents, floods and windstorms) were nearly identical.

Comparing the two periods 1995–1999 and 2000–2004, the average numbers of deaths due to geophysical disasters and extreme temperatures increased, even discounting 2004's tsunami and 2003's heatwave in Europe. Conversely, numbers killed by floods and windstorms decreased over this period, even if Hurricane Mitch in 1998 and Venezuela's floods in 1999 are excluded. The same period saw an increase of 40 per cent in people killed by industrial accidents.

Table 7 Total number of people reported affected, by type of phenomenon and by year (1995 to 2004) in thousands

	1995	1996	1997	1998	1999	2000	2001	2002	2003	2004	Total
Avalanches/landslides	1,122	9	34	209	15	208	67	771	459	13	2,908
Droughts/famines	30,431	5,836	8,016	24,495	38,647	176,477	86,757	338,536	70,274	7,780	787,250
Earthquakes/tsunamis	3,029	2,018	634	1,888	3,893	2,458	19,307	549	3,956	3,058	40,791
Extreme temperatures	535	n.a.	615	36	725	28	213	104	1,840	2,140	6,236
Floods	198,233	178,451	44,956	290,073	150,167	62,506	34,500	167,186	166,828	116,583	1,409,482
Forest/scrub fires	12	6	53	167	19	39	6	26	9	20	356
Volcanic eruptions	26	7	7	8	34	119	78	298	25	53	654
Windstorms	13,771	28,144	13,594	26,784	21,153	15,459	30,645	110,709	10,781	15,920	286,962
Other natural disasters[1]	n.a.	n.a.	29	n.a.	1	17	n.a.	ndr	ndr	n.a.	48
Subtotal hydro-meteorological disasters	244,105	212,446	67,297	341,765	210,727	254,734	152,189	617,333	250,191	142,455	2,493,242
Subtotal geophysical disasters	3,055	2,025	641	1,896	3,928	2,577	19,386	847	3,981	3,110	41,445
Total natural disasters	247,160	214,471	67,939	343,661	214,655	257,312	171,574	618,180	254,171	145,566	2,534,687
Industrial accidents	27	16	163	63	3	17	19	2	555	157	1,023
Miscellaneous accidents	19	18	20	52	12	15	30	56	14	102	340
Transport accidents	3	3	3	4	5	6	3	5	4	48	85
Total technological disasters	50	36	186	119	21	38	53	63	574	307	1,447
Total	247,210	214,507	68,125	343,780	214,675	257,350	171,627	618,243	254,745	145,872	2,536,134

Source: EM-DAT, CRED, University of Louvain, Belgium

[1] Insect infestations and waves/surges.

Note: n.a. signifies no data available; ndr signifies no disaster reported. For more information, see section on caveats in introductory text.

In 2004, floods affected over 116 million people – 80 per cent of the year's total for all disasters. Windstorms affected nearly 16 million people – 11 per cent of the total.

Over the decade, hydrometeorological disasters accounted for 98 per cent of all people affected by disasters.

During 2004, 12 times as many people were affected by transport accidents, compared to the average over the previous nine years.

International Federation
of Red Cross and Red Crescent Societies

Table 8 Total amount of disaster estimated damage, by type of phenomenon and by year (1995 to 2004) in millions of US dollars (2004 prices)

	1995	1996	1997	1998	1999	2000	2001	2002	2003	2004	Total
Avalanches/landslides	13	n.a.	19	n.a.	n.a.	185	75	13	53	n.a.	358
Droughts/famines	7,158	1,444	481	522	7,768	6,927	4,033	1,535	729	1,341	31,939
Earthquakes/tsunamis	165,146	636	5,798	438	35,704	156	10,623	1,279	9,765	36,483	266,029
Extreme temperatures	1,034	n.a.	3,534	4,287	1,134	136	213	n.a.	11,550	n.a.	21,888
Floods	32,310	30,006	15,081	33,778	15,095	11,700	3,327	24,703	15,095	12,840	193,935
Forest/scrub fires	167	2,071	20,011	702	556	1,154	75	96	2,664	3	27,500
Volcanic eruptions	1	20	9	n.a.	n.a.	n.a.	16	9	n.a.	n.a.	55
Windstorms	30,250	15,041	8,836	19,451	26,834	10,581	11,474	1,347	17,591	47,434	188,841
Other natural disasters[1]	129	n.a.	4	2	n.a.	132	n.a.	ndr	ndr	n.a.	267
Subtotal hydro-meteorological disasters	71,060	48,562	47,967	58,743	51,387	30,815	19,198	27,694	47,682	61,619	464,727
Subtotal geophysical disasters	165,147	656	5,807	438	35,704	156	10,639	1,289	9,765	36,483	266,084
Total natural disasters	**236,208**	**49,218**	**53,774**	**59,181**	**87,090**	**30,971**	**29,837**	**28,983**	**57,448**	**98,102**	**730,812**
Industrial accidents	772	1,451	449	149	3	n.a.	11	n.a.	n.a.	800	3,635
Miscellaneous accidents	273	1,471	n.a.	22	2	477	n.a.	53	n.a.	n.a.	2,298
Transport accidents	850	249	12	34	225	n.a.	n.a.	n.a.	n.a.	408	1,778
Total technological disasters	**1,896**	**3,170**	**461**	**205**	**231**	**477**	**11**	**53**	**n.a.**	**1,208**	**7,711**
Total	**238,104**	**52,387**	**54,235**	**59,386**	**87,321**	**31,448**	**29,848**	**29,036**	**57,448**	**99,310**	**738,523**

Source: EM-DAT, CRED, University of Louvain, Belgium

[1] Insect infestations and waves/surges.

Note: n.a. signifies no data available; ndr signifies no disaster reported. For more information, see section on caveats in introductory text.

In 2004, the greatest reported damage was caused by windstorms (US$ 47 billion) followed by earthquakes and tsunamis (US$ 36 billion) and floods (US$ 13 billion).

Over the decade, earthquakes and tsunamis caused most damage (US$ 266 billion). Costs per reported earthquake were significantly higher than per windstorm, even excluding the US$ 163 billion bill left by 1995's Kobe earthquake.

ANNEX 1

Table 9 Total number of reported disasters, by type of phenomenon and by continent (1995 to 2004)

	Africa	Americas	Asia	Europe	Oceania	HHD²	MHD²	LHD²	Total
Avalanches/landslides	11	44	112	19	8	24	153	17	194
Droughts/famines	120	48	85	14	9	30	127	119	276
Earthquakes/tsunamis	17	50	154	50	8	53	201	25	279
Extreme temperatures	8	37	44	63	2	63	80	11	154
Floods	277	267	432	199	35	297	638	275	1,210
Forest/scrub fires	12	63	22	46	9	84	62	6	152
Volcanic eruptions	4	23	13	2	6	13	33	2	48
Windstorms	69	305	320	94	68	404	389	63	856
Other natural disasters¹	14	3	10	1	2	2	17	11	30
Subtotal hydro-meteorological disasters	511	767	1,025	436	133	904	1,466	502	2,872
Subtotal geophysical disasters	21	73	167	52	14	66	234	27	327
Total natural disasters	**532**	**840**	**1,192**	**488**	**147**	**970**	**1,700**	**529**	**3,199**
Industrial accidents	45	43	313	72	0	72	351	50	473
Miscellaneous accidents	84	63	212	67	4	90	269	71	430
Transport accidents	650	277	742	207	11	241	1,147	499	1,887
Total technological disasters	**779**	**383**	**1,267**	**346**	**15**	**403**	**1,767**	**620**	**2,790**
Total	**1,311**	**1,223**	**2,459**	**834**	**162**	**1,373**	**3,467**	**1,149**	**5,989**

Source: EM-DAT, CRED, University of Louvain, Belgium

¹ Insect infestations and waves/surges.

² HHD stands for high human development, MHD for medium human development and LHD for low human development. See note on UNDP's Human Development Index country status in the section on data definitions in the introduction to this annex.

Floods were the most common natural disaster over the past decade, particularly in Africa, Asia and Europe.

Windstorms were the most common disaster in the Americas and Oceania. Half of earthquake and tsunami disasters occurred in Asia. Africa accounted for over 40 per cent of all reported droughts and famines. But half of Africa's reported disasters were transport accidents.

Over the decade, HHD countries were most afflicted by windstorms (29 per cent of all their disasters), while transport accidents were the most common disasters in MHD countries (33 per cent) and LHD countries (43 per cent).

Table 10 Total number of people reported killed, by type of phenomenon and by continent (1995 to 2004)

	Africa	Americas	Asia	Europe	Oceania	HHD²	MHD²	LHD²	Total
Avalanches/landslides	251	1,742	6,219	416	128	370	7,576	810	8,756
Droughts/famines	4,551	59	270,923	n.a.	88	n.a.	927	274,694	275,621
Earthquakes/tsunamis	3,114	2,990	292,050	20,727	2,200	8,231	304,237	8,761	321,229
Extreme temperatures	200	2,325	9,817	32,888	1	32,986	11,378	867	45,231
Floods	9,176	38,000	44,219	1,414	33	3,599	76,093	13,150	92,842
Forest/scrub fires	114	83	125	107	9	146	288	4	438
Volcanic eruptions	254	52	3	n.a.	4	20	39	254	313
Windstorms	1,385	25,271	33,958	720	250	4,514	52,391	4,679	61,584
Other natural disasters¹	n.a.	3	448	n.a.	n.a.	n.a.	451	n.a.	451
Subtotal hydro-meteorological disasters	15,677	67,483	365,709	35,545	509	41,615	149,104	294,204	484,923
Subtotal geophysical disasters	3,368	3,042	292,053	20,727	2,204	8,251	304,276	9,015	321,542
Total natural disasters	**19,045**	**70,525**	**657,762**	**56,272**	**2,713**	**49,866**	**453,380**	**303,219**	**806,465**
Industrial accidents	2,810	279	7,956	918	ndr	385	8,655	2,923	11,963
Miscellaneous accidents	2,781	2,784	7,592	1,416	46	2,806	9,320	2,493	14,619
Transport accidents	24,028	8,364	29,465	5,762	511	7,587	39,676	20,867	68,130
Total technological disasters	**29,619**	**11,427**	**45,013**	**8,096**	**557**	**10,778**	**57,651**	**26,283**	**94,712**
Total	**48,664**	**81,952**	**702,775**	**64,368**	**3,270**	**60,644**	**511,031**	**329,502**	**901,177**

Source: EM-DAT, CRED, University of Louvain, Belgium

¹ Insect infestations and waves/surges.
² HHD stands for high human development, MHD for medium human development, and LHD for low human development. See note on UNDP's Human Development Index country status in the section on data definitions in the introduction to this annex.
Note: n.a. signifies no data available; ndr signifies no disaster reported. For more information, see section on caveats in introductory text.
Over the decade, the biggest killers per continent (not including conflict- and disease-related deaths) were transport accidents in Africa (49 per cent of all those killed by disasters); floods in the Americas (46 per cent); earthquakes and tsunamis in Asia (42 per cent) and Oceania (67 per cent); and extreme temperatures in Europe (51 per cent).
Deaths from industrial and transport accidents were significantly higher in Asia and Africa than in other continents.
Analysing the figures by level of human development, HHD countries lost most lives to extreme temperatures (54 per cent); MHD countries to earthquakes and tsunamis (60 per cent); and LHD countries to droughts and famines (83 per cent).

Table 11 Total number of people reported affected, by type of phenomenon and by continent (1995 to 2004) in thousands

	Africa	Americas	Asia	Europe	Oceania	HHD[2]	MHD[2]	LHD[2]	Total
Avalanches/landslides	3	204	2,685	14	1	15	2,887	7	2,908
Droughts/famines	122,984	15,183	639,187	7,063	2,833	8,415	658,759	120,075	787,250
Earthquakes/tsunamis	378	3,584	34,619	2,175	35	2,791	36,465	1,535	40,791
Extreme temperatures	0	4,072	893	771	500	579	5,458	200	6,236
Floods	21,636	9,717	1,372,252	5,784	93	6,507	1,371,298	31,677	1,409,482
Forest/scrub fires	8	159	58	113	17	147	207	2	356
Volcanic eruptions	139	298	187	n.a.	29	60	465	130	654
Windstorms	3,893	17,051	258,119	6,636	1,264	18,099	263,465	5,397	286,962
Other natural disasters[1]	n.a.	1	47	n.a.	n.a.	n.a.	19	29	48
Subtotal hydro-meteorological disasters	148,524	46,387	2,273,241	20,382	4,708	33,761	2,302,093	157,388	2,493,242
Subtotal geophysical disasters	517	3,882	34,806	2,175	65	2,851	36,930	1,665	41,445
Total natural disasters	149,041	50,269	2,308,047	22,557	4,773	36,612	2,339,023	159,053	2,534,687
Industrial accidents	6	577	369	71	ndr	120	897	5	1,023
Miscellaneous accidents	124	10	183	11	12	17	211	111	340
Transport accidents	12	8	61	4	n.a.	9	25	52	85
Total technological disasters	141	594	612	87	12	146	1,133	167	1,447
Total	149,183	50,864	2,308,659	22,644	4,785	36,758	2,340,156	159,220	2,536,134

Source: EM-DAT, CRED, University of Louvain, Belgium

[1] Insect infestations and waves/surges.
[2] HHD stands for high human development, MHD for medium human development, and LHD for low human development.
Development Index country status in the section on data definitions in the introduction to this annex.
Note: n.a. signifies no data available; ndr signifies no disaster reported. For more information, see section on caveats in introductory text.
Over the decade, Africans were most affected by droughts and famines (accounting for 82 per cent of all disaster-affected Africans); Americans by windstorms
(34 per cent); Asians by floods (59 per cent); while droughts affected most Europeans (31 per cent) and most people from Oceania (59 per cent).
Analysing the figures by level of human development, HHD countries were most affected by windstorms (accounting for 49 per cent of all disaster-affected
people); MHD countries were most affected by floods (59 per cent); and LHD countries by droughts and famines (75 per cent). In MHD countries, industrial
accidents accounted for 79 per cent of those affected by technological disasters.

International Federation
of Red Cross and Red Crescent Societies

Table 12 Total amount of disaster estimated damage, by type of phenomenon and by continent (1995 to 2004) in millions of US dollars (2004 prices)

	Africa	Americas	Asia	Europe	Oceania	HHD²	MHD²	LHD²	Total
Avalanches/landslides	n.a.	194	138	26	n.a.	7	350	n.a.	358
Droughts/famines	445	3,447	14,435	11,993	1,620	15,940	15,596	403	31,939
Earthquakes/tsunamis	5,633	9,931	219,912	30,554	n.a.	215,646	50,383	n.a.	266,029
Extreme temperatures	1	5,449	3,529	12,696	213	18,234	3,655	n.a.	21,888
Floods	1,440	21,956	125,636	43,433	1,471	62,211	108,776	22,948	193,935
Forest/scrub fires	4	2,645	22,378	2,062	412	4,938	22,562	n.a.	27,500
Volcanic eruptions	9	22	1	23	n.a.	23	23	9	55
Windstorms	941	102,461	63,264	19,265	2,909	146,853	34,887	7,101	188,841
Other natural disasters¹	6	129	n.a.	n.a.	132	132	131	4	267
Subtotal hydro-meteorological disasters	2,837	136,280	229,380	89,475	6,756	248,315	185,956	30,456	464,727
Subtotal geophysical disasters	5,642	9,953	219,913	30,577	0	215,669	50,406	9	266,084
Total natural disasters	**8,479**	**146,233**	**449,292**	**120,051**	**6,756**	**463,984**	**236,362**	**30,466**	**730,812**
Industrial accidents	811	1,278	828	719	ndr	2,024	1,401	210	3,635
Miscellaneous accidents	5	1,700	24	569	n.a.	2,232	61	5	2,298
Transport accidents	67	129	1,156	426	n.a.	550	811	418	1,778
Total technological disasters	**883**	**3,106**	**2,008**	**1,714**	**n.a.**	**4,805**	**2,273**	**633**	**7,711**
Total	**9,362**	**149,340**	**451,301**	**121,765**	**6,756**	**468,789**	**238,634**	**31,099**	**738,523**

Source: EM-DAT, CRED, University of Louvain, Belgium

¹ Insect infestations and waves/surges
² HHD stands for high human development, MHD for medium human development, and LHD for low human development. See note on UNDP's Human Development Index country status in the section on data definitions in the introduction to this annex.
Note: n.a. signifies no data available; ndr signifies no disaster reported. For more information, see section on caveats in introductory text.
Amounts of estimated damage must be approached with caution due to low reporting rates and methodological weaknesses.
Over the decade, earthquakes and tsunamis proved the costliest disasters for Africa (accounting for 60 per cent of total disaster damage), Asia (49 per cent) and HHD countries (46 per cent).
Floods proved costliest for Europe (36 per cent) and countries of medium and low human development (46 and 74 per cent respectively).
Windstorms proved costliest for the Americas (69 per cent) and Oceania (43 per cent).

	Total number of people reported killed (1985–1994)	Total number of people reported affected (1985–1994)	Total number of people reported killed (1995–2004)	Total number of people reported affected (1995–2004)	Total number of people reported killed (2004)	Total number of people reported affected (2004)
Africa	**168,532**	**146,331,465**	**48,812**	**149,183,339**	**4,308**	**9,000,583**
Algeria	492	96,707	3,899	328,175	104	28,061
Angola	1,152	3,697,320	1,175	540,785	118	358,795
Benin	357	1,265,814	265	801,305	ndr	ndr
Botswana	191	2,325,625	23	149,236	n.a.	4,960
Burkina Faso	75	2,900,396	95	110,220	72	20
Burundi	332	5,668	219	1,177,335	3	25,620
Cameroon	3,625	812,877	789	6,271	ndr	ndr
Canary Is. (ES)	ndr	ndr	100	852	62	122
Cape Verde	n.a.	n.a.	18	46,306	n.a.	n.a.
Central African Republic	87	418	186	93,414	28	12,748
Chad	1,788	1,901,210	161	932,451	30	15
Comoros	29	85,650	256	300	ndr	ndr
Congo	663	16,550	100	67,163	42	32
Congo, DR of[1]	1,759	28,009	2,562	284,503	351	346
Côte d'Ivoire	154	7,237	416	193	49	30
Djibouti	165	320,539	52	546,125	51	100,000
Egypt	2,193	198,004	2,013	9,487	301	121
Equatorial Guinea	15	313	2	3,650	n.a.	2,650
Eritrea[2]	28	1,615,700	105	2,881,025	n.a.	8,000
Ethiopia[2]	9,698	37,339,942	1,036	51,778,186	45	72
Gabon	122	10,132	50	11	19	11
Gambia	100	n.a.	80	52,906	2	6,137
Ghana	225	8,966	597	1,171,000	24	40
Guinea	702	30,096	419	220,186	33	50
Guinea-Bissau	264	24,681	220	102,500	3	1,000
Kenya	2,482	9,200,494	1,355	15,976,596	221	2,342,228
Lesotho	40	350,000	1	1,103,751	ndr	ndr
Liberia	n.a.	1,000,000	80	7,000	ndr	ndr
Libyan AJ	310	121	130	61	27	51
Madagascar	629	2,274,429	933	4,804,172	409	1,032,434
Malawi	541	21,438,145	703	4,192,647	27	17
Mali	389	326,979	3,791	52,267	57	10
Mauritania	2,428	489,468	97	823,591	n.a.	n.a.
Mauritius	162	14,307	6	2,050	ndr	ndr
Morocco	201	151	2,260	404,315	716	13,596

	Total number of people reported killed (1985–1994)	Total number of people reported affected (1985–1994)	Total number of people reported killed (1995–2004)	Total number of people reported affected (1995–2004)	Total number of people reported killed (2004)	Total number of people reported affected (2004)
Mozambique	107,324	9,560,244	1,428	4,640,944	11	16
Namibia	120	250,000	21	1,217,748	n.a.	25,000
Niger	3,278	2,863,924	135	3,718,599	14	8
Nigeria	11,389	3,906,324	8,789	642,849	454	35,569
Reunion (FR)	79	10,261	2	3,700	ndr	ndr
Rwanda	317	81,892	301	1,339,410	ndr	ndr
Saint Helena (GB)	ndr	ndr	n.a.	300	ndr	ndr
Sao Tome and Principe	181	1,063	ndr	ndr	ndr	ndr
Senegal	431	39,025	2,265	606,981	62	1,191
Seychelles	ndr	ndr	8	12,867	3	4830
Sierra Leone	514	3,000	899	200,025	34	n.a.
Somalia	3,643	662,408	3,012	4,552,499	416	306,610
South Africa	1,878	4,816,218	2,120	4,516,840	138	4,015,146
Sudan	2,727	15,741,276	1,272	9,195,208	72	45
Swaziland	30	482,228	52	709,559	22	242,500
Tanzania	1,367	1,440,292	2,199	10,024,911	21	180,003
Togo	50	463,117	3	220,405	ndr	ndr
Tunisia	109	98,716	385	27,134	93	43
Uganda	940	1,001,748	983	1,272,402	151	56,058
Zambia	2,301	2,518,034	333	5,541,423	2	196,398
Zimbabwe	456	14,605,747	411	12,069,500	21	n.a.
Americas	**72,841**	**34,800,277**	**81,952**	**50,863,711**	**8,269**	**4,267,665**
Anguilla (GB)	ndr	ndr	n.a.	150	ndr	ndr
Antigua and Barbuda	2	8,030	5	76,684	ndr	ndr
Argentina	508	6,387,834	617	889,771	213	6,534
Aruba (NL)	ndr	ndr	ndr	ndr	ndr	ndr
Bahamas	104	1,700	3	10,500	2	9,000
Barbados	n.a.	230	1	3,000	1	1,000
Belize	n.a.	n.a.	66	145,170	ndr	ndr
Bermuda	28	40	22	n.a.	ndr	ndr
Bolivia	625	887,093	854	756,555	58	55,025
Brazil	3,173	5,752,885	2,453	12,890,074	275	155,490
Canada	554	53,541	407	574,934	10	1,000
Cayman Is. (GB)	ndr	ndr	1	300	1	n.a.
Chile	901	1,972,475	399	586,604	3	9,502
Colombia	25,693	759,849	2,684	3,031,098	143	540,049
Costa Rica	121	396,426	134	873,853	10	3,336
Cuba	878	1,610,351	262	7,925,683	4	247,250

	Total number of people reported killed (1985–1994)	Total number of people reported affected (1985–1994)	Total number of people reported killed (1995–2004)	Total number of people reported affected (1995–2004)	Total number of people reported killed (2004)	Total number of people reported affected (2004)
Dominica	n.a.	710	15	3,991	n.a.	100
Dominican Republic	401	1,214,085	1,509	1,090,345	781	24,292
Ecuador	1,778	492,703	802	414,973	ndr	ndr
El Salvador	1,414	823,035	1,927	2,098,883	68	52
Falkland Is. (GB)	ndr	ndr	ndr	ndr	ndr	ndr
French Guiana (FR)	ndr	ndr	n.a.	70,000	ndr	ndr
Grenada	n.a.	1,000	39	60,210	39	60,000
Guadeloupe (FR)	5	12,084	25	1,052	1	153
Guatemala	987	161,340	1,103	368,192	37	20,079
Guyana	n.a.	281	10	645,400	ndr	ndr
Haiti	3,531	3,653,686	6,717	548,273	5,422	353,377
Honduras	843	192,084	14,830	3,819,187	115	137,530
Jamaica	132	1,432,312	26	353,626	16	350,126
Martinique (FR)	10	4,510	n.a.	600	ndr	ndr
Mexico	11,198	848,987	3,677	2,396,835	72	4,090
Montserrat (GB)	11	12,040	32	13,000	ndr	ndr
Netherlands Antilles (NL)	n.a.	n.a.	17	40,004	ndr	ndr
Nicaragua	354	1,021,184	3,521	1,573,150	29	5,969
Panama	274	54,960	46	64,833	16	22,748
Paraguay	n.a.	125,575	508	505,494	390	300
Peru	13,424	4,336,698	3,450	5,651,987	242	2,145,123
Puerto Rico (US)	760	2,534	167	121,453	39	3,514
St Kitts and Nevis	1	1,330	5	12,980	ndr	ndr
St Lucia	49	750	n.a.	375	n.a.	n.a.
St Vincent and the Grenadines	3	1,560	n.a.	1,104	n.a.	1,004
Suriname	169	13	10	n.a.	ndr	ndr
Trinidad and Tobago	11	1,030	3	2,377	3	1,760
Turks and Caicos Is. (GB)	n.a.	770	43	200	n.a.	200
United States	3,930	2,480,326	5,027	2,482,766	198	101,332
Uruguay	20	26,740	98	27,547	n.a.	2,000
Venezuela	949	57,496	30,426	720,495	81	5,730
Virgin Is. (GB)	n.a.	10,000	n.a.	3	ndr	ndr
Virgin Is. (US)	ndr	ndr	11	10,000	n.a.	n.a.
Asia	**359,324**	**1,536,059,526**	**702,775**	**2,308,658,878**	**236,102**	**131,955,871**
Afghanistan	2,591	508,423	10,052	7,000,376	97	5,663
Armenia[3]	91	1,300,798	16	319,156	1	n.a.

	Total number of people reported killed (1985–1994)	Total number of people reported affected (1985–1994)	Total number of people reported killed (1995–2004)	Total number of people reported affected (1995–2004)	Total number of people reported killed (2004)	Total number of people reported affected (2004)
Azerbaijan[3]	91	20	563	2,484,196	ndr	ndr
Bahrain	10	n.a.	143	n.a.	ndr	ndr
Bangladesh	170,977	208,830,481	10,817	93,142,451	1,485	36,893,105
Bhutan	39	65,600	200	1,000	n.a.	n.a.
Brunei Darussalam	ndr	ndr	ndr	ndr	ndr	ndr
Cambodia	687	1,309,400	586	15,427,614	n.a.	n.a.
China, PR of[4]	28,351	673,792,465	31,348	1,293,273,729	2,543	53,167,165
East Timor[5]			4	3,508	ndr	ndr
Georgia[3]	565	266,762	68	1,238,560	1	90
Hong Kong (CN)[4]	300	13,651	105	4,638	ndr	ndr
India	47,027	543,253,682	83,620	702,027,610	18,410	33,861,550
Indonesia	7,791	5,504,285	171,419	3,916,245	164,397	742,082
Iran, Islamic Rep. of	43,258	1,784,582	33,052	64,219,732	682	8,083
Iraq	821	500	171	816,007	61	8,000
Israel	90	360	102	1,897	ndr	ndr
Japan	1,824	617,898	6,218	3,223,620	273	421,569
Jordan	66	18,369	114	330,274	12	12
Kazakhstan[3]	90	30,004	231	651,002	71	164
Korea, DPR of	774	22,967	270,634	10,803,470	185	241,555
Korea, Rep. of	2,105	765,101	2,555	925,579	24	9,768
Kuwait	ndr	ndr	2	200	ndr	ndr
Kyrgyzstan[3]	220	255,400	212	11,486	68	105
Lao, PDR	746	1,569,462	185	3,008,905	ndr	ndr
Lebanon	70	105,575	48	555	ndr	ndr
Macau (CN)[4]	n.a.	3,986	ndr	ndr	ndr	ndr
Malaysia	809	117,687	611	145,716	85	77,101
Maldives	n.a.	24,149	143	27,314	133	27,314
Mongolia	145	600,000	185	2,371,712	ndr	ndr
Myanmar	1,289	582,505	627	419,958	337	37,530
Nepal	5,048	1,420,792	3,489	1,453,676	290	800,086
Oman	ndr	ndr	104	104	21	13
Pakistan	6,144	20,983,415	6,192	9,224,032	272	13,475
Palestine (West Bank/Gaza)[6]	ndr	ndr	14	20	ndr	ndr
Philippines	22,885	41,282,818	7,832	20,388,186	2,098	3,284,086
Qatar	ndr	ndr	ndr	ndr	ndr	ndr
Saudi Arabia	2,066	5,000	1,157	17,807	256	670
Singapore	27	237	n.a.	1,200	ndr	ndr
Sri Lanka	811	6,078,866	36,096	5,781,189	35,405	1,219,306

	Total number of people reported killed (1985–1994)	Total number of people reported affected (1985–1994)	Total number of people reported killed (1995–2004)	Total number of people reported affected (1995–2004)	Total number of people reported killed (2004)	Total number of people reported affected (2004)
Syrian Arab Republic	46	n.a.	304	668,568	28	211
Taiwan (CN)	710	24,176	3,592	774,336	79	8,873
Tajikistan[3]	1,718	146,512	199	3,342,898	n.a.	5,180
Thailand	3,485	7,460,080	10,140	29,308,220	8,428	586,699
Turkmenistan[3]	n.a.	420	51	n.a.	ndr	ndr
United Arab Emirates	n.a.	100	183	41	43	2
Uzbekistan[3]	10	50,400	168	1,123,988	37	n.a.
Viet Nam	5,295	16,354,058	8,147	30,516,182	239	536,349
Yemen[7]	252	908,540	1,076	261,921	41	65
Yemen, Arab Rep.[7]	ndr	ndr				
Yemen, DPR[7]	ndr	ndr				
Europe	**41,566**	**8,366,611**	**64,368**	**22,643,594**	**1,182**	**524,179**
Albania	196	3,242,801	28	220,909	18	2,525
Andorra	ndr	ndr	ndr	ndr	ndr	ndr
Austria	41	30	263	70,494	ndr	ndr
Azores (PT)	172	n.a.	74	1,215	ndr	ndr
Belarus[3]	n.a.	40,000	92	23,468	ndr	ndr
Belgium	266	1,413	235	4,742	23	200
Bosnia and Herzegovina[8]	ndr	ndr	60	351,080	n.a.	278,000
Bulgaria	71	8,179	17	1,740	ndr	ndr
Channel Is. (GB)	ndr	ndr	ndr	ndr	ndr	ndr
Croatia[8]	61	25	87	3,400	ndr	ndr
Cyprus	n.a.	n.a.	59	4,347	n.a.	10
Czech Republic[9]	ndr	ndr	84	302,146	ndr	ndr
Czechoslovakia[9]	51	n.a.				
Denmark	55	100	9	2,072	1	2,072
Estonia[3]	912	140	22	30	ndr	ndr
Faroe Is. (DK)	ndr	ndr	ndr	ndr	ndr	ndr
Finland	n.a.	n.a.	35	48	24	15
France	672	9,972	15,670	3,904,896	39	54
Germany[10]	ndr	ndr	5,609	477,461	n.a.	150
Germany, Dem. Rep.[10]	339	105,854	ndr	ndr	ndr	ndr
Germany, Fed. Rep. of[10]	ndr	ndr	ndr	ndr	ndr	ndr
Gibraltar (GB)	ndr	ndr	ndr	ndr	ndr	ndr
Greece	1,285	47,288	544	215,897	54	7
Greenland (DK)	ndr	ndr	ndr	ndr	ndr	ndr

	Total number of people reported killed (1985–1994)	Total number of people reported affected (1985–1994)	Total number of people reported killed (1995–2004)	Total number of people reported affected (1995–2004)	Total number of people reported killed (2004)	Total number of people reported affected (2004)
Holy See	ndr	ndr	ndr	ndr	ndr	ndr
Hungary	47	59	198	147,582	n.a.	393
Iceland	n.a.	280	34	282	ndr	ndr
Ireland	386	3,500	n.a.	1,000	ndr	ndr
Isle of Man (GB)	ndr	ndr	ndr	ndr	ndr	ndr
Italy	922	32,813	5,101	240,907	28	207
Latvia[3]	ndr	ndr	36	n.a.	ndr	ndr
Liechtenstein	ndr	ndr	ndr	ndr	ndr	ndr
Lithuania[3]	6	780,000	62	n.a.	ndr	ndr
Luxembourg	n.a.	n.a.	20	n.a.	ndr	ndr
Macedonia, FYR of[8]	196	10,015	42	107,906	15	100,000
Malta	12	n.a.	299	4	16	4
Moldova[3]	50	50,580	10	2,604,457	ndr	ndr
Monaco	ndr	ndr	ndr	ndr	ndr	ndr
Netherlands	80	12,656	1,306	253,251	ndr	ndr
Norway	272	n.a.	252	6,142	18	12
Poland	297	294	942	241,113	n.a.	600
Portugal	234	2,542	2,155	3,138	2	n.a.
Romania	329	25,311	499	256,823	67	17,141
Russian Federation[3]	2,605	871,541	6,396	2,797,409	408	14,435
San Marino	ndr	ndr	ndr	ndr	ndr	ndr
Serbia and Montenegro[8]	1	6,000	140	79,754	12	38
Slovakia[9]	ndr	ndr	87	58,593	3	10,554
Slovenia[8]	ndr	ndr	1	1,305	1	605
Soviet Union[3]	27,172	2,078,222				
Spain	577	19,101	750	6,056,340	26	1,700
Sweden	47	122	64	162	ndr	ndr
Switzerland	62	7,220	111	1,810	ndr	ndr
Turkey	2,358	392,447	20,123	1,831,913	340	88,962
Ukraine[3]	183	410,412	593	2,079,067	66	5,334
United Kingdom	1,200	205,038	2,259	290,691	21	1,161
Yugoslavia[8]	409	2,656				
Oceania	**1,155**	**13,944,488**	**3,270**	**4,785,060**	**35**	**124,213**
American Samoa (US)	25	n.a.	6	23,063	n.a.	23,060
Australia	371	12,307,078	304	3,364,571	6	4,385
Cook Is.	13	3,200	19	1,644	ndr	ndr
Fiji	85	511,372	92	309,327	16	10,600

	Total number of people reported killed (1985–1994)	Total number of people reported affected (1985–1994)	Total number of people reported killed (1995–2004)	Total number of people reported affected (1995–2004)	Total number of people reported killed (2004)	Total number of people reported affected (2004)
French Polynesia (FR)	10	n.a.	13	511	ndr	ndr
Guam (US)	1	6,115	233	22,064	4	500
Kiribati	ndr	ndr	n.a.	84,000	ndr	ndr
Marshall Is.	n.a.	6,000	ndr	ndr	ndr	ndr
Micronesia, Fed. States of	5	203	48	37,456	1	6,008
Nauru	ndr	ndr	ndr	ndr	ndr	ndr
New Caledonia (FR)	2	n.a.	2	1,100	ndr	ndr
New Zealand	23	13,672	28	8,610	4	5,350
Niue (NZ)	n.a.	200	1	702	1	702
Northern Mariana Is. (US)	ndr	ndr	ndr	ndr	ndr	ndr
Palau	ndr	ndr	1	12,004	ndr	ndr
Papua New Guinea	389	375,302	2,456	815,270	n.a.	19,600
Samoa	21	283,000	1	n.a.	1	n.a.
Solomon Is.	139	239,674	n.a.	1,905	ndr	ndr
Tokelau (NZ)	n.a.	1,832	ndr	ndr	ndr	ndr
Tonga	1	3,103	n.a.	23,021	n.a.	n.a.
Tuvalu	n.a.	850	18	n.a.	ndr	ndr
Vanuatu	64	188,367	48	79,812	2	54,008
Wallis and Futuna (FR)	6	4,520	ndr	ndr	ndr	ndr
Total	**643,418**	**1,739,502,367**	**901,177**	**2,536,134,582**	**249,896**	**145,872,511**

Source: EM-DAT, CRED, University of Louvain, Belgium

[1] Democratic Republic of the Congo since 1997. Previously: Zaire.

[2] Prior to 1993, Ethiopia was considered one country; after this date separate countries: Eritrea and Ethiopia.

[3] Prior to 1991, the Soviet Union was considered one country; after this date separate countries. The former western republics of the USSR (Belarus, Estonia, Latvia, Lithuania, Moldova, Russian Federation, Ukraine) are included in Europe; the former southern republics (Armenia, Azerbaijan, Georgia, Kazakhstan, Kyrgyzstan, Tajikistan, Turkmenistan, Uzbekistan) are included in Asia.

[4] Since July 1997, Hong Kong has been included in China; Macau has been included in China since December 1999.

[5] Since May 2002, East Timor has been an independent country.

[6] Since September 1993 and the Israel-PLO Declaration of Principles, the Gaza Strip and the West Bank have had a Palestinian government. Direct negotiations to determine the permanent status of these territories began in September 1999 but are not yet concluded.

[7] Prior to May 1990, Yemen was divided into Arab and People's Democratic Republics; after this date it has been considered one country.

[8] Prior to 1992, Yugoslavia was considered one country; after this date separate countries: Bosnia and Herzegovina, Croatia, Serbia and Montenegro, Slovenia, FYR of Macedonia.

[9] Prior to 1993, Czechoslovakia was considered one country; after this date, separate countries: Czech Republic and Slovakia.

International Federation
of Red Cross and Red Crescent Societies

[10] Prior to October 1990, Germany was divided into Federal and Democratic Republics; after this date it has been considered one country.

Note: n.a. signifies no data available; ndr signifies no disaster reported. For more information, see section on caveats in introductory text.

From 1995 to 2004, the total number of deaths reported from natural and technological disasters amounted to over 900,000. This represents a 40 per cent increase over the decade 1985–1994.

Two disasters substantially contributed to this figure: the famine in the Democratic People's Republic of Korea from 1995 to 1999 (270,000 deaths) and the Indian Ocean tsunami of 2004 (224,495 deaths, including 163,795 in Indonesia, 35,399 in Sri Lanka, 16,389 in India and 8,345 in Thailand).

Over the decade, if the tsunami's reported deaths and missing people are not considered, nine countries reported death tolls greater than 10,000: Afghanistan, Bangladesh, China, France, Honduras, India, Iran, Turkey and Venezuela.

On average over the past decade, more than 250 million people were reported affected by disasters globally every year. Half of these were in China and more than a quarter in India.

Worldwide, the number of people affected by disasters has climbed by 46 per cent, compared to the decade 1985–1994.

Table 14 Refugees and asylum seekers by country/territory of origin (1998 to 2004)

	1998	1999	2000	2001	2002	2003	2004
Africa	**2,880,950**	**3,072,800**	**3,254,300**	**2,923,000**	**2,907,700**	**3,102,100**	**3,225,000**
Algeria	3,000	5,000	–	10,000	–	–	1,900
Angola[1]	303,300	339,300	400,000	445,000	402,000	312,000	223,100
Benin	–	–	–	–	–	–	100
Burundi[1]	281,000	311,000	421,000	375,000	395,000	349,000	481,800
Cameroon	–	–	–	2,000	–	–	4,400
Central African Republic	–	–	–	22,000	14,000	41,000	31,700
Chad	15,000	13,000	53,000	35,000	–	3,000	54,100
Comoros	–	–	–	–	–	–	500
Congo, DR of[1]	136,000	229,000	342,000	355,000	393,000	422,000	468,200
Congo	20,000	25,000	22,000	30,000	15,000	14,000	28,300
Côte d'Ivoire[1]	–	–	–	–	22,000	51,000	47,700
Djibouti	3,000	1,000	1,000	–	–	–	100
Egypt	–	–	–	–	–	–	2,800
Equatorial Guinea	–	–	–	–	–	–	500
Eritrea[1]	323,100	323,100	356,400	305,000	285,000	277,000	123,800
Ethiopia[1]	39,600	53,300	36,200	13,000	15,500	14,500	49,900
Gambia	–	–	–	–	–	–	500
Ghana	11,000	10,000	10,000	10,000	10,000	10,000	11,700
Guinea	–	–	–	5,000	–	–	2,300
Guinea-Bissau	11,150	5,300	1,500	–	–	–	100
Kenya	8,000	5,000	–	–	–	–	11,800
Liberia[1]	310,000	249,000	196,000	215,000	255,300	381,800	317,100
Malawi	–	–	–	–	–	–	2,900
Mali	3,000	2,000	–	–	–	–	200
Mauritania[1]	30,000	45,000	45,000	50,000	40,000	20,000	28,700
Morocco	–	–	–	–	–	–	124,800
Mozambique	–	–	–	–	–	–	300
Namibia	–	1,000	–	–	–	–	1,400
Niger	–	–	–	–	–	–	200
Nigeria	–	–	–	10,000	15,000	17,000	30,800
Rwanda[1]	12,000	27,000	52,000	60,000	36,000	40,000	47,800
Senegal	10,000	10,000	10,000	10,000	11,000	13,000	12,500
Sierra Leone[1]	480,000	454,000	419,000	185,000	115,000	61,000	30,000
Somalia	414,600	415,600	370,000	300,000	282,900	263,300	323,400
South Africa	–	–	–	–	–	–	600
Sudan[1]	352,200	423,200	392,200	440,000	471,000	595,000	703,300
Tanzania	–	–	–	–	–	–	4,400
Togo	3,000	3,000	2,000	–	–	4,000	7,200
Tunisia	–	–	–	–	–	–	100
Uganda	12,000	15,000	20,000	20,000	25,000	28,000	31,500
Western Sahara	100,000	105,000	105,000	110,000	105,000	191,000	–*
Zambia	–	–	–	–	–	–	400

	1998	1999	2000	2001	2002	2003	2004
Zimbabwe[1]	–	–	–	–	–	2,500	12,100
East Asia and Pacific	**763,200**	**864,100**	**1,056,000**	**1,078,500**	**1,172,100**	**1,236,100**	**1,370,200**
Cambodia	51,000	15,100	16,400	16,000	16,000	16,000	15,700
China (Tibet)	128,000	130,000	130,000	151,000	160,900	139,900	149,800
East Timor	–	120,000	120,000	80,000	28,000	–	1,200
Fiji	–	–	–	–	–	–	1,100
Indonesia	8,000	8,000	6,150	5,500	5,100	23,400	24,100
Korea, DPR of	–	–	50,000	50,000	100,000	101,700	101,900
Lao PDR	12,100	13,900	400	–	–	15,000	14,000
Malaysia	–	–	–	–	–	–	400
Mongolia	–	–	–	–	–	–	200
Myanmar	238,100	240,100	380,250	450,000	509,100	584,800	681,500
Philippines	45,000	45,000	57,000	57,000	57,000	57,200	66,200
Thailand	–	–	–	–	–	–	1,300
Viet Nam	281,000	292,000	295,800	295,000	296,000	298,100	312,800
South and Central Asia	**2,928,700**	**2,906,750**	**3,832,700**	**4,961,500**	**3,878,600**	**2,839,500**	**2,413,400**
Afghanistan	2,628,600	2,561,050	3,520,350	4,500,000	3,532,900	2,533,200	2,085,800
Bangladesh	–	–	–	–	–	–	10,300
Bhutan	115,000	125,000	124,000	126,000	127,000	128,700	120,500
India	15,000	15,000	17,000	17,000	18,000	17,000	31,400
Kazakhstan	–	–	100	–	–	–	600
Kyrgyzstan	–	–	–	–	–	–	300
Nepal	–	–	–	–	–	–	1,400
Pakistan	–	–	–	10,000	–	6,700	18,200
Sri Lanka	110,000	110,000	110,000	144,000	148,100	106,400	87,400
Tajikistan	15,100	62,500	59,750	55,000	52,600	47,500	56,200
Uzbekistan	45,000	33,200	1,500	–	–	–	1,300
Middle East	**4,397,700**	**3,987,050**	**5,426,500**	**4,428,000**	**3,244,500**	**3,220,200**	**3,348,100**
Iran	30,800	31,200	30,600	34,000	24,800	21,000	30,300
Iraq	555,800	534,450	409,300	300,000	237,400	268,200	337,700
Israel	–	–	–	–	–	–	900
Jordan	–	–	–	–	–	–	900
Kuwait	–	–	–	–	–	–	100
Lebanon	–	–	4,400	–	1,200	–	1,500
Libyan AJ	–	–	–	–	–	–	300
Palestinian Territory, Occupied[2]	3,811,100	3,931,400	4,982,100	4,123,000	2,981,100	2,927,000	2,972,100
Saudi Arabia	–	–	–	–	–	–	100
Syrian Arab Rep.	–	–	100	–	–	4,000	3,500
Yemen	–	–	–	–	–	–	700
Europe	**1,241,300**	**1,238,100**	**755,900**	**674,000**	**517,500**	**438,600**	**284,100**
Albania	–	–	–	–	–	–	4,600
Armenia	180,000	188,400	–	9,000	–	–	4,300
Azerbaijan	218,000	230,000	–	–	–	–	12,8000

	1998	1999	2000	2001	2002	2003	2004
Belarus	–	–	–	–	–	–	1,600
Bosnia and Herzegovina	80,350	250,000	234,600	210,000	156,100	121,200	32,900
Bulgaria	–	–	–	–	–	–	1,400
Croatia	329,000	336,000	314,700	272,000	250,000	208,900	70,400
Czech Republic	–	–	–	–	–	–	1,000
Estonia	–	–	–	–	–	–	200
Georgia	23,000	2,800	22,400	21,000	11,400	6,600	22,900
Hungary	–	–	–	–	–	–	1,300
Latvia	–	–	–	–	–	–	200
Lituania	–	–	–	–	–	–	300
Macedonia, FYR of	–	–	–	23,000	3,000	–	1,500
Moldova	–	–	–	–	–	–	2,500
Poland	–	–	–	–	–	–	800
Portugal	–	–	–	–	–	–	200
Romania	–	–	–	–	–	–	3,300
Russian Federation	500	12,350	22,700	18,000	27,900	25,600	50,700
Serbia and Montenegro	136,900	376,400	148,900	60,000	52,200	52,800	34,300
Slovenia	–	–	4,400	–	–	–	–
Turkey	11,300	11,800	12,600	43,000	16,900	17,600	30,700
Ukraine	–	–	–	10,000	–	5,900	6,200
Americas and Caribbean	**442,550**	**393,800**	**366,750**	**428,000**	**454,200**	**319,000**	**387,200**
Argentina	–	–	–	–	–	–	1,100
Bolivia	–	–	–	–	–	–	200
Brazil	–	–	–	–	–	–	1,400
Chile	–	–	–	–	–	–	700
Colombia	600	–	2,300	23,000	42,900	230,700	284,300
Costa Rica	–	–	–	–	–	–	400
Cuba	300	850	1,200	3,000	31,500	26,500	27,500
Dominican Republic	–	–	–			–	100
Ecuador	–	–	–	–	–	–	500
El Salvador[3]	250,150	253,000	235,500	217,000	203,000	4,500	8,100
Grenada	–	–	–	–	–	–	100
Guatemala[3]	251,300	146,000	102,600	129,000	129,000	10,200	12,900
Guyana	–	–	–	–	–	–	1,000
Haiti	600	23,000	20,600	25,000	30,800	23,800	21,100
Honduras	–	–	–	–	–	–	1,900
Jamaica	–	–	–	–	–	–	400
Mexico	–	–	–	11,000	–	20,700	5,500
Nicaragua[3]	18,000	18,000	3,800	13,000	15,800	2,600	9,800
Peru	350	1,700	750	–	1,200	–	4,300
St Lucia	–	–	–	–	–	–	200

International Federation of Red Cross and Red Crescent Societies

	1998	1999	2000	2001	2002	2003	2004
St Vincent and the Grenadines	–	–	–	–	–	–	200
Trinidad and Tobago	–	–	–	–	–	–	200
United States	–	–	–	–	–	–	300
Uruguay	–	–	–	–	–	–	100
Venezuela	–	–	–	–	–	–	4,900
Total	**12,733,150**	**12,511,350**	**14,692,150**	**14,493,000**	**12,174,600**	**11,163,500**	**11,028,000**

Source: US Committee for Refugees

Note: – indicates zero or near zero.

* This territory is now controlled by Morocco. Hence USCR is listing Morocco as being the source responsible.

[1] These figures are provisional, as accurate estimates were unavailable at the time of publication.

[2] See note 2, Table 15.

[3] The Nicaraguan Adjustment and Central American Relief Act of 1997 (NACARA) covers many long-pending Salvadorean and Guatemalan asylum applicants. Those who apply under NACARA are granted permanent residence at a rate of 96 per cent. Those denied can still pursue asylum pursuant to a federal court settlement. USCR, therefore, considers that these populations have a durable solution and should no longer be counted as people in need of international protection.

More than half of the world's 11 million refugees and asylum seekers in 2004 were Palestinians (nearly 3 million), Afghans (over 2 million) or Sudanese (700,000) – despite the repatriation of hundreds of thousands of Afghans during the year. The numbers of refugees and asylum seekers from Colombia, Liberia, Myanmar (Burma) and Sudan increased during the year, while the numbers from Afghanistan, Angola, Bosnia and Herzegovina, Croatia, East Timor and Sierra Leone decreased.

Compared to 2003, the total number of refugees and asylum seekers decreased in 2004 due to continuing large repatriations to several countries, notably Afghanistan (mostly from Iran and Pakistan, but some from the Russian Federation), Iraq (mostly from Iran), Liberia (from Guinea and elsewhere), Sierra Leone (from Guinea and Liberia), Burundi, Angola (from Zambia and DR Congo) and Eritrea (from Sudan). But the decline also reflected stringent new migration controls in Australia, Europe and the United States, and stricter asylum standards and procedures.

Table 15 Refugees and asylum seekers by host country/territory (1998 to 2004)

	1998	1999	2000	2001	2002	2003	2004
Africa	**2,924,000**	**3,147,000**	**3,346,000**	**3,002,000**	**3,030,000**	**3,245,500**	**3,167,100**
Algeria	84,000	84,000	85,000	85,000	85,000	170,000	102,000
Angola	10,000	15,000	12,000	12,000	12,000	13,000	14,900
Benin	3,000	3,000	4,000	5,000	6,000	5,000	5,900
Botswana	–	1,000	3,000	4,000	4,000	4,500	3,800
Burkina Faso	–	–	–	–	–	–	1,000
Burundi	5,000	2,000	6,000	28,000	41,000	42,000	60,700
Cameroon	3,000	10,000	45,000	32,000	17,000	25,000	65,000
Central African Rep.	47,000	55,000	54,000	49,000	50,000	51,000	30,600
Chad	10,000	20,000	20,000	15,000	16,000	156,000	260,000
Congo, DR of	220,000	235,000	276,000	305,000	274,000	241,000	188,900
Congo	20,000	40,000	126,000	102,000	118,000	91,000	71,700
Côte d'Ivoire	128,000	135,000	94,000	103,000	50,000	74,000	74,200
Djibouti	23,000	23,000	22,000	22,000	23,000	36,000	18,000
Egypt	46,000	47,000	57,000	75,000	78,000	69,000	85,800
Eritrea	3,000	2,000	1,000	2,000	3,000	4,000	4,700
Ethiopia	251,000	246,000	194,000	114,000	115,000	112,000	116,000
Gabon	1,000	15,000	15,000	20,000	20,000	19,000	19,100
Gambia	13,000	25,000	15,000	15,000	10,000	10,000	11,000
Ghana	15,000	12,000	13,000	12,000	41,000	48,000	48,100
Guinea	514,000	453,000	390,000	190,000	182,000	223,000	145,200
Guinea-Bissau	5,000	5,000	6,000	7,000	7,000	10,000	7,700
Kenya	192,000	254,000	233,000	243,000	221,000	219,000	249,300
Liberia	120,000	90,000	70,000	60,000	65,000	60,000	38,600
Libyan AJ	28,000	11,000	11,000	33,000	12,000	–	12,400
Malawi	–	–	–	6,000	13,000	12,000	7,000
Mali	5,000	7,000	7,000	9,000	4,000	7,000	12,300
Mauritania	20,000	25,000	25,000	25,000	25,000	26,500	26,600
Morocco	–	–	–	–	2,000	–	2,300
Mozambique	–	1,000	2,000	5,000	7,000	8,000	5,500
Namibia	2,000	8,000	20,000	31,000	26,000	15,000	16,900
Niger	3,000	2,000	1,000	1,000	–	–	400
Nigeria	5,000	7,000	10,000	7,000	7,000	10,000	9,500
Rwanda	36,000	36,000	29,000	35,000	32,000	37,000	36,100
Senegal	30,000	42,000	41,000	43,000	45,000	23,000	23,200
Sierra Leone	10,000	7,000	3,000	15,000	60,000	70,000	55,000
Somalia	–	–	–	–	–	–	700
South Africa	29,000	40,000	30,000	22,000	65,000	104,000	142,900
Sudan	360,000	363,000	385,000	307,000	287,000	280,000	145,900
Swaziland	–	–	–	1,000	1,000	–	1,000
Tanzania	329,000	413,000	543,000	498,000	516,000	480,000	602,300
Togo	11,000	10,000	11,000	11,000	11,000	12,000	11,700
Tunisia	–	–	–	–	–	–	100

International Federation
of Red Cross and Red Crescent Societies

	1998	1999	2000	2001	2002	2003	2004
Uganda	185,000	197,000	230,000	174,000	221,000	231,500	252,300
Zambia	157,000	205,000	255,000	270,000	247,000	239,000	173,900
Zimbabwe	1,000	1,000	2,000	9,000	10,000	8,000	6,900
East Asia and Pacific	**559,200**	**657,300**	**791,700**	**815,700**	**874,700**	**953,400**	**1,035,700**
Australia	15,000	17,000	16,700	21,800	25,000	22,800	14,600
Cambodia	200	100	50	1,000	300	100	700
China[1]	281,800	292,800	350,000	345,000	396,000	396,000	401,500
Hong Kong[1]	n.a.	n.a.	n.a.	n.a.	–	–	–
Indonesia	100	120,000	120,800	81,300	28,700	300	200
Japan	500	400	3,800	6,400	6,500	7,900	8,800
Korea, Rep. of	–	–	350	600	–	1700	2,200
Malaysia	50,600	45,400	57,400	57,500	59,000	75,700	101,200
Nauru	–	–	–	800	100	200	100
New Zealand	–	–	3,100	2,700	1,700	1,200	20,600
Papua New Guinea	8,000	8,000	6,000	5,400	5,200	7,800	7,800
Philippines	300	200	200	200	200	2,200	2,200
Thailand	187,700	158,400	217,300	277,000	336,000	421,500	460,800
Viet Nam	15,000	15,000	16,000	16,000	16,000	16,000	15,000
South and Central Asia	**1,708,700**	**1,689,000**	**2,655,600**	**2,702,800**	**2,188,600**	**1,872,900**	**1,618,800**
Afghanistan	–	–	–	–	–	–	100
Bangladesh	53,100	53,100	121,600	122,000	122,200	119,900	150,000
India	292,100	292,000	290,000	345,800	332,300	316,900	270,300
Kazakhstan	4,100	14,800	20,000	19,500	20,600	15,300	15,800
Kyrgyzstan	15,000	10,900	11,000	9,700	8,300	8,200	4,200
Nepal	118,000	130,000	129,000	131,000	132,000	134,600	130,600
Pakistan	1,217,400	1,127,000	2,019,000	2,018,000	1,518,000	1,219,000	985,800
Sri Lanka	–	–	–	–	–	–	100
Tajikistan	5,500	4,700	12,400	4,600	3,500	3,200	3,700
Turkmenistan	500	18,500	14,200	14,000	13,700	14,100	13,300
Uzbekistan	3,000	38,000	38,400	38,000	38,000	41,700	44,900
Middle East	**5,814,100**	**5,849,000**	**6,035,300**	**6,830,200**	**5,290,300**	**4,353,100**	**4,267,700**
Gaza Strip	773,000	798,400	824,600	852,600	879,000	923,000	952,000
Iran	1,931,000	1,835,000	1,895,000	2,558,000	2,208,500	1,335,000	1,046,000
Iraq	104,000	129,400	127,700	128,100	134,700	131,500	96,600
Israel	–	400	4,700	4,700	2,100	1,000	700
Jordan[2]	1,463,800	1,518,000	1,580,000	1,643,900	155,000	163,700	168,300
Kuwait	52,000	52,000	52,000	50,000	65,000	65,000	51,800
Lebanon[2]	368,300	378,100	383,200	389,500	409,000	256,000	252,400
Qatar	–	–	–	–	–	–	100
Saudi Arabia	128,300	128,600	128,500	128,500	245,400	240,900	240,700
Syrian Arab Rep.[2]	369,800	379,200	389,000	397,600	482,400	497,000	701,700
United Arab Emirates	200	–	–	–	–	–	200

	1998	1999	2000	2001	2002	2003	2004
West Bank	555,000	569,700	583,000	607,800	627,500	665,000	683,000
Yemen	68,700	60,000	67,600	69,500	81,700	75,000	74,200
Europe	**1,728,400**	**1,909,100**	**1,153,300**	**972,800**	**877,400**	**884,500**	**595,300**
Albania	25,000	5,000	500	400	100	100	100
Armenia	229,000	240,000	–	11,000	11,000	11,000	11,200
Austria	16,500	16,600	6,100	10,800	30,900	17,600	7,400
Azerbaijan	235,300	222,000	3,600	7,000	11,400	10,300	9,800
Belarus	16,500	2,900	3,200	3,100	3,600	3,400	3,400
Belgium	25,800	42,000	46,400	41,000	30,300	33,000	24,500
Bosnia and Herzegovina	40,000	60,000	38,200	33,200	34,200	22,500	22,700
Bulgaria	2,800	2,800	3,000	2,900	1,200	800	5,200
Croatia	27,300	24,000	22,500	21,900	8,100	4,200	3,700
Cyprus	200	300	300	1,300	1,800	5,300	10,600
Czech Republic	2,400	1,800	4,800	10,600	6,300	3,900	2,700
Denmark	6,100	8,500	10,300	12,200	5,200	2,800	3,400
Finland	2,300	3,800	2,600	2,100	1,200	2,300	1,400
France	17,400	30,000	26,200	12,400	27,600	34,900	–
Georgia	300	5,200	7,600	7,900	4,200	3,900	2,600
Germany	198,000	285,000	180,000	116,000	104,000	90,800	89,200
Greece	2,800	7,500	800	6,500	1,800	5,200	10,200
Hungary	3,200	6,000	4,200	2,900	1,200	1,500	8,000
Iceland	–	100	50	–	–	–	–
Ireland	6,900	8,500	7,700	9,500	6,500	5,800	10,800
Italy	6,800	24,900	13,700	9,600	5,200	5,600	5,600
Lithuania	100	100	150	300	200	100	600
Macedonia, FYR of	7,300	17,400	9,000	3,600	2,700	2,300	2,200
Malta	–	–	–	–	–	200	1,200
Moldova	–	–	–	300	300	100	200
Netherlands	47,000	40,000	29,600	31,000	17,200	14,600	12,800
Norway	2,500	9,500	8,600	13,200	5,900	11,000	11,000
Poland	1,300	1,300	2,300	1,800	300	1,500	8,700
Portugal	1,400	1,700	1,600	50	–	–	400
Romania	900	900	2,100	200	100	200	2,400
Russian Federation	161,900	104,300	36,200	28,200	17,400	161,300	150,000
Serbia and Montenegro	480,000	476,000	484,200	400,000	353,000	291,100	76,500
Slovak Republic	300	400	400	3,100	4,500	4,700	3,300
Slovenia	7,300	5,000	12,000	2,700	400	100	600
Spain	2,500	4,500	1,100	1,000	200	200	5,900
Sweden	16,700	20,200	18,500	18,500	24,900	25,600	19,400
Switzerland	40,000	104,000	62,600	57,900	44,200	38,300	31,200
Turkey	12,000	9,100	9,900	12,600	10,000	9,500	7,800
Ukraine	8,600	5,800	5,500	6,000	3,600	3,100	6,400
United Kingdom	74,000	112,000	87,800	69,800	79,200	55,700	22,200

International Federation
of Red Cross and Red Crescent Societies

	1998	1999	2000	2001	2002	2003	2004
Americas and the Caribbean	**739,950**	**737,000**	**562,100**	**597,000**	**76,500**	**543,500**	**563,800**
Argentina	1,100	3,300	1,000	3,100	2,700	2,300	3,900
Bahamas	100	100	100	100	–	–	–
Belize	3,500	3,000	1,700	–	1,000	900	800
Bolivia	350	400	–	400	400	500	500
Brazil	2,400	2,300	2,700	4,050	3,700	3,900	3,800
Canada	46,000	53,000	54,400	70,000	78,400	70,200	54,800
Chile	100	300	300	550	400	500	700
Colombia	200	250	250	200	200	200	200
Costa Rica	23,100	22,900	7,300	10,600	12,800	13,600	10,600
Cuba	1,100	1,000	1,000	1,000	1,000	800	800
Dominican Republic	600	650	500	500	300	500	1,000
Ecuador	250	350	1,600	4,300	9,100	16,500	45,100
El Salvador	100	–	–	–	–	200	200
Guatemala	800	750	700	700	700	800	700
Honduras	100	–	–	–	–	–	–
Jamaica	50	50	50	–	–	–	–
Mexico	7,500	8,500	6,500	6,200	4,000	2,900	4,500
Nicaragua	150	500	300	–	–	300	300
Panama	1,300	600	1,300	1,500	1,700	2,000	1,900
Paraguay	–	–	–	50	–	–	–
Peru	–	700	750	750	900	800	1,000
United States[3]	651,000	638,000	481,500	492,500	638,000	244,200	232,800
Uruguay	–	150	50	100	100	100	100
Venezuela	150	200	100	400	1,100	182,300	200,100
Total	**13,566,400**	**13,988,000**	**14,543,700**	**14,921,000**	**12,337,500**	**11,852,900**	**9,798,400**

Source: US Committee for Refugees

Note: – indicates zero or near zero; n.a. not available, or reported estimates unreliable.

[1] As of 1997, figures for Hong Kong are included in total for China.

[2] In the light of persistent protection gaps, USCR concluded in 2003 that the inclusion clause of Article 1D of the UN Refugee Convention brings Palestinian refugees under the Convention's application. Accordingly, USCR changed its statistical approach in 2003 by applying the Convention's definition of refugee status – including its cessation – to this population rather than UNRWA's registration criteria as before. The numbers in Lebanon were adjusted to reflect the acquisition of citizenship in Lebanon and other countries.

[3] Includes asylum applications pending in the United States; USCR estimates the number of individuals represented per case.

Significant new outflows in 2004 included nearly 200,000 new Iraqi refugees and asylum seekers in Syria. Over 100,000 more Sudanese fled to Chad, about 100,000 Nepalese were India (although precise data were not available and some had come the year before). Refugees and asylum seekers continued to stream from Myanmar into Thailand (48,000), Bangladesh (30,000) and Malaysia (15,000). New refugees fled from DR Congo to Burundi (19,000) and South Africa (18,000), while some returned from Congo (Brazzaville). Iran and Pakistan continue to host the largest populations of refugees – more than 2 million between them.

USCR adjusted the number of Burundians in Tanzania upwards to reflect new analysis of the durability of protection for more than 100,000 'long stayers', and made the same calculations for 40,000 Chadians in Cameroon. USCR adjusted the number of Western Saharan refugees in Algeria downwards by 67,000 to reflect new data. A joint UNHCR-host government re-registration exercise reduced the count of former Yugoslav refugees in Serbia and Montenegro by more than 200,000, as many were found to have naturalized, returned or resettled, some earlier than 2004. USCR also reduced the count of Eritreans in Sudan, although the number is believed to be substantially more than UNHCR's figures.

Table 16 Significant populations of internally displaced people (1998 to 2004)

	1998	1999	2000	2001	2002	2003	2004
Africa[1]	**8,958,000**	**10,355,000**	**10,527,000**	**10,935,000**	**15,230,000**	**13,099,000**	**12,162,000**
Algeria	200,000	100,000	100,000	100,000	100,000	100,000	400,000
Angola	1,500,000	1,500,000	2,000,000	2,000,000	2,000,000	1,000,000	60,000
Burundi	500,000	800,000	600,000	600,000	400,000	400,000	145,000
Central African Republic	–	–	–	5,000	10,000	200,000	200,000
Congo, DR	300,000	800,000	1,500,000	50,000	2,000,000	3,200,000	2,329,000
Congo	250,000	500,000	30,000	2,000,000	100,000	60,000	48,000
Côte d'Ivoire	–	–	2,000	5,000	500,000	500,000	500,000
Eritrea	100,000	250,000	310,000	90,000	75,000	75,000	59,000
Ethiopia	150,000	300,000	250,000	100,000	90,000	90,000	132,000
Ghana	20,000	–	–	–	–	–	–
Guinea	–	–	60,000	100,000	20,000	20,000	82,000
Guinea-Bissau	200,000	50,000	–	–	–	–	–
Kenya	200,000	100,000	100,000	200,000	230,000	230,000	360,000
Liberia	75,000	50,000	20,000	80,000	100,000	500,000	464,000
Nigeria	3,000	5,000	–	50,000	50,000	57,000	200,000
Rwanda	500,000	600,000	150,000		–	–	–
Senegal	10,000	–	5,000	5,000	5,000	17,000	–
Sierra Leone	300,000	500,000	700,000	600,000	–	–	3,000
Somalia	250,000	350,000	300,000	400,000	350,000	350,000	400,000
Sudan	4,000,000	4,000,000	4,000,000	4,000,000	4,000,000	4,800,000	5,300,000
Uganda	400,000	450,000	400,000	500,000	600,000	1,400,000	1,330,000
Zimbabwe	–	–	–	50,000	100,000	100,000	150,000
East Asia and Pacific	**1,150,000**	**1,577,000**	**1,670,000**	**2,266,000**	**1,349,000**	**1,400,000**	**1,160,000**
Cambodia	22,000	–	–	–	–	–	–
East Timor	–	300,000	–	–	–	–	–
Indonesia	–	440,000	800,000	1,400,000	600,000	600,000	500,000
Korea, DPR of	–	–	100,000	100,000	100,000	50,000	50,000
Myanmar	1,000,000	600,000	600,000	600,000	600,000	600,000	550,000
Papua New Guinea	6,000	5,000	–	1,000	–	–	–
Philippines	122,000	200,000	140,000	135,000	45,000	150,000	60,000
Solomon Islands	–	32,000	30,000	30,000	4,000	–	–
Europe	**3,685,000**	**3,993,000**	**3,539,000**	**2,785,000**	**2,560,000**	**2,455,800**	**2,244,500**
Armenia	60,000	–	–	50,000	50,000	50,000	50,000
Azerbaijan	576,000	568,000	575,000	572,000	576,000	571,000	528,000
Bosnia and Herzegovina	836,000	830,000	518,000	439,000	368,000	327,200	327,200
Croatia	61,000	50,000	34,000	23,000	17,000	12,600	12,600
Cyprus	265,000	265,000	265,000	265,000	265,000	265,000	150,000
Georgia	275,000	280,000	272,000	264,000	262,000	260,000	260,000
Macedonia, FYR of	–	–	–	21,000	9,000	–	2,700

	1998	1999	2000	2001	2002	2003	2004
Russian Federation	350,000	800,000	800,000	474,000	371,000	368,000	339,000
Serbia and Montenegro	257,000	600,000	475,000	277,000	262,000	252,000	225,000
Turkey[1]	1,000,000	600,000	600,000	400,000	380,000	350,000	350,000
Americas and Caribbean	**1,755,000**	**1,886,000**	**2,176,000**	**2,465,000**	**2,518,000**	**2,742,000**	**2,912,000**
Colombia	1,400,000	1,800,000	2,100,000	2,450,000	2,500,000	2,730,000	2,900,000
Haiti	–	–	–	–	6,000	–	–
Mexico	15,000	16,000	16,000	15,000	12,000	12,000	12,000
Peru	340,000	70,000	60,000	–	–	–	–
Middle East[1]	**1,575,000**	**1,917,000**	**1,700,000**	**1,670,000**	**2,646,000**	**2,346,000**	**1,648,000**
Palestinian Territory, Occupied	–	17,000	–	20,000	26,000	–	–
Iraq	1,000,000	900,000	700,000	700,000	1,100,000	800,000	1,000,000
Israel	–	200,000	200,000	200,000	250,000	276,000	10,000
Jordan	–	–	–	–	800,000	800,000	168,000
Lebanon	450,000	350,000	350,000	250,000	300,000	300,000	300,000
Syrian Arab Rep.	125,000	450,000	450,000	500,000	170,000	170,000	170,000
South and Central Asia	**2,130,000**	**1,617,000**	**1,542,000**	**2,402,000**	**2,023,000**	**1,511,000**	**1,205,000**
Afghanistan[1]	1,000,000	500,000	375,000	1,000,000	700,000	200,000	167,000
Bangladesh	50,000	50,000	60,000	100,000	60,000	61,000	65,000
India	520,000	507,000	507,000	500,000	600,000	650,000	500,000
Nepal[1]	–	–	–	–	100,000	100,000	100,000
Pakistan[1]	–	–	–	2,000	–	–	17,000
Sri Lanka	560,000	560,000	600,000	800,000	563,000	500,000	353,000
Uzbekistan	–	–	–	–	–	–	3,000
Total	**19,253,000**	**21,345,000**	**21,154,000**	**22,523,000**	**26,326,000**	**23,553,800**	**21,331,500**

Source: US Committee for Refugees

Note: – indicates zero or near zero; n.a. not available, or reported estimates unreliable.

[1] Estimates of the size of internally displaced populations are frequently subject to great margins of error and are often imprecise, particularly in these countries and regions.

Estimated numbers of global internally displaced people (IDPs) dropped in 2004 to just over 21 million. Internal displacement declined most dramatically in Angola, from 1 million IDPs in 2003 to less than 100,000 in 2004; and in DR Congo, where IDPs decreased by about 700,000 to a total of just over 2.3 million (also, 2003's total is believed to be an overestimate).

During 2004, internal displacement increased by half a million people in Sudan (totalling 5.3 million) and by 200,000 in Iraq (totalling 1 million). Internally displaced populations of half a million or more remained in Azerbaijan, Côte d'Ivoire, India, Indonesia, Myanmar and Uganda. As in 2003, well over half the world's IDPs were in Africa.

USCR decided to cease counting descendants of IDPs who were not themselves displaced. This reduced the counts in Jordan (800,000 to 168,000) and Israel (276,000 to 10,000) – where the displacement occurred in 1948 – and in Cyprus (265,000 to 150,000). New analysis of old data increased the count of IDPs in Algeria (100,000 to 400,000) even though actual displacement there did not increase.

International Federation
of Red Cross and Red Crescent Societies

A global and
local network

This annex contains contact details for the members of the International Red Cross and Red Crescent Movement (the International Federation, ICRC and National Societies) and the International Federation's network of regional and country delegations. Information correct as of 20 May 2005.

National Red Cross and Red Crescent Societies are listed alphabetically by International Organization for Standardization Codes for the Representation of Names of Countries, English spelling.

International Federation of Red Cross and Red Crescent Societies
P.O. Box 372
1211 Geneva 19
Switzerland
Tel. +41 22 7304222
Fax +41 22 7330395
E-mail secretariat@ifrc.org
Web http://www.ifrc.org

International Committee of the Red Cross
19 avenue de la Paix
1202 Geneva
Switzerland
Tel. +41 22 7346001
Fax +41 22 7332057
E-mail icrc.gva@gwn.icrc.org
Web http://www.icrc.org

Red Cross/European Union Office
Rue Belliard 65, Box 7
1040 – Brussels
Belgium
Tel. +32 2 2350680
Fax +32 2 2305465
E-mail infoboard@redcross-eu.net

Office of the Permanent Observer for the International Federation of Red Cross and Red Crescent Societies to the United Nations
800 Second Avenue
Third floor
New York, NY 10019
United States
Tel. +1 212 3380161
Fax +1 212 3389832
E-mail ifrcny02@ifrc.org

National Red Cross and Red Crescent Societies

Afghan Red Crescent Society
Afshar
P.O. Box 3066
Shar-e-Now
Kabul
Afghanistan
Tel. +93 702 80698
Fax +93 229 0097

Albanian Red Cross
Rruga "Muhammet Gjollesha"
Sheshi "Karl Topia"
C.P. 1511
Tirana
Albania
Tel. +355 42 57532
Fax +355 42 25855

Algerian Red Crescent
15 bis, Boulevard Mohammed V
Alger 16000
Algeria
Tel. +213 21 633952
Fax +213 21 633690
E-mail cra@algeriainfo.com

Photo opposite page: In the first two weeks following the tsunami, the Red Cross Red Crescent network responded in an unprecedented way to the needs of the affected populations.

Yoshi Shimizu/ International Federation

Andorra Red Cross
Prat de la Creu 22
Andorra la Vella
Andorra
Tel. +376 808225
Fax +376 808240
E-mail creuroja@creuroja.ad
Web http://www.creuroja.ad

Angola Red Cross
Rua 1° Congresso no 27
Caixa Postal 927
Luanda
Angola
Tel. +244 2 336543
Fax +244 2 372868
E-mail cruzvermelha@
        netangola.com

Antigua and Barbuda Red Cross Society
Old Parham Road
P.O. Box 727
St. Johns, Antigua W.I.
Antigua and Barbuda
Tel. +1 268 4620800
Fax +1 268 4609595
E-mail redcross@candw.org

Argentine Red Cross
Hipólito Yrigoyen 2068
1089 Buenos Aires
Argentina
Tel. +54 114 9527200
Fax +54 114 9527715
E-mail info@cruzroja.org.ar
Web http://www.cruzroja.org.ar

Armenian Red Cross Society
21 Paronian Street
375015 Yerevan
Armenia
Tel. +374 10 539443
Fax +374 10 539217
E-mail redcross@redcross.am

Australian Red Cross
155 Pelham Street
P.O. Box 196
Carlton, VIC
Australia
Tel. +61 3 93451800
Fax +61 3 93482513
E-mail redcross@redcross.org.au
Web http://www.redcross.org.au

Austrian Red Cross
Wiedner Hauptstrasse 32
Postfach 39
1041 Wien
Austria
Tel. +43 1 58900 0
Fax +43 1 58900 199
E-mail oerk@redcross.or.at
Web http://www.roteskreuz.at

Red Crescent Society of Azerbaijan
S. Safarov Street 2
Baku, Nesimi district
PC 370010
Azerbaijan
Tel. +994 12 938481
Fax +994 12 931578
E-mail redcrescent@azdata.net

The Bahamas Red Cross Society
John F. Kennedy Drive
P.O. Box N-8331
Nassau
Bahamas
Tel. +1 242 3237370
Fax +1 242 3237404
E-mail redcross@bahamas.net.bs

Bahrain Red Crescent Society
P.O. Box 882
Manama
Bahrain
Tel. +973 293171
Fax +973 291797
E-mail hilal@batelco.com.bh

Bangladesh Red Crescent Society
684-686 Bara Maghbazar
G.P.O. Box 579
Dhaka – 1217
Bangladesh
Tel. +880 2 9330188
Fax +880 2 9352303
E-mail bdrcs@bangla.net
Web http://www.bdrcs.org

The Barbados Red Cross Society
Red Cross House
Jemmotts Lane
P.O. Box 300
Bridgetown
Barbados
Tel. +1 246 4333889
Fax +1 246 4262052
E-mail bdosredcross@caribsurf.com

Belarusian Red Cross
35, Karl Marx Str.
220030 Minsk
Belarus
Tel. +375 17 2272620
Fax +375 17 2272620
E-mail brc@home.by

Belgian Red Cross
96, rue de Stalle
Bruxelles
Belgium
Tel. +32 2 3713111
Fax +32 2 6460439 French;
        6456041 Flemish
E-mail info@redcross-fr.be
        documentatie@redcross-fl.be
Web http://www.redcross.be

Belize Red Cross Society
1 Gabourel Lane
P.O. Box 413
Belize City
Belize
Tel. +501 2 273319
Fax +501 2 230998
E-mail bzercshq@btl.net

International Federation
of Red Cross and Red Crescent Societies

Red Cross of Benin

B.P. No. 1
Porto-Novo
Benin
Tel. +229 212886
Fax +229 214927
E-mail crbenin@leland.bj

Bolivian Red Cross

Avenida Simón Bolívar N° 1515
Casilla N° 741
La Paz
Bolivia
Tel. +591 2 202930
Fax +591 2 359102
E-mail cruzrobo@caoba.entelnet.bo
Web http://www.come.to/
        cruzroja.org.bo

The Red Cross Society of Bosnia and Herzegovina

Titova 7
71000 Sarajevo
Bosnia and Herzegovina
Tel. +387 33 200147
Fax +387 33 200 148
E-mail rcsbihhq@bih.net.ba

Botswana Red Cross Society

135 Independance Avenue
P.O. Box 485
Gaborone
Botswana
Tel. +267 3952465
Fax +267 312352
E-mail brcs@info.bw

Brazilian Red Cross

Praça Cruz Vermelha No. 10/12
20230-130 Rio de Janeiro RJ
Brazil
Tel. +55 21 22210658
Fax +55 21 5071594
E-mail cvbrasileira@terra.com.br

Brunei Darussalam Red Crescent Society

P.O. Box 3065
KA1131 Kuala Belait
Brunei Darussalam
Tel. +673 2 380635
Fax +673 2 382797
E-mail bdrcs@netcad.com.bn

Bulgarian Red Cross

76, James Boucher Boulevard
1407 Sofia
Bulgaria
Tel. +359 2 8164700
Fax +359 2 8656937
E-mail secretariat@redcross.bg
Web http://www.redcross.bg

Burkinabe Red Cross Society

01 B.P. 4404
Ouagadougou 01
Burkina Faso
Tel. +226 361340
Fax +226 363121
E-mail croixrouge.bf@fasonet.bf

Burundi Red Cross

Comit, National
B.P. 324
Bujumbura
Burundi
Tel. +257 216246
Fax +257 211101
E-mail croixrou@cbinf.com

Cambodian Red Cross Society

17, Vithei de la Croix-Rouge
        Cambodgienne
Phnom Penh
Cambodia
Tel. +855 23 212876
Fax +855 23 212875
E-mail communications@
        crc.org.kh

Cameroon Red Cross Society

Rue Henri Dunant 2005
B.P. 631
Yaoundé
Cameroon
Tel. +237 2224177
Fax +237 2224177
E-mail croixrouge@camnet.com

The Canadian Red Cross Society

170 Metcalfe Street, Suite 300
Ottawa
Ontario K2P 2P2
Canada
Tel. +1 613 7401900
Fax +1 613 7401911
E-mail cancross@redcross.ca
Web http://www.redcross.ca

Red Cross of Cape Verde

Rua Andrade Corvo
Caixa Postal 119
Praia
Cape Verde
Tel. +238 2611701
Fax +238 2614174
E-mail cruzvermelhasg@
        mail.cvtelecom.cv

Central African Red Cross Society

Avenue Koudoukou Km, 5
B.P. 1428
Bangui
Central African Republic
Tel. +236 612509
Fax +236 613561
E-mail sida_crca@yahoo.fr

Red Cross of Chad

B.P. 449
N'Djamena
Chad
Tel. +235 523434
E-mail crftchad@intnet.td

Chilean Red Cross

Avenida Santa María No. 150
  Providencia
Comuna Providencia
Correo 21, Casilla 246 V
Santiago de Chile
Chile
Tel. +56 2 7771448
Fax +56 2 7370270
E-mail cruzroja@entelchile.net
Web http://www.cruzroja.cl

Red Cross Society of China

No. 8 Beixinqiao Santiao
East City District
Beijing
China
Tel. +86 10 84025890
Fax +86 10 64029928
E-mail rcsc@chineseredcross.org.cn
Web http://www.chineseredcross.
  org.cn

Colombian Red Cross Society

Avenida 68 N° 66-31
1110 Santafé de Bogotá D.C.
Colombia
Tel. +57 1 4376339
Fax +57 1 4376365
E-mail mundo@
  cruzrojacolombiana.org
Web http://www.
  cruzrojacolombiana.org/
  cruzroja.html

Congolese Red Cross

8 rue Lucien Fourneau
Face Ministère de la Santé et
  Fonction Publique
Brazzaville
Congo
Tel. +242 688249
E-mail croixrouge_congobzv@
  yahoo.fr

Red Cross of the Democratic Republic of the Congo

41, Avenue de la Justice
Zone de la Gombe
B.P. 1712
Kinshasa I
Congo, D.R. of the
Tel. +243 1234897
Fax +243 8804151
E-mail secretariat@crrdc.aton.cd

Cook Islands Red Cross

P.O. Box 888
Rarotonga
Cook Islands
Tel. +682 22598
Fax +682 22598
E-mail nikratt@redcross.org.ck

Costa Rican Red Cross

Calle 14, Avenida 8
Apartado 1025
1000 San José
Costa Rica
Tel. +506 2337033
Fax +506 2337628
E-mail info@cruzroja.or.cr
Web http://www.cruzroja.or.cr

Red Cross Society of Côte d'Ivoire

P.O. Box 1244
Abidjan 01
Côte d'Ivoire
Tel. +225 20321335
Fax +225 20324381
E-mail crci@afnet.net

Croatian Red Cross

Ulica Crvenog kriza 14
10000 Zagreb
Croatia
Tel. +385 1 4655814
Fax +385 1 4655365
E-mail redcross@hck.hr
Web http://www.hck.hr

Cuban Red Cross

Calle 20#707
C.P. 10300
Cuidad de la Habana
Cuba
Tel. +53 7 228272
Fax +53 7 228272
E-mail crsn@infomed.sld.cu

Czech Red Cross

Thunovska 18
CZ-118 04 Praha 1
Czech Republic
Tel. +420 2 51104111
Fax +420 2 51104271
E-mail sochorova.linda@cck-cr.cz

Danish Red Cross

Blegdamsvej 27
P.O. Box 2600
DK-2100 Copenhagen Ö
Denmark
Tel. +45 35259200
Fax +45 35259292
E-mail drk@drk.dk
Web http://www.redcross.dk

Red Crescent Society of Djibouti

B.P. 8
Djibouti
Tel. +253 352270
Fax +253 352451
E-mail crd@intnet.dj

Dominica Red Cross Society

Federation Drive
Goodwill
Dominica
Tel. +1 767 4488280
Fax +1 767 4487708
E-mail redcross@cwdom.dm

Dominican Red Cross
Calle Juan E. Dunant No. 51
Ens. Miraflores
Apartado Postal 1293
Santo Domingo, D.N.
Dominican Republic
Tel. +1 809 3344545
Fax +1 809 2385252
E-mail cruzrojadom@codetel.net.do

Ecuadorian Red Cross
Antonio Elizalde E 4-31
    y Av. Colombia (esq.)
Casilla 1701
2119 Quito
Ecuador
Tel. +593 2 2954587
Fax +593 2 2570424
E-mail quitocr@attglobal.net
Web http://www.cruzroja-
    ecuador.org

Egyptian Red Crescent Society
Abd El Razek Al Sanhoury Street,
8th District, Nasr City
7516 Cairo
Egypt
Tel. +20 2 6703979
Fax +20 2 6703967
E-mail erc@brainy1.ie-eg.com

Salvadorean Red Cross Society
17 C. Pte. y Av. Henri Dunant
Apartado Postal 2672
San Salvador
El Salvador
Tel. +503 22192200
Fax +503 72227758
E-mail secretaria.ejecutiva@
    cruzrojasal.sv
Web http://www.elsalvador.
    cruzroja.org

Red Cross of Equatorial Guinea
Alcalde Albilio Balboa 92
Apartado postal 460
Malabo
Equatorial Guinea
Tel. +240 9 3701
Fax +240 9 3701
E-mail crge@intnet.gq

Estonia Red Cross
Eha Street 8
Tallinn
Estonia
Tel. +372 6411644
Fax +372 6411641
E-mail haide.laanemets@recross.ee

Ethiopian Red Cross Society
Ras Desta Damtew Avenue
P.O. Box 195
Addis Ababa
Ethiopia
Tel. +251 1 519074
Fax +251 1 512643
E-mail ercs@telecom.net.et

Fiji Red Cross Society
22 Gorrie Street
GPO Box 569
Suva
Fiji
Tel. +679 3314133
Fax +679 3303818
E-mail redcross@connect.com.fj

Finnish Red Cross
Tehtaankatu 1a
P.O. Box 168
FIN-00141 Helsinki
Finland
Tel. +358 9 12931
Fax +358 9 1293226
E-mail forename.surname@
    redcross.fi
Web http://www.redcross.fi

French Red Cross
1, Place Henry-Dunant
F-75384 Paris Cedex 08
France
Tel. +33 1 44431100
Fax +33 1 44431101
E-mail communication@
    croix-rouge.net
Web http://www.croix-rouge.fr

Gabonese Red Cross Society
Place de l'Indépendance
Derrière le Mont de Cristal
Boîte Postale 2274
Libreville
Gabon
Tel. +241 766159
Fax +241 766160
E-mail gab.cross@
    internetgabon.com

The Gambia Red Cross Society
Kanifing Industrial Area
P.O. Box 472
Banjul
Gambia
Tel. +220 4392405
Fax +220 4394921
E-mail redcrossgam@gamtel.gm

Red Cross Society of Georgia
15, Krilov St.
380002 Tbilisi
Georgia
Tel. +995 32 961534
Fax +995 32 96098
E-mail redcross@redcross.ge

German Red Cross
General Sekretariat
Carstennstrasse 58
D-12205 Berlin
Germany
Tel. +49 30 85404-0
Fax +49 30 85404470
E-mail drk@drk.de
Web http://www.rotkreuz.de

Ghana Red Cross Society
Ministries Annex Block A3
Off Liberia Road Extension
P.O. Box 835
Accra
Ghana
Tel. +233 21 662298
Fax +233 21 661491
E-mail grcs@idngh.com

Hellenic Red Cross
Rue Lycavittou 1
Athens 106 72
Greece
Tel. +30 210 3621681
Fax +30 210 3615606
E-mail ir@redcross.gr
Web http://www.redcross.gr

Grenada Red Cross Society
Upper Lucas Street
P.O. Box 551
St. George's
Grenada
Tel. +1 473 4401483
Fax +1 473 4401829
E-mail grercs@caribsurf.com

Guatemalan Red Cross
3a Calle 8-40, Zona 1
Guatemala, C.A.
Guatemala
Tel. +502 25322027
Fax +502 25324649
E-mail crg@guate.net
Web http://www.guatemala.
    cruzroja.org

Red Cross Society of Guinea
B.P. 376
Conakry
Guinea
Tel. +224 13405237
Fax +224 414255
E-mail belly1961@yahoo.fr

Red Cross Society of Guinea-Bissau
Parça Herios Avacionais
Bissau
Guinea-Bissau
Tel. +245 201361
Fax +245 205202
E-mail cvgb@mail.gtelecom.gv

The Guyana Red Cross Society
Eve Leary
P.O. Box 10524
Georgetown
Guyana
Tel. +592 22 65174
Fax +592 22 52525
E-mail redcross@sdnp.org.gy
Web http://www.sdnp.org.gy/
    redcross/

Haitian National Red Cross Society
1, rue Eden
Bicentenaire
CRH-B.P. 1337
Port-au-Prince
Haiti
Tel. +509 5109813
Fax +509 2231054
E-mail croroha@haitiworld.com

Honduran Red Cross
7a Calle
    entre 1a. y 2a. Avenidas
Comayagüela D.C.
Honduras
Tel. +504 2378876
Fax +504 2380185
E-mail honducruz@datum.hn
Web http://www.honduras.
    cruzroja.org/

Hungarian Red Cross
Arany J nos Utca 31
Budapest V.
Hungary
Tel. +36 1 3741338
Fax +36 1 3741312
E-mail intdept@hrc.hu

Icelandic Red Cross
Efstaleiti 9
103 Reykjavik
Iceland
Tel. +354 5704000
Fax +354 5704010
E-mail central@redcross.is
Web http://www.redcross.is

Indian Red Cross Society
Red Cross Building
1 Red Cross Road
110001 New Delhi
India
Tel. +91 112 3716424
Fax +91 112 3717454
E-mail indcross@vsnl.com
Web http://www.indianredcross.org

Indonesian Red Cross Society
Jl. Jenderal Datot Subroto Kav. 96
P.O. Box 2009
Jakarta
Indonesia
Tel. +62 21 7992325
Fax +62 21 7995188

Red Crescent Society of the Islamic Republic of Iran
Rashid Yasemi Street
Valiasr Avenue
Tehran
Iran, Islamic Republic of
Tel. +98 21 8662618
Fax +98 21 8662652
E-mail intdep@rcs.ir

Iraqi Red Crescent Society
Al-Mansour
P.O. Box 6143
Baghdad
Iraq
Tel. +964 1 8862191
Fax +964 1 5372519

International Federation
of Red Cross and Red Crescent Societies

Irish Red Cross Society

16, Merrion Square
Dublin 2
Ireland
Tel. +353 1 6765135
Fax +353 1 6614461
E-mail info@redcross.ie
Web http://www.redcross.ie

Italian Red Cross

Via Toscana, 12
00187 Roma – RM
Italy
Tel. +39 06 47591
Fax +39 06 4759223
E-mail webmaster@cri.rupa.it
Web http://www.cri.it

Jamaica Red Cross

Central Village, Spanish Town
St. Catherine
Kingston 5
Jamaica
Tel. +1 876 9847860
Fax +1 876 9848272
E-mail jrcs@infochan.com

Japanese Red Cross Society

1-3 Shiba Daimon, 1-Chome,
    Minato-ku
Tokyo-105-8521
Japan
Tel. +81 3 34377087
Fax +81 3 34358509
E-mail kokusai@jrc.or.jp
Web http://www.jrc.or.jp

Jordan National Red Crescent Society

Madaba Street
P.O. Box 10001
Amman 11151
Jordan
Tel. +962 64 773141
Fax +962 64 750815
E-mail jrc@cyberia.jo

Kazakh Red Crescent Society

Kunaev Street 86
480100 Almaty
Kazakhstan, Republic of
Tel. +73272 916291
Fax +73272 918172
E-mail Kazrc2@yahoo.co.k

Kenya Red Cross Society

Nairobi South "C"
Belle Vue, off Mombasa Road
P.O. Box 40712
Nairobi
Kenya
Tel. +254 20 603593
Fax +254 20 603589
E-mail info@kenyaredcross.org

Kiribati Red Cross Society

P.O. Box 213
Bikenibeu
Tarawa
Kiribati
Tel. +686 28128
Fax +686 21416
E-mail redcross@tskl.net.ki

Red Cross Society of the Democratic People's Republic of Korea

Ryonwa 1, Central District
Pyongyang
Korea, Democratic People's
    Republic of
Tel. +850 2 18333
Fax +850 2 3814644

The Republic of Korea National Red Cross

32 – 3ka, Namsan-dong
Choong-Ku
Seoul 100 – 043
Korea, Republic of
Tel. +82 2 37053705
Fax +82 2 37053667
E-mail international@redcross.or.kr
Web http://www.redcross.or.kr

Kuwait Red Crescent Society

Al-Jahra Street, Shuweek
P.O. Box 1359
Kuwait
Tel. +965 4818084
Fax +965 4839114
E-mail krcs@kuwait.net

Red Crescent Society of Kyrgyzstan

10, prospekt Erkindik
720040 Bishkek
Kyrgyzstan
Tel. +996 312 624857
Fax +996 312 662181
E-mail redcross@elcat.kg

Lao Red Cross

Impasse XiengNhune
Avenue Sethathirath
B.P. 650
Vientiane
Lao People's Democratic Republic
Tel. +856 21 242467
Fax +856 21 212128
E-mail lrchqod@laotel.com

Latvian Red Cross

1, Skolas Street
Riga, LV-1010
Latvia
Tel. +371 7336651
Fax +371 7336652
E-mail secretariat@redcross.lv

Lebanese Red Cross

Rue Spears
Beyrouth
Lebanon
Tel. +961 1 372802
Fax +961 1 378207
E-mail redcross@dm.net.lb
Web http://www.dm.net.lb/
    redcross/

Lesotho Red Cross Society
23 Mabile Road
Old Europe
Maseru 100
Lesotho
Tel. +266 22 313911
Fax +266 22 310166
E-mail redcross@redcross.org.ls

Liberian Red Cross Society
National Headquarters
107 Lynch Street
P.O. Box 20-5081
1000 Monrovia 20
Liberia
Fax +231 330125
E-mail lnrc@Liberia.net

Libyan Red Crescent
General Secretariat
P.O. Box 541
Benghazi
Libyan Arab Jamahiriya
Tel. +218 61 9095202
Fax +218 61 9095829
E-mail libyan_redcrescent@
        libyamail.net

Liechtenstein Red Cross
Heiligkreuz 25
FL-9490 Vaduz
Liechtenstein
Tel. +423 2322294
Fax +423 2322240
E-mail info@lieredcross.li

Lithuanian Red Cross Society
Gedimino ave. 3a
2600 Vilnius
Lithuania
Tel. +370 52 628037
Fax +370 52 619923
E-mail international@redcross.lt
Web http://www.redcross.lt

Luxembourg Red Cross
44 Bd Joseph II
L – 2014 Luxembourg
Tel. +352 450202
Fax +352 457269
E-mail siege@croix-rouge.lu
Web http://www.croix-rouge.lu/

The Red Cross of The Former Yugoslav Republic of Macedonia
No. 13
Bul. Koco Racin
91000 Skopje
Macedonia, The Former Yugoslav
        Republic of
Tel. +389 23 114355
Fax +389 23 230542
E-mail mrc@redcross.org.mk

Malagasy Red Cross Society
1, rue Patrice Lumumba Tsaralalana
B.P. 1168
Antananarivo
Madagascar
Tel. +261 20 2222111
Fax +261 20 2266739
E-mail crm@dts.mg

Malawi Red Cross Society
Red Cross House
Presidential Way
Area 14
Lilongwe
Malawi
Tel. +265 1 775208
Fax +265 1 775590
E-mail mrcs@eomw.net

Malaysian Red Crescent Society
JKR 32, Jalan Nipah
Off Jalan Ampang
55000 Kuala Lumpur
Malaysia
Tel. +60 3 42578122
Fax +60 3 4533191
E-mail mrcs@po.jaring.my
Web http://www.redcrescent.
        org.my/

Mali Red Cross
Route Koulikoro
B.P. 280
Bamako
Mali
Tel. +223 244569
Fax +223 240414
E-mail crmalienne@afribone.net.ml

Malta Red Cross Society
104 St Ursula Street
Valletta VLT 05
Malta
Tel. +356 21222645
Fax +356 21243664
E-mail redcross@redcross.org.mt
Web http://www.redcross.org.mt

Mauritanian Red Crescent
Avenue Gamal Abdel Nasser
B.P. 344
Nouakchott
Mauritania
Tel. +222 5251249
Fax +222 5291221
E-mail crm@toptechnology.mr

Mauritius Red Cross Society
Ste. Thérèse Street
Curepipe
Mauritius
Tel. +230 6763604
Fax +230 6748855
E-mail redcross@
        mauritiusredcross.com

Mexican Red Cross
Calle Luis Vives 200
Colonia Polanco
México, D.F. 11510
Mexico
Tel. +52 55 10844510
Fax +52 55 10844514
E-mail dirgral@
        cruzrojamexicana.org

International Federation
of Red Cross and Red Crescent Societies

Micronesia Red Cross

P.O. Box 2405, Kolonia
Pohnpei
Micronesia, Federated States of
Tel. +691 3207077
Fax +691 3206531
E-mail mrcs@mail.fm

Red Cross Society of the Republic of Moldova

67a, Ulitsa Asachi
MD-277028 Chisinau
Moldova, Republic of
Tel. +373 2 729644
Fax +373 2 729700
E-mail moldova-RC@mdl.net

Red Cross of Monaco

27, Boulevard de Suisse
98000 Monte Carlo
Monaco
Tel. +377 97 976800
Fax +377 93 159047
E-mail redcross@croix-rouge.mc
Web http://www.croix-rouge.mc

Mongolian Red Cross Society

Central Post Office
Post Box 537
Ulaanbaatar 13
Mongolia
Tel. +976 11 312578
Fax +976 11 320934
E-mail redcross@magicnet.mn

Moroccan Red Crescent

Palais Mokri
Takaddoum
B.P. 189
Rabat
Morocco
Tel. +212 37 650898
Fax +212 37 653280
E-mail crm@iam.net.ma

Mozambique Red Cross Society

Avenida Agostinho Neto 284
Caixa Postal 2986
Maputo
Mozambique
Tel. +258 1 490943
Fax +258 1 497725
E-mail cvm@redcross.org.mz

Myanmar Red Cross Society

Red Cross Building
42 Strand Road
Yangon
Myanmar
Tel. +95 1 383680
Fax +95 1 383675
E-mail mrcshs-ec@redcross.org.mm

Namibia Red Cross

Red Cross House
Erf 2128, Independence Avenue
Katutura
P.O. Box 346
Windhoek
Namibia
Tel. +264 61 235226
Fax +264 61 228949
E-mail enquiries@redcross.org.na

Nepal Red Cross Society

Red Cross Marg
Kalimati
P.O. Box 217
Kathmandu
Nepal
Tel. +977 1 4270650
Fax +977 1 4271915
E-mail nrcs@nrcs.org
Web http://www.nrcs.org

The Netherlands Red Cross

Leeghwaterplein 27
2502 KC The Hague
Netherlands
Tel. +31 70 4455666
Fax +31 70 4455777
E-mail hq@redcross.nl
Web http://www.rodekruis.nl

New Zealand Red Cross

69 Molesworth Street
Thorndon
Wellington 6038
New Zealand
Tel. +64 4 4723750
Fax +64 4 4730315
E-mail national@redcross.org.nz
Web http://www.redcross.org.nz

Nicaraguan Red Cross

Reparto Belmonte
Carretera Sur, km 7
Apartado 3279
Managua
Nicaragua
Tel. +505 2 650380
Fax +505 2 651643
E-mail crnsalud@ibw.ni
Web http://www.nicaragua.
cruzroja.org

Red Cross Society of Niger

B.P. 11386
N° 655, rue NB 045
Niamey
Niger
Tel. +227 733037
Fax +227 732461
E-mail crniger@intnet.ne

Nigerian Red Cross Society

11, Eko Akete Close
Off St. Gregory's Road
South West Ikoyi
P.O. Box 764
Lagos
Nigeria
Tel. +234 1 7738955
Fax +234 1 2691599
E-mail nrcs@nigerianredcross.org

Norwegian Red Cross

Hausmannsgate 7
Postbox 1 – Gronland
0133 Oslo
Norway
Tel. +47 22054000
Fax +47 22054040
E-mail documentation.
        center@redcross.no
Web http://www.redcross.no

Pakistan Red Crescent Society

Sector H-8
Islamabad
Pakistan
Tel. +92 51 9257404
Fax +92 51 9257408
E-mail hilal@comsats.net.pk
Web http://www.prcs.org.pk

Palau Red Cross Society

P.O. Box 6043
Koror 96940
Republic of Palau
Tel. +680 4885780
Fax +680 4884540
E-mail palredcross@palaunet.com

Red Cross Society of Panama

Albrook, Areas Revertidas
Calle Principal
Edificio # 453
Apartado 668
Zona 1
Panama
Tel. +507 3151389
Fax +507 3151401
E-mail cruzroja@pan.gbnet.cc
Web http://www.panama.
        cruzroja.org

Papua New Guinea Red Cross Society

Taurama Road
Port Moresby
P.O. Box 6545
Boroko
Papua New Guinea
Tel. +675 3258577
Fax +675 3259714
E-mail hqpngrcs@online.net.pg

Paraguayan Red Cross

Brasil 216 esq. José Berges
Asunción
Paraguay
Tel. +595 21 222797
Fax +595 21 211560
E-mail crpveids@uninet.com.py
Web http://www.cruzroja.org.py

Peruvian Red Cross

Av. Arequipa N° 1285
Lima
Peru
Tel. +51 1 2658783
Fax +51 1 2658783
E-mail cruzrojaperuana@
        cruzroja.org.pe
Web http://www.cruzroja.org.pe

The Philippine National Red Cross

Bonifacio Drive
Port Area
P.O. Box 280
Manila 2803
Philippines
Tel. +63 2 5278386
Fax +63 2 5270857
E-mail pnrcnhq@redcross.org.ph

Polish Red Cross

Mokotowska 14
P.O. Box 47
00-950 Warsaw
Poland
Tel. +48 22 3261286
Fax +48 22 6284168
E-mail head.office@pck.org.pl
Web http://www.pck.org.pl

Portuguese Red Cross

Campo Grande, 28-6th
1700-093 Lisboa
Portugal
Tel. +351 21 3905571
Fax +351 21 7822454
E-mail internacional@
        cruzvermelha.org.pt

Qatar Red Crescent Society

P.O. Box 5449
Doha
Qatar
Tel. +974 4 435111
Fax +974 4 439950
E-mail info@qrcs.net

Romanian Red Cross

Strada Biserica Amzei, 29
Sector 1
Bucarest
Romania
Tel. +40 21 2129862
Fax +40 21 3128452
E-mail crr@crucearosie.ro

The Russian Red Cross Society

Tcheryomushkinski Proezd 5
117036 Moscow
Russian Federation
Tel. +7 095 1265771
Fax +7 095 2302867
E-mail mail@redcross.ru

Rwandan Red Cross

B.P. 425, Kacyiru
Kigali
Rwanda
Tel. +250 585446
Fax +250 585449
E-mail rrc@rwandate11.com

International Federation
of Red Cross and Red Crescent Societies

Saint Kitts and Nevis Red Cross Society

National Headquarters
Horsford Road
P.O. Box 62
Basseterre
Saint Kitts and Nevis
Tel. +1 869 4652584
Fax +1 869 4668129
E-mail skbredcr@caribsurf.com

Saint Lucia Red Cross

Vigie
P.O. Box 271
Castries St Lucia, W.I.
Saint Lucia
Tel. +1 758 4525582
Fax +1 758 4537811
E-mail sluredcross@candw.lc

Saint Vincent and the Grenadines Red Cross

Halifax Street
Minister of Education Compound
Kingstown
P.O. Box 431
Saint Vincent and the Grenadines
Tel. +1 784 4561888
Fax +1 784 4856210
E-mail svgredcross@caribsurf.com

Samoa Red Cross Society

P.O. Box 1616
Apia
Samoa
Tel. +685 23686
Fax +685 22676
E-mail samoaredcross@samoa.ws

Red Cross of the Republic of San Marino

Via Scialoja, Cailungo
Republic of San Marino 47031
Tel. +37 8 994360
Fax +37 8 994360
E-mail crs@omniway.sm
Web http://www.tradecenter.sm/crs

Sao Tome and Principe Red Cross

Avenida 12 de Julho No.11
B.P. 96
Sao Tome
Sao Tome and Principe
Tel. +239 12 22469
Fax +239 12 22305
E-mail cvstp@sol.stome.telepac.net

Saudi Arabian Red Crescent Society

General Headquarters
Riyadh 11129
Saudi Arabia
Tel. +966 1 4740027
Fax +966 1 4740430
E-mail redcrescent@zajil.net

Senegalese Red Cross Society

Boulevard F. Roosevelt
B.P. 299
Dakar
Senegal
Tel. +221 8233992
Fax +221 8225369
E-mail crsnational@sentoo.sn

The Red Cross of Serbia and Montenegro

Simina 19
11000 Belgrade
Serbia and Montenegro
Tel. +381 11 2623564
Fax +381 11 2622965
E-mail indep@jck.org.yu
Web http://www.jck.org/yu

Seychelles Red Cross Society

Place de la République
B.P. 53
Victoria, Mahé
Seychelles
Tel. +248 324646
Fax +248 321663
E-mail redcross@seychelles.net
Web http://www.seychelles.net/
    redcross

Sierra Leone Red Cross Society

6 Liverpool Street
P.O. Box 427
Freetown
Sierra Leone
Tel. +232 22 222384
Fax +232 22 229083
E-mail slrcs@sierratel.sl

Singapore Red Cross Society

Red Cross House
15 Penang Lane
Singapore 238486
Tel. +65 6 3360269
Fax +65 6 3374360
E-mail redcross@starhub.net.sg
Web http://www.redcross.org.sg

Slovak Red Cross

Grösslingova 24
814 46 Bratislava
Slovakia
Tel. +421 2 52967518
Fax +421 2 52923576
E-mail us.sms@redcross.sk

Slovenian Red Cross

Mirje 19
P.O. Box 236
SI-61000 Ljubljana
Slovenia
Tel. +386 1 2414300
Fax +386 1 2414344
E-mail rdeci.kriz@rks.si

The Solomon Islands Red Cross

P.O. Box 187
Honiara
Solomon Islands
Tel. +677 22682
Fax +677 25299
E-mail sirc@solomon.com.sb

Somali Red Crescent Society

c/o ICRC Box 73226
Nairobi
Kenya
Tel. +252 1 216049 Mogadishu
    +254 2 2713785 Nairobi
Fax +252 5943880 Mogadishu
    +254 2 2718 862 Nairobi
E-mail srcsnai@iconnect.co.ke
Web http://www.bishacas.org

The South African Red Cross Society

1st Floor, Helen Bowden Bldg
Beach Road, Granger Bay
P.O. Box 50696, Waterfront
Cape Town 8002
South Africa
Tel. +27 21 4186640
Fax +27 21 4186644
E-mail sarcs@redcross.org.za
Web http://www.redcross.org.za

Spanish Red Cross

Rafael Villa, s/n Vuelta Ginés
    Navarro
28023 El Plantio
Madrid
Spain
Tel. +34 91 3354637
Fax +34 91 3354455
E-mail informa@cruzroja.es
Web http://www.cruzroja.es

The Sri Lanka Red Cross Society

307, 2/1 T.B. Jayah Mawatha
P.O. Box 375
Colombo 10
Sri Lanka
Tel. +94 11 2691095
Fax +94 11 5367462
E-mail nhq@slrcs.org

The Sudanese Red Crescent

P.O. Box 235
Khartoum
Sudan
Tel. +249 83 772011
Fax +249 83 772877
E-mail srcs@sudanmail.com

Suriname Red Cross

226 Gravenberchstraat 2
Postbus 2919
Paramaribo
Suriname
Tel. +597 498410
Fax +597 464780
E-mail surcross@sr.net

Baphalali Swaziland Red Cross Society

104 Johnstone Street
P.O. Box 377
Mbabane
Swaziland
Tel. +268 4042532
Fax +268 4046108
E-mail thabsile@redcross.org.sz

Swedish Red Cross

Hornsgatan 54
Box 17563
SE-118 91 Stockholm
Sweden
Tel. +46 8 4524600
Fax +46 8 4524601
E-mail int@redcross.se
Web http://www.redcross.se

Swiss Red Cross

Rainmattstrasse 10
Postfach
3001 Bern
Switzerland
Tel. +41 31 3877111
Fax +41 31 3877122
E-mail info@redcross.ch
Web http://www.redcross.ch

Syrian Arab Red Crescent

Al Malek Aladel Street
Damascus
Syrian Arab Republic
Tel. +963 11 4429662
Fax +963 11 4425677
E-mail SARC@net.sy

Red Crescent Society of Tajikistan

120, Omari Khayom St.
734017 Dushanbe
Tajikistan
Tel. +7 3772 240374
Fax +7 3772 245378
E-mail rcstj@yahoo.com

Tanzania Red Cross National Society

Ali Hassan Mwinyi Road,
Plot 294/295
P.O. Box 1133
Dar es Salaam
Tanzania, United Republic of
Tel. +255 22 2150881
Fax +255 22 2150147
E-mail logistics@raha.com

The Thai Red Cross Society

Terd Prakiat Building, 4th Floor
1871 Henry Dunant Road
Bangkok 10330
Thailand
Tel. +66 2 2564037
Fax +66 2 2553064
E-mail wmaster@redcross.or.th
Web http://www.redcross.or.th

Togolese Red Cross

51, rue Boko Soga
Amoutivé
B.P. 655
Lome
Togo
Tel. +228 2212110
Fax +228 2215228
E-mail crtsiege@laposte.tg

Tonga Red Cross Society

P.O. Box 456
Nuku'Alofa
South West Pacific
Tonga
Tel. +676 21360
Fax +676 21508
E-mail redcross@kalianet.to

The Trinidad and Tobago Red Cross Society

7A, Fitz Blackman Drive
Wrightson Road
P.O. Box 357
Port of Spain
Trinidad and Tobago
Tel. +1 868 6278128
Fax +1 868 6278215
E-mail ttrcs@carib-link.net

Tunisian Red Crescent

19, Rue d'Angleterre
Tunis 1000
Tunisia
Tel. +216 71 325572
Fax +216 71 320151
E-mail hilal.ahmar@planet.tn

Turkish Red Crescent Society

Atac Sokak 1 No. 32
Yenisehir, Ankara
Turkey
Tel. +90 312 4302300
Fax +90 312 4300175
E-mail international@kizilay.org.tr
Web http://www.kizilay.org.tr

Red Crescent Society of Turkmenistan

48 A. Novoi str.
744000 Ashgabat
Turkmenistan
Tel. +993 12 395511
Fax +993 12 351750
E-mail nrcst@online.tm

The Uganda Red Cross Society

Plot 28/30 Lumumba Avenue
Kampala
Uganda
Tel. +256 41 258701
Fax +256 41 258184
E-mail sgurcs@redcross.org

Ukrainian Red Cross Society

30, Pushkinskaya St.
252004 Kiev
Ukraine
Tel. +380 44 2350157
Fax +380 44 2465658
E-mail international@redcross.
   org.ua
Web http://www.redcross.org.ua

Red Crescent Society of the United Arab Emirates

P.O. Box 3324
Abu Dhabi
United Arab Emirates
Tel. +9 712 6419000
Fax +9 712 6420101
E-mail hilalrc@emirates.net.ae

British Red Cross

44 Moorfields
London EC2Y 9AL
United Kingdom
Tel. +44 20 78777000
Fax +44 20 75622013
E-mail information@redcross.
   org.uk
Web http://www.redcross.org.uk

American Red Cross

2025 E Street NW, 8th Floor
NW 8088C
Washington, DC 20006
United States of America
Tel. +1 202 3035279
Fax +1 202 3030054
E-mail postmaster@usa.redcross.org
Web http://www.redcross.org

Uruguayan Red Cross

Avenida 8 de Octubre, 2990
11600 Montevideo
Uruguay
Tel. +598 2 4802112
Fax +598 2 4800714
E-mail cruzroja@adinet.com.uy
Web http://www.uruguay.
   cruzroja.org

Red Crescent Society of Uzbekistan

30, Yusuf Hos Hojib St.
700031 Tashkent
Uzbekistan
Tel. +988 712 563741
Fax +988 712 561801
E-mail RCUZ@uzpak.uz
Web http://www.redcrescent.uz

Vanuatu Red Cross Society

P.O. Box 618
Port Vila
Vanuatu
Tel. +678 27418
Fax +678 22599
E-mail redcross@vanuatu.com.vu

Venezuelan Red Cross

Avenida Andrés Bello, 4
Apartado 3185
Caracas 1010
Venezuela
Tel. +58 212 5714380
Fax +58 212 5761042
E-mail dirnacsoc@cantv.net
Web http://www.venezuela.
   cruzroja.org

Red Cross of Viet Nam

82, Nguyen Du Street
Hanoï
Viet Nam
Tel. +844 8 225157
Fax +844 9 424285
E-mail vnrchq@netnam.org.vn
Web http://www.vnrc.org.vn

Yemen Red Crescent Society
Head Office, Building No. 10
26 September Street
P.O. Box 1257
Sanaa
Yemen
Tel. +967 1 283132
Fax +967 1 283131

Zambia Red Cross Society
2837 Los Angeles Boulevard
Longacres
P.O. Box 50001 Ridgeway 15101
Lusaka
Zambia
Tel. +260 1 253661
Fax +260 1 252219
E-mail zrcs@zamnet.zm

Zimbabwe Red Cross Society
10 St. Annes Road
Avondale
Harare
Zimbabwe
Tel. +263 4 335490
Fax +263 4 335490
E-mail zrcs@ecoweb.co.zw

International Federation regional delegations

Yaoundé
Rue Mini-Prix Bastos
BP 11507
Yaoundé
Cameroon
Tel. +237 2217437
Fax +237 2217439
E-mail ifrccm04@ifrc.org

Beijing
4-1-133, Jian Guo Men Wai
Diplomatic Compound
Beijing 100600
China
Tel. +8610 65327164
Fax +8610 65327166

Suva
77 Cakobau Road
P.O. Box 2507
Government Building
Suva
Fiji
Tel. +679 311855
Fax +679 311406
E-mail ifrcfj00@ifrc.org

Budapest
Zolyomi Lepcso Ut 22
1124 Budapest
Hungary
Tel. +361 2483300
Fax +361 2483322
E-mail ifrchu01@ifrc.org

New Delhi
C-1/35 Safdarjung Development
    Area
New Delhi 110 016
India
Tel. +9111 26858671
Fax +9111 26857567
E-mail ifrcin01@ifrc.org

Amman
Al Shmeisani
Maroof Al Rasafi Street
Building No. 19
P.O. Box 830511 / Zahran
Amman
Jordan
Tel. +962 6 5681060
Fax +962 6 5694556
E-mail ifrcjo01@ifrc.org

Almaty
86, Kunaeva Street
480100 Almaty
Kazakhstan, Republic of
Tel. +732 72 918838
Fax +732 72 914267
E-mail ifrckz01@ifrc.org

Nairobi
Woodlands Road
    (off State House Road)
P.O. Box 41275
Nairobi
Kenya
Tel. +254 20 2714255
Fax +254 20 2718415
E-mail ifrcke01@ifrc.org

Panama
Clayton, Ciudad del Saber # 804 A/B
Ciudad de Panamá
Panama, Republic of Panama
Tel. +507 317 1300
Fax +507 317 1304
E-mail ifrcpa50@ifrc.org

Lima
Los Naranjos 351
San Isidro, Lima
Peru
Tel. +511 2219006
Fax +511 4413607
E-mail ifrcpe07@ifrc.org

International Federation
of Red Cross and Red Crescent Societies

Dakar

VDN x Ancienne Piste, Mermoz
    Pyrotechnie
Boîte Postale 25956
Dakar – Fann
Senegal
Tel. +221 869 36 40
Fax +221 860 20 02
E-mail ifrcsn20@ ifrc.org

Bangkok

Asoke Towers 219/8-10
4th Floor, Sukhumvit 21
Soi Asoke
Wattana
Bangkok 10110
Thailand
Tel. +662 6408211
Fax +662 6408220
E-mail ifrcth023@ifrc.org

Harare

42 Bates Street
Milton Park
Harare
Zimbabwe
Tel. +2634 705166
Fax +2634 708784
E-mail ifrczw01@ifrc.org

International Federation country delegations

Afghanistan

Estgah Dawa Khana
Shash Darak, House 61
Kabul
Afghanistan
Tel. +873 382280530
Fax +873 382280534
E-mail hod.kabuldel@wireless.
    ifrc.org

Angola

Caixa Postal 3324
Rua 1 Congresso de MPLA 27/ 27
Luanda
Angola
Tel. +2442 393652
Fax +2442 372868
E-mail ifrcao01@ifrc.org

Armenia

21 Paronyan Str.
Yerevan 375015
Armenia
Tel. +374 10 539443
Fax +374 10 539217
E-mail ifrcam03@ifrc.org

Azerbaijan

S. Safarov Street 2
Baku, Nesimi District
PC 370010
Azerbaijan
Tel. +99412 983772
Fax +99412 985501
E-mail ifrcaz01@ifrc.org

Bangladesh

c/o Bangladesh Red Crescent
    Society
684-686 Bara Magh Bazar
Dhaka – 1217
Bangladesh
Tel. +8802 8315401
Fax +8802 9341631
E-mail ifrcbd@citecho.net

Belarus

Ulitsa Mayakovkosgo 14
Minsk 220006
Belarus
Tel. +375172 217237
Fax +375172 219060
E-mail ifrcby01@ifrc.org

Burundi

Avenue des Etats-Unis 3674A
B.P. 324
Bujumbura
Burundi
Tel. +257 242 401
Fax +257 211 101
E-mail ifrcbi01@ifrc.org

Cambodia

17 Deo, Street Croix-Rouge
Central Post Office/P.O. Box 620
Phnom Penh
Cambodia
Tel. +855 23 210162
Fax +855 23 210163
E-mail ifrckh01@ifrc.org

Chad

Sudanese Refugees Operation
    Delegation
c/o Croix-Rouge du Tchad
B.P. 449
N'Djamena
Chad
Tel. + 235 52 23 39
Fax +235 52 23 99
E-mail ifrccd13@ifrc.org

Congo, Democratic Republic of the
41, avenue de la Justice
Gombe
Kinshasa
Congo, Dem. Rep. of the
Tel. +243 98 31 14 45
Fax +243 88 01 94
E-mail kinshasdel@wireless.ifrc.org

Côte d'Ivoire
II Plateau Polyclinique
Lôt N° 41/Ilôt N° 4
Villa Duplex
Abidjan-Cocody
Côte d'Ivoire
Tel. +225 22 40 44 66
Fax +225 22 40 44 59
E-mail ifrcci36@ifrc.org

East Timor
Bidau-Santana Rua de Cristo Rei s/n
Dili
East Timor
Tel. +670 390 322778
Fax +670 390 322778
E-mail ifrc_east_timor01@ifrc.org

El Salvador
c/o Salvadorean Red Cross Society
Apartado Postal 1401
17 calle Poniente y
    Av. Henry Dunant
Centro de Gobierno, San Salvador
El Salvador
Tel. +503 2222166
Fax +503 2811932
E-mail ifrcsv11@ifrc.org

Eritrea
c/o Red Cross Society of Eritrea
Andnet Street
P.O. Box 575
Asmara
Eritrea
Tel. +2911 150550
Fax +2911 151859
E-mail ifrc2@gemel.com.er

Ethiopia
Ras Desta Damtew Avenue
P.O. Box 195
Addis Ababa
Ethiopia
Tel. +2511 514571
Fax +2511 512888
E-mail ifrcet04@ifrc.org

Gabon
c/o Croix-rouge Gabonaise
Place de l'Indépendance
    Derrière le Mont de Cristal
Boîte Postale 2274
Libreville
Gabon
Tel. +241 747000
Fax +241 747900
E-mail ifrcga01@ifrc.org

Georgia
54, Chavchavadze Ave., Apt. 18
380079 Tbilisi
Georgia
Tel. +99532 922248
Fax +99532 922248
E-mail ifrcge01@ifrc.org

Guatemala
c/o Guatemala Red Cross
3A Calle 8-40, Zona 1, 2no Nivel
Guatemala, C.A.
Guatemala
Tel. +502 2537351
Fax +502 2380091
E-mail fedecng@intelnet.net.gt

Guinea
Coleah, route du Niger
    (derrière la station Shell)
    Près de l'Ambassade
    de Yougoslavie
B.P. No 376
Conakry
Guinea
Tel. +224 413825
Fax +224 414255
E-mail ifrc.gn01@ifrc.org

Haiti
Angle Avenue Christophe 119
    et Rue 7
Port-au-Prince
B.P. 15322, Pétion-Ville
Haiti
Tel. +509 510 2629
Fax +59 244 1907

India
Red Cross Building
1 Red Cross Road
110001 New Delhi
India
Tel. +9111 23324203
Fax +9111 23324235
E-mail ifrcin65@ifrc.org

Indonesia
c/o Indonesian Red Cross Society
P.O. Box 2009
Jakarta
Indonesia
Tel. +6221 79191841
Fax +6221 79180905
E-mail ifrcid01@ifrc.org

Iran
c/o Iranian Red Crescent Society
Ostad Nejatollahi Avenue
Tehran
Islamic Republic of Iran
Tel. +98 21 889 0567
Fax +98 21 889 5346
E-mail ifrcir01@ifrc.org

Iraq
P.O. Box 830511/Zahran
Amman
Jordan
Tel. +962 6 5681060
Fax +962 6 5694556
E-mail ifrciq10@ifrc.org

International Federation
of Red Cross and Red Crescent Societies

Korea, DPR

c/o Red Cross Society of
the DPR Korea
Ryonwa 1, Central District
Pyongyang
Korea, Democratic People's
Republic of
Tel. +8502 3814350
Fax +8502 3813490

Laos

c/o Lao Red Cross
P.O. Box 2948
Setthatirath Road, Xiengnhune
Vientiane
Lao People's Democratic Republic
Tel. +856 21215762
Fax +856 21215935
E-mail laocas@laotel.com

Lebanon

Mar Takla – Haymieh
N. Dagher Building
Beirut
Lebanon
Tel. +961 1 365 374
Fax +961 1 365 046
E-mail ifrclb03@ifrc.org

Lesotho

c/o Lesotho Red Cross
23 Mabile Rd.
Maseru 100
Lesotho
Tel. +266 22 313 911
Fax +266 3310166
E-mail ifrcsa19@ifrc.org

Liberia

c/o Liberian Red Cross Society
National Headquarters
107, Lynch Street
P.O. Box 5081
Monrovia
Liberia
Tel. +231 6 553 195
E-mail ifrclr01@ifrc.org

Malawi

c/o Malawi Red Cross Society
Red Cross House
Presidential Way
Area 14
Lilongwe
Malawi
Tel. +265 1 772650
Fax +265 1 7755907
E-mail ifrcmw01@ifrc.org

Mongolia

c/o Red Cross Society of Mongolia
Central Post Office
Post Box 537
Ulaanbaatar
Mongolia
Tel. +97611 321684
Fax +97611 321684
E-mail ifrcmongol@magicnet.mn

Mozambique

c/o Mozambique Red Cross
Society
Av. Agostinho Neto 284
Maputo
Mozambique
Tel. + 258 1492278
Fax +258 01498219
E-mail ifrcmz01@ifrc.org

Myanmar

c/o Myanmar Red Cross Society
Red Cross Building
42 Strand Road
Yangon
Myanmar
Tel. +951 383 686
Fax +951 383 682
E-mail ifrc@ifrc-myanmar.org.mm

Nicaragua

c/o Nicaraguan Red Cross
Reparto Belmonte, Carretera Sur
Km 71/2
Apartado Postal P-48 Las Piedrecitas
Managua
Nicaragua
Tel. +505 2650186
Fax +505 2652069

Nigeria

c/o Nigerian Red Cross Society
11, Eko Akete Close
Off St. Gregory's Road
South West Ikoyi
P.O. Box 764
Lagos
Nigeria
Tel. +2341 2695228
Fax +2341 2695229
E-mail ifrcng02@ifrc.org

Pakistan

c/o Pakistan Red Crescent Society
National Headquarters
Sector H-8
Islamabad
Pakistan
Tel. +9251 9257122
Fax +9251 4430745
E-mail ifrcpk08@ifrc.org

Palestine

P.O.Box 18646
Jerusalem 91184
Israel
Tel. +972 2 2400485
Fax +972 2 2400484
E-mail ifrcpal01@ifrc.org

Papua New Guinea

c/o PNG Red Cross Society
P.O. Box 6545
Boroko
Papua New Guinea
Tel. +675 3112277
Fax +675 3230731

Russian Federation

c/o Russian Red Cross Society
Tcheryomushkinski Proezd 5
117036 Moscow
Russian Federation
Tel. +7095 9375267
Fax +70959375263
E-mail moscow@ifrc.org

Rwanda

c/o Rwandan Red Cross
B.P. 425, Kacyiru
Kigali
Rwanda
Tel. +250 585447
Fax +250 585447
E-mail ifrcrw03@ifrc.org

Serbia and Montenegro

Simina Ulica Broj 21
11000 Belgrade
Serbia and Montenegro
Tel. +381 11 3282202
Fax +381 11 3281791
E-mail telecom@ifrc.org.yu

Sierra Leone

c/o Sierra Leone Red Cross Society
6, Liverpool Street
P.O. Box 427
Freetown
Sierra Leone
Tel. +23222 227772
Fax +23222 228180
E-mail ifrcsl01@ifrc.org

Somalia

c/o Regional Delegation Nairobi
Woodlands Road,
    off State House Road
P.O. Box 41275
Nairobi
Kenya
Tel. +254 20 2728294
Fax +254 20 2718415
E-mail ifrcso01@ifrc.org

South Africa

c/o South African Red Cross
1st Floor, Helen Bowden Bldg
Beach Road, Granger Bay
P.O. Box 50696, Waterfront
Cape Town 8002
South Africa
Tel. +27 82 4503984
Fax +27 21 4186644
E-mail ifrcsa15@ifrc.org

Sri Lanka

3rd floor, 307 T B Jayah Mawatha
LK Colombo
Sri Lanka
Tel. +9411 4715977
Fax +9411 4715978
E-mail ifrclk01@srilanka.net

Sudan

Al Mak Nimir Street/
    Gamhouria Street
Plot No 1, Block No 4
P.O. Box 10697
East Khartoum
Sudan
Tel. 249 1 83 771033
Fax +24911 770484
E-mail ifrcsd01@ifrc.org

Swaziland

c/o Baphalali Swaziland Red Cross
    Society
104 Johnstone Street
P.O. Box 377
Mbabane
Swaziland
Tel. +268 404 61 08
Fax +268 404 6108
E-mail ifrcsw01@ifrc.org

Tajikistan

c/o Tajikistan Red Crescent Society
120, Omar Khayom St.
734017 Dushanbe
Tajikistan
Tel. +992372 245981
Fax +992372 248520
E-mail ifrcdsb@ifrc.org

Tanzania

c/o Tanzania Red Cross Society
Ali Hassan Mwinyi Road
Plot No. 294/295
P.O. Box 1133
Dar es Salaam
Tanzania, United Republic of
Tel. +255 22 2116514
Fax +255 22 2117308
E-mail ifrctz02@ifrc.org

Turkey

Cemal Nadir Sokak, No.9
Cankaya
Ankara 06680
Turkey
Tel. +90312 441 42 92
Fax +90312 441 3866
E-mail ifrctr06@ifrc.org

Uganda

c/o Uganda Red Cross Society
P.O.Box 494
    (Plot 2830, Lumumba Ave.)
Uganda
Tel. + 256 41 231480
Fax +256 41 258184
E-mail ifrcug01@ifrc.org

International Federation
of Red Cross and Red Crescent Societies

Viet Nam

15 Thien Quang Street
Hanoï
Viet Nam
Tel. +844 9422983
Fax +844 9422987
E-mail ifrc@hn.vnn.vn

Zambia

c/o Zambia Red Cross Society
2837 Los Angeles Boulevard
Longacres
P.O. Box 50001 Ridgeway 15101
Lusaka
Zambia
Tel. +260 1 254074
Fax +260 1 251599
E-mail ifrczmb01@ifrc.org

Zimbabwe

c/o Zimbabwe Red Cross Society
10 St. Annes Road
Avondale
Harare
Zimbabwe
Tel. +263 4 335490
Fax +263 4 335490
E-mail ifrcsa09@ifrc.org

Index

International Federation
of Red Cross and Red Crescent Societies

International Federation
of Red Cross and Red Crescent Societies

INDEX